OX42

West Sussex Within Living Memory

Compiled by the West Sussex
Federation of Women's Institutes

GW00647859

Published jointly by
Countryside Books, Newbury
and the WSFWI, Chichester

First published 1993
© West Sussex Federation of Women's Institutes 1993

COUNTRYSIDE BOOKS
3 Catherine Road
Newbury, Berkshire

ISBN 1 85306 253 7

The cover photograph shows Westergate Street,
Aldingbourne in about 1912.

Designed by Mon Mohan
Produced through MRM Associates Ltd, Reading
Printed in England

Contents

Foreword

The beauty of the Downs, the fascination of the coastline, the charm of woodland and the farming area all epitomise the county of West Sussex. Many changes have taken place within living memory, as motorways have altered the character of villages and towns and railway branch lines have disappeared.

How fortunate that we have been able to capture so many experiences in this book, with memories of life before the important international airport and speed ridden roads. Then horses worked the fields and extended families lived in the same village. It is fascinating to read these anecdotes and to learn how people coped with the problems of everyday life. Gone are the days when a WI committee consisted of five ladies, three school teachers and two women, as reported in the early minutes. Today many of the old crafts and skills are being revived and taught by those who can remember them.

We are proud in West Sussex to know that the first institute formed in England was at Singleton in 1915. This rural area has perhaps seen fewer changes over the decades than many other parts of our county. We now look forward, wondering how many more changes lie ahead for those who live in and love the County of West Sussex.

Thelma Smellie
County Federation Chairman

Acknowledgements

West Sussex Federation of Women's Institutes wish to thank the very many WI members who sent contributions for this book, through their Institutes and independently. We appreciate the tremendous interest shown in the project.

Unfortunately we were not able to include extracts from every article sent to us; this would have meant some duplication of content, in addition to which we had to take account the space available in the eventual publication.

All the contributions, without exception, were of value in deciding the shape and content of this book. We are grateful for them all.

I would like to thank Jean Cross, Sandra Williams and Elaine Simpson for their help with the typing of the handwritten manuscripts. Special thanks are due to Sylvia Eatherden for her delightful line drawings, Joyce Lee for the map of West Sussex and Beryl Ware for her help with proof reading.

Pauline Roberts
Co-ordinator

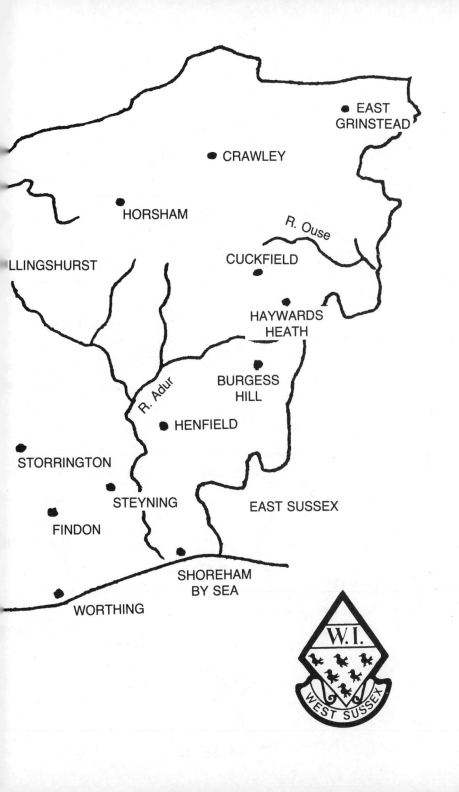

List of Contributing WIs

Contributions were recieved from the following West Sussex Institutes:

Aldingbourne, Aldwick, Aldwick West, Angmering, Angmering Green, Ardingly, Ashurst, Bepton, Billingshurst, Birdham, Bosham, Boxgrove, Broadbridge Heath, Broadwater Green, Burgess Hill St Andrews, Camelsdale, Chichester, Chidham, Chilgrove and The Mardens, Clapham and Patching, Clayton, Coldwaltham and Watersfield, Crawley, Crawley Down Afternoon, Cuckfield, Cuckfield Evening, Donnington, Durrington, East Preston Green, East Preston Village, Felpham Southdown, Felpham Village, Felpham Way, Fernhurst, Ferring, Ferring Village, Findon Downs, Findon Village, Fishbourne, Fishbourne Evening, Fittleworth, Forestside and Stanstead, Funtington and West Stoke, Goring-By-Sea, Gossops Green, Handcross, Henfield, Heyshott, High Salvington, Horsted Keynes, Hunston, Kingscote, Kirdford, Lancing, Lavant, Lower Beeding, Loxwood, Lurgashall, Mannings Heath, Midhurst and West Lavant, North Bersted Village, North Emsworth, North Lancing and Coombes, North Mundham, Pagham, Partridge Green Colvin, Petworth, Pound Hill, Pulborough Meadows, Roffey, Roffey Greenfields, Rogate, Rose Green, Rudgwick, Rustington, Scaynes Hill, Selsey, Shoreham by Sea, Shoreham Greenways, Sidlesham, Sompting Seadown, Sompting Village, Southwater Weald, Southwick, Steyning, Storrington, Storrington Downs, Sullington Windmills, Thakeham, Warnham, Washington, West Chiltington, West Chiltington Hayling, Westergate, West Hoathly, West Wittering, Wisborough Green, Woodmancote, Worth and Yapton.

With apologies for any omissions. Some entries were sent in by members without mentioning the name of their Institute.

TOWN & COUNTRY LIFE

SOME TOWNS AND VILLAGES REMEMBERED

⟳

It isn't really so long since a lamplighter could be seen on the streets of Worthing, since you could take your Christmas dinner along to the baker's opposite the blacksmith in Findon and have it cooked for you, or since a horse-drawn fire engine raced through the streets of Midhurst. Memories of just some towns and villages during the first half of the 20th century show how much life has changed since then.

WORTHING BETWEEN THE WARS

'When I went to live in Worthing in 1923 there were little goat carts on the sea front giving rides to children and the old people used to go out in big leather bath chairs which were pulled by men. The old lady living opposite me went out every afternoon at three o'clock.

People bathed from bathing machines. These were looked after by a fat old lady and taken down by a horse to the shallow water so that would-be bathers could get straight out of them into the water without having to walk on the pebbles.

The lifeboat was also taken by horse down to the sea. The lifeboat station was near where the Cavendish Hotel now stands (the small look-out turret still exists) and the lifeboat had to be pulled over the stones to be launched by the pier.

We used to go horse riding on the Downs and when we went along the north side of Chanctonbury Ring the horses would shy and slip – there seemed to be an eerie atmosphere which always affected them in the same place. It was very quiet up there. No birds ever sang in the Ring.

For Sunday school outings we went in open-topped charabancs. These had a hood at the back which could be pulled forward over us if it rained. We did not go far – perhaps to the Downs by Long Furlong – but the drives and picnics were great occasions and we always played games after tea before returning home. Some of the children were very poor and when I first taught in the Sunday school in 1923 the children from Surrey Street, ages six to eight, came with bare feet.

We often went driving into the country. When going to Midhurst we had to pass through Cowdray Park which had gates. A little girl, who always wore a big white apron, lived in the Lodge and for a penny or twopence she would come out and open them to let us in.

Worthing was much smaller in those days – a population of 3,500 in 1923. We used to walk from Tarring village across corn fields to Goring church – it was all open country.

If we went to Coldwaltham we had to open and close the gates at either end of the common land on Greatham Brooks between Greatham Bridge and Widneys, which was a farmhouse in those days. The twisty Old London Road was the main road – there was no bypass and very few houses, just several smallholdings.'

'The Worthing I remember was a compact little town where most people not only knew each other, but also each other's parents, grandparents and other relations. It was a friendly little place with shops where they knew, from week to week, what you were likely to want.

The Front was its shop window, with the pier and an ornate bandstand at the south end of Steyne Gardens. By the entrance to the pier was "Bubbles", a round object filled with coloured ping-pong balls. When enough customers were waiting, each was given a cane with a wire cup on the end. When told "Go!" these were held out over the centre and a rush of air blew all the balls into the air. You got a prize if you managed to catch three. Also there, and most impressive, was the goat carriage – a perfect replica of a ceremonial carriage of the day drawn by a magnificent, immaculately groomed white goat with big curving horns. You longed for a ride but only occasionally got one because it cost a whole sixpence, two weeks' pocket money.

To the west the town ended at Wallace Avenue, to the east at the south end of Brougham Road. Just before Brougham Road there was a cottagey-looking terrace, an almshouse called Pearson's Retreat, and we used to see the old people who lived there sitting at their front doors to enjoy the sun. To the north the extent was Chesswood Road and Newland Road (Grandpa used to warn anyone buying a house, "Don't buy one in Newland Road, it'll flood whenever the Teville stream rises.").

Steyne Gardens, in the centre of the town, were still guarded by iron railings and locked at night, until the middle of the Second World War when the railings, with many others, were taken "to make munitions".

Near the Steyne Gardens they built Steyne Gardens Methodist chapel, largely through the efforts of local people, who were invited to "Buy a Brick". Since Grandpa was one of the organisers all his family did so, and at the base of the west wall can be seen the initials of all of his seven children.

In the 1880s they were just beginning to put up substantial houses each side of what was then Heene Lane (Heene had originally been a village on its own). The council wished to change the name, but my future employer, Mr Charles (of Charles, Malcolm & Wilson), who lived there, objected and said so. "Oh, come!" said one councillor, "How can we leave a thoroughfare with such fine substantial houses as a 'lane'?" Little Mr Charles got up and said gently, "Has the last speaker never heard of Park Lane?" But he was outvoted just the same, and the change unfortunately took place.

There was plenty of recreation available in the town. It had its own football team, there were concerts (amateur and professional) and at least three tennis clubs – the Northcourt, the Shelley and the Pavilion. We belonged to the Shelley, which used to hold tennis teas every Saturday.

Mrs Rose Wilmot was President at that time and came up with the idea, favoured by a number of other members too, of a club to meet on winter evenings to keep the members together when there was no tennis. "What will it be *for*?" someone asked. Mrs Wilmot replied, "Social intercourse in the winter." She happened to be a widow, and a rather deaf member at the back heard her and said, reproachfully, "Oh, Rosie!" The club, christened The Bonhomie Club, did materialise and cards, chess and ping-pong were played.

A bit later, when I was working in an office, the Women's League of Health & Beauty was started. Quite a few of us joined, and changed at the office into white shirts and little black satin shorts – which caused considerable interest, amusement, and requests for front row seats from the male members of staff.

When, between the wars, so much nursery land was given up for building, new streets were often named by the vendor and this accounts for some of the names. For instance, the area to the west of Wallace Avenue was developed in the 1920s and one road was built on my father's uncle's nursery. His youngest son was named Gerald, hence Gerald Road. The rather exotic names of other roads in the area are accounted for in the same way – Phrosso, Aglaia and Eirene were the children of the man who owned that piece of land. Moat Way does not commemorate some medieval moat, merely that the owner's name was Moat. I think, however, that Smugglers Farm and Smugglers Walk may be assumed to be authentic – I never heard of any owner named Smuggler!'

'I remember the traffic was gentle before the war and flowed either side of an avenue of stately trees in the centre of Brighton Road opposite Steyne Gardens. There were four entrance gates and the gardens were for the use of the residents of the houses on either side, but the southern end was public with an ornate bandstand which was removed when one was built on the seafront. This new one gave great delight to young and old alike with military or modern bands playing all summer. Many of the artists appearing went on to make a name for themselves, Geoff Love being one when he was a singer with Jan Ralfini and his band.

There was also a very well known and loved "Tram-O-Car". This was a single decker, electric powered bus service which ran along the length of the seafront then down to West Worthing station and back to Splash Point. It trundled along at a leisurely pace but, without the volume of today's traffic, possibly completed its journey in half the time of today's bus service.

Hubbard's was opened in South Street. This was a large privately owned modern department store, now recognised as Debenhams, but in pre-war days it was quite exclusive with a hand picked staff of young ladies who were offered accommodation in the firm's property in an adjoining Bedford Row.

South Street was a wide main road running from the town centre to the sea. The centre was the Old Town Hall, housing on top a large clock by which all Worthing residents set their timepieces. Down the middle of the road stood horse troughs for the use of the horse-drawn taxis and other vehicles. I must admit they were hardly used during my youth.'

'When I started school in Worthing in the 1920s, I can remember my mother meeting me in the afternoon, and on our way home we would see the lamplighter come along on his bicycle and light each gas street light with a hook on a long pole. The boys would climb the lamp post and swing on the bar that was there to lean the ladder against when the lamp needed attention.

We often stood and watched the man delivering blocks of ice with large hooks to the butcher and fishmonger, as there were no freezers in those days. There was a slaughterhouse near where we lived in East Worthing, and once a week we would see the cattle being driven with a stick along the road from the railway station to the abattoir.'

FINDON IN THE 1920s

'I was born in Findon in 1912 when there were three racing stables and estates such as Muntham Court, Cissbury House, Findon Place and Park Farm. Many men were employed at the stables as jockey lads and grooms, and on the estates as gardeners, gamekeepers,

13

carpenters, blacksmiths, carters and grooms for the farm horses and hunters, and also as chauffeurs and under-chauffeurs.

There was a chimney sweep, and if there were any children in the house involved, they had the job of being outside and giving a shout when they saw the brush come out of the chimney top. From the same family came the road or lengthman who was to be seen every working day somewhere in the village with his wheelbarrow, brush and shovel, keeping the ditches clear and the roads swept clean which, remembering that there were many horses and cows about, was no mean feat. The blacksmith's brother Alf did odd jobs, one of which was to fetch water from the well of the Gun Inn, carrying two buckets on a wooden yoke on his shoulders.

Women were employed indoors as cooks, ladies' maids and parlour maids. On the farms they worked in the dairies, as did Mrs Short and her daughter at Short's Farm, part of which is now our newsagent and post office. The Shorts' son delivered milk to our doors, using pint and half pint measures which hooked on to the side of the churn. One woman (known as Old Mother Upton) went stonepicking – that is, clearing the flints from the ploughed fields.

In the Square there were three shops. The butcher had a slaughter-house at the rear. My father's grocery and general store, with drapery in a small part of it, adjoined the then post office, which was run by my grandmother and my aunt. My father was the postmaster, since the ladies at that time were not acceptable in that role. Opposite the blacksmith's forge there was a bakery where at Christmas time the villagers could take their dinners to be cooked. It was demolished in the 1950s. There were three brothers named Brown: Ted the blacksmith, Arthur, a greengrocer who grew most of his produce on his smallholding adjoining his wooden shop, and Walter who had a cycle shop.

In the High Street a Mr Tyler was a saddler and harnessmaker, and in his shop he had a life sized wooden horse which was quite a startling sight with its glaring glass eyes. His wife had a small shop selling among other things dog leads, and baskets which were made by a blind man in Worthing. Next door was a shoe and repair shop where three young men were employed, and further on was a tailor, Mr Mills, who made breeches for the jockey lads, and an ironmonger.

There was a coal merchant with his coalyard in Cross Lane, and Ockenden's Timber Yard up at Nepcote, where six out of the seven boys in the family worked in the firm; they were also undertakers, builders and decorators. Many of the flint walls in the district were built and maintained by this firm.

Often shops were originally the front parlours of houses, as was the first post office, and as many were family businesses it was quite usual for a wife to be in the desk and keeping the books, as they did in the grocer's and butcher's.

In 1934 four shops with living accommodation were built opposite The Black Horse public house; a fishmonger and greengrocery, a butcher, a hairdresser and a cafe. There was a private car hire service (one car) run from what was part of the stables of the Village House Hotel, and where you could take your wireless accumulators to be recharged – a definite must by the early 1930s!'

LANCING IN THE 1930s AND 1940s

'As a child in the 1930s I often used to visit my grandparents who lived in a large house (now demolished and replaced by block of flats) near Lancing station. My grandfather, Charles Frederick Pycroft, ran Belvedere Nurseries, a substantial market garden business. I remember helping him at the end of the day when picking was finished, to carry the baskets of fruit and vegetables across the road to the station. They were loaded onto the train for overnight despatch to Covent Garden. Next day we collected the empty baskets to be filled again.

When the lord of the manor died there were heavy death duties to be paid and the family sold off a lot of land in Lancing. My grandfather was one of a small consortium who bought some of the land, and houses for the railway workers who moved into the village in large numbers in the 1930s were built on it. One of the roads, Belvedere Avenue, was named after my grandfather's nurseries.'

'In 1929 my husband was among several hundred railway workers transferred from Ashford in Kent to Lancing. There were few houses to let here, so men had to go into lodgings while the wives waited for houses to be built, the men coming home for weekends. Houses were built in Myrtle Road, Wembley and Anweir Avenues and later in First, Second, etc., Avenues. All the land had previously been market gardens or orchards with thousands of daffodils under the trees, so beautiful in the spring.

Until 1930, Lancing had a population of under 2,000, most of whom were employed in market gardening. When we moved here, the railway company paid our removal expenses and granted us 100% mortgages. The company then deducted £1 5s 0d each week from the men's wages as mortgage repayments. Many of the older residents resented our invasion of their quiet village, and told us so. I protested to one lady who complained that we had not chosen to come, but had been sent, to which she replied, "But they need not have sent you here!"

In 1930 North Road had only four small shops in it, all on the left going north. One, the shoe repairer's, has only recently closed after three generations in the same family. Opposite these shops was the school consisting of three classrooms for children up to eight years of age. An older school (now the church hall) was situated in North Lancing near the church. There were acres of glasshouses and fields of chrysanthemums and the Luxor Cinema (now a carpet store) was built on a field in which onions were always grown. In those days Boundstone Lane was very picturesque with the trees meeting overhead, the only houses being four cottages near Crowshaw recreation ground which are still there today. Where Warren Court now stands there were huge trees and a children's heart hospital, a branch of the Great Ormond Street Children's Hospital in London.'

'My husband's parents lived in Lancing during the war and we used to come from Surrey to stay whenever we could. We were sure of getting a good night's sleep in Lancing! When we arrived at the station the staff always asked us where we were going to stay. In those days the level crossing gates were operated by hand by a man turning a huge wheel. Defences of barbed wire and concrete blocks were all along the seafront; traces of the concrete blocks can still be seen today.

My parents in law had one of the first beach huts built in Lancing opposite Lancing Park. This was about 1944. It was constructed from ammunition boxes and unlike many other beach huts it survived the hurricane of 1987 and is still used by members of the family.

My mother in law bought our rations at the general store, Potter Baileys, and at the local bakery, Virginia's, where queues would form when something good was on offer. The return fare from Lancing to Worthing was sevenpence.

It was here, one Christmas after the war, I first saw television. It was Bertram Mills' Christmas Circus and I remember the little ones looking round the back of the set to try to discover where the elephants had gone!'

'When I first came to West Sussex in 1948 from Manchester, I was impressed with the cleanliness of the county, especially Worthing, where the beaches were swept clean of seaweed every day after high tide: the local farmers came down with horses and carts and gathered up the seaweed for manure.

An uncle who had just come back from India settled in Lancing as his son was at Lancing College. Lancing was a sleepy village in those days and our uncle loved to take us up on the Downs: I thought it was heaven! Bicycles were the means of getting about, and we often cycled to Bramber castle and even as far as Storrington along winding country lanes. "Brooklands" was an infill tip, and I watched it being slowly transformed into a lake. On Sundays you could not buy anything in the food line. They were much stricter here than in Manchester. If you arrived on holiday on Saturday night and wished to buy a loaf of bread or a packet of crackers on the Sunday, no shopkeeper would break the law to sell them to you.

Just after the war Lancing had two cinemas. Seats cost one shilling and sixpence. People generally walked there, and to the local dances. The highlight of the year for us was the Christmas pantomime put on by Lancing Repertory Players (an amateur company, still flourishing). Reg Green, the manager of a local store, always played the Dame and slipped in lots of references to local people. Everyone went along to find out if they were mentioned! At Christmas a shop near the station used to sell branches cut from Christmas trees at sixpence each. They were all laid out against the station fence. I remember buying three and carrying them home on the top of the pram with my two babies inside. I wired the branches together to make a tree six feet tall which looked very grand and expensive.

The summer carnival was an annual event with lots of floats – the dramatic society entered one, and the students from Worthing Hospital; the coalman's cart was there and a lady in pony and trap. The carnival procession was preceded by a large banner and people collected money from the watching crowds – for charity, of course.'

GORING-BY-SEA AND FERRING

'Born at Goring-by-Sea in 1906, I remember going to school aged five years and sometimes seeing a man playing an organ with a monkey prancing about on top which would take pennies when offered. There was also a muffin man, with muffins covered with a baize cloth on a tray on his head. Roads were safe in those days with only an occasional horse and cart.

My family were farmers and market gardeners. Produce from farms and gardens went to Brighton market once a week by horse and cart, starting at 4 pm for market at 5 am. Grapes went by train to Covent Garden and we understood that some went to the royal table. The few acres of asparagus were manured with seaweed brought from the shore, heavy loads of which were pulled up the beach by beautiful shire horses.'

'Until comparatively recently Ferring was composed of a very few cottages surrounding the Saxon church, with scattered farms, larger houses and more cottages further afield – and elm trees. Before the Second World War the practice began of building holiday homes here, often little more than shacks, but mostly the intensive building was done post war.

What a change it must be to the tranquil, far-away-from-it-all piece of rural Sussex it once was, with no electricity and consequently no street lights, no main drains and no public transport – although the trains did pass behind the village. In fact, a mile and a half from the nearest station, residents could hear the call "Goring-by-Sea, Goring-by-Sea" as the train pulled in there. How quiet it used to be! Except for the rooks. They were a noisy nuisance once, so much so that each autumn a rook shoot was organised to keep the numbers under control. Many a local household had, if not four and twenty, quite a number of black birds in a pie at that time each year. Another local practice was to go wooding along the seashore to collect the drift-wood for fires.

Fishing, farming and gardening were the main occupations of the village men and the women remember taking meals to the labourers in the fields, especially at harvest time. Cattle roamed along the lanes, which were rough tracks made from chalk from the pits on Highdown or gravel from the nearby quarry.

The Hon Mrs Lionel Guest had a herd of pedigree Jersey cows, all milk being bought direct from the farms and often warm. To hear the old residents talk of the area they knew as children, it seems a place remote and quiet. So remote and quiet that the Prince of Wales, before becoming briefly Edward VIII, rented a house in the village to entertain his current lady friend Mrs Dudley Ward.'

SELSEY TO THE 1950s

'Of disasters we have fortunately had only one in Selsey. In the year 1876 about 700 acres of land had been reclaimed from Pagham Harbour by the building of an embankment 407 yards long. The cost of maintenance of the sluices etc amounted to several hundreds of pounds a year. Then, for the whole of the week previous to the 15th December 1910, great storms and gales raged round the coast. At 10 pm on the 15th the storm reached its height and suddenly, with a roar which could be heard miles away, the embankment broke, making a breach 30 to 40 yards wide, flooding 2,000 acres in less than an hour.

The water rushed inland and poured a torrent half a mile wide across farms three miles from the western coast. There it joined, through a sluice gate, with an arm of the sea which had flooded in from the east and was only prevented from cutting Selsey completely

18

off by the narrow dyke which formed the Ferry. Even here the water was over the ankles of persons wishing to enter or leave the village. A writer in the *Daily News* (19th Dec 1910) says, "The sea has conquered once again, and since Friday, Selsey has been an island in the English Channel."

This flood was a great catastrophe and ruined and altered a great deal of arable and pasture land. Many persons had narrow escapes from drowning and many cottages were damaged (the population at this time was about 1,500). The Hundred of Manhood and Selsey Tramway track for some two miles was submerged, and for about four months the stage coach met passengers at the point where the track was submerged, took them by road to the point where the track emerged again and the passengers again joined the tramway.

Vegetables and fruit at Selsey were almost entirely home produced, with meat available in this fashion. Someone, say Mr Arnell, wished to kill a pig. Therefore Mr Arnell notified the general store (which was also the butcher's shop) and after keeping a joint himself, the villagers that week purchased pork. The next week perhaps, Farmer Rushbridge killed a bullock, and the same process was repeated. This rotary system prevented too much meat from being available. There was no refrigeration, and the pork had to be smoked and the beef salted if it was not to be eaten at once.

No spiritous drinks could be obtained in the village and no off-licences existed so many of the housewives brewed their own beer from malt and hops. This, according to many old people was a far superior drink to the beer sold today.

There were two bakeries in the village, one behind the shop and the other in the cellar of The Neptune. The bread was taken to the general stores for sale.

Clothes were very often bought from mail-order houses after being chosen from catalogues. Sometimes the carter brought them or the material on approval from Chichester. A great many dresses, pinafores and children's clothes were made at home.

The cottages, as can be seen from those that remain, were rather dark because of the low-hanging thatch and the rooms were small. In spite of this, large families were brought up in them (ten or twelve children being quite a common number).

Up to about 1910 there were very few shops and everything that could not be obtained in Selsey came in via the carter or through the post.

Wages were very low, sometimes only about eleven shillings per week, but vegetables were home grown and many people kept pigs and chickens and caught rabbits. Until 1898 there was no doctor available in the village, the nearest being four miles away in

Sidlesham. In 1898 Dr Eldred came as the first Selsey doctor.

Prior to 1897 coal deliveries were by sea. The barge tied up at the beach and as soon as it arrived all available men ran down to the beach to unload. The coal was taken round to the cottages by cart and shot out at the gate and then taken in bucket by bucket. Even house removals were sometimes done by sea.'

MIDHURST BEFORE THE FIRST WORLD WAR

'Mr Goldring's family moved to Midhurst from London in 1901 when he was four. His father opened a shop in the town selling vegetables, flowers, seeds etc. Because roads were made only of local stone flattened by a steam roller there was mud everywhere. Behind West Street there was a slaughterhouse and a brewery. As there was no drainage all the dirty water drained down to the pond. Cattle were driven along the road to the slaughterhouse, adding to the mess left by the horses. The local gas works by the wharf supplied gas for homes and street lighting. There were constant smells from all these buildings. The family took water from a well in the yard, his father pumping it up to a cistern in the house. If someone was ill deep straw would be put down in the road so that the clatter of hooves and carts was muffled.

A bicycle was essential if you had no horse and there were three cycle shops in the town. One shop owner – Matt Burnet – was terrified of fire so he slept all day and worked at night. If you wanted your bike mended, you left it outside his house and picked it up in the morning!

All the local tradesmen had horses and carts as did the postmen. Milkmen had floats carrying churns and householders provided jugs to be filled by various sized measures. The fire engine was drawn by three horses which had to be fetched from different stables. After the street alarm sounded it could take half an hour for the horses to be harnessed etc. As a result fires in the surrounding villages usually burned out by the time the brigade arrived.

Children played in the streets with whip tops, hoops and marbles. Mr Goldring remembered breaking a shop window once with his top.

Local pubs opened at 6 am till late at night. Shopkeepers stayed open until 10 pm and welcomed customers as they left the pubs. The Bricklayers Arms had a quoits pitch with heavy steel rings.

Dr Bailey had a De Dion Bouton car and employed a chauffeur to drive him out to the villages. Goodwood Week was the highlight of the year when the town was crowded with vehicles. Cabs, victorias, four in hands (these would have had a groom and a manservant complete with horn) – in fact anything which would carry people to the races, a huge social occasion. Local children wrote down car numbers as they were still a novelty. The Royal Train went through Midhurst station en route for Singleton.

The Rev Frank Tatchell, Vicar of Midhurst from 1906–1935 was a very eccentric character. His sermons rarely lasted more than three minutes. Instead he paid a curate £100 a year to take the services while he went travelling, taking only an umbrella and a small black bag (he bought new clothes when necessary rather than carry them). He provided steel-tipped clogs for poor local children and boots for tramps. He would also invite tramps and middle class citizens to dinner at the rectory together. He created a garden at the back of his house and invited everyone to use it. He had a bandstand erected at Closewalks, a local park, and put in seats, statues and even peacocks for people to enjoy. He sent all the school teachers to Paris for a week's holiday because he believed everyone should travel. He was popular with some people and unpopular with others, but he was definitely one of the town's benefactors.'

LOWER BEEDING

'In the village of Lower Beeding in the early 1900s the church choir played a very large part in village life. In the 1920s girls were actually admitted to the choir, along with the boys and men – to the horror apparently of one particular resident! The vicar at that time (who was in fact there for over 30 years) was very musical and encouraged the choir to enter competitions as far afield as Bognor.

There were three large estates in the village at that time and the families kept a great number of staff, who, of course, attended church twice every Sunday. This often entailed a walk of a mile and a half each way. When walking to church or school the village children would be expected to bow or curtsy to any members of the gentry.

On Christmas night at South Lodge (one of the large estates) all the workers were summoned to the big house where each was given a present and refreshments. This was followed by music and dancing and they were led in such dances as Sir Roger de Coverley by the two daughters of the house. One can imagine the merriment at such an occasion. Another highlight was a day trip to Brighton once a year in an open charabanc, with a canvas hood to put up should the weather be inclement.

There were many flourishing activities in the village. The stoolball team played every Thursday afternoon and an open waggon conveyed the team to surrounding villages when playing away. There was folk dancing once a week and of course Scout, Brownie and Guide troops. A whist drive and dance was held in the village hall each week during the winter and there was always a Fancy Dress Dance at Christmas time.

As with the present day, the WI of course has played a major role in village life in Lower Beeding, where it has flourished since 1918.'

HENLEY COMMON IN THE 1920s

'I am over 70 years of age now, and many of my early childhood memories are centred around Henley Common, about two miles north of Midhurst. My maternal grandmother lived there, where her family by the name of Cole firstly managed the forge. They ran a pony and trap business, mainly as a "taxi" service, especially when the Edward VII Sanatorium was built on top of the hill and many visitors needed transport from Haslemere station. Goodwood Races was also a very busy time for them.

I well remember the old workhouse at the bottom of Budgenor Hill, Easebourne, where the old men used to lean over the wall hoping passers-by would drop a penny or two into their caps. If a married couple finished up there, the rule was that they had to live in separate wards, men in one place, women in another, which even as a child always seemed to me to be very heartless.

In the little hamlet of Henley, there was a mission hall served by a lay preacher, Mr C Willcock. I believe the foundation stone was laid in 1885 (it was converted to a private dwelling in 1966). He lived a very frugal and spartan life, and walked miles through the woods tending his scattered flock and visiting the charcoal burners. Even in the depth of freezing cold winters he would have no food cooked on a Sunday because "it was the Lord's Day".

Later, my grandmother moved across the common to an old cottage, one of a pair, with a pond outside. As was usual in those days, the front door opened straight into the living room, with a big black coal range on which all the cooking was done, with a bread oven. Leading from this was the dairy, with a long marble slab on which the milk was kept, where butter was churned and cheese made, with that lingering never-to-be-forgotten slightly sour lactic smell. No fridges in those days, of course. A pig was always kept in the sty outside so there was usually bacon and hams hanging from the ceiling, and water was drawn in a bucket from the outside well.

I was one of three sisters and I remember it as an enormous treat to go down for, say, Easter weekend, sleeping on the floor upstairs on a big mattress, and waking up to find an Easter egg in a china eggcup left for each of us by the bed.

I suppose I was then about five or six. Bliss, eating chocolate *before* breakfast!

To me the setting was idyllic, but looking back I can see there were many hardships which the older folk had to cope with, and certainly life for them was far from being a bed of roses.'

WEST CHILTINGTON IN THE 1950s

'We came to live in West Chiltington in 1958, after exploring Dell Quay and Graffham. Our area (known as Roundabout) was then in Storrington parish, separated from the "Old Village" by more than a mile of twisting lanes and sunken hollows (hollow-ways). There were very few houses along this road except for those at The Common. This was no longer a common, although one elderly local man remembered as a child seeing flocks of sheep driven across it to the famous Findon Sheep Fair; an old lady used to turn her geese out to graze in the morning and call them back in the evening; and the locals were allowed to skate on Monkhead Pond during severe winters. Hayling Pond near the church was drained soon after we arrived, and our whole area is now completely developed.

We "inherited" a gardener, a real countryman, who could turn his hand to anything. He was with us for three years until his death, and only then did we learn that he had had a wooden leg. He helped us to win prizes at the local Flower Show, which in those days had a separate section for entries from households with a gardener.

Those were the days of open log fires and chimney sweeps, the village blacksmith and travelling knife grinders. French onion sellers arrived on bicycles, and "carpet men" from Morocco would appear at the front door with their rugs and woven goods.

One day we returned from shopping to discover a Canadian man and woman walking round our garden. He told us that he had been a soldier billeted in our house during the war, and that he wanted his wife to see it. Canadian soldiers had been camped in Monkmead Woods, which in 1958 was still known as The Camp, and the concrete plinths on which the army huts were built are still in existence. Several dug-outs remained (the last one was only recently covered up and made safe), and large amounts of small arms ammunition were scattered around, to be discovered in later years by boys with metal detectors. I understand the soldiers camped in the woods along Nyetimber Lane were Polish. In among the lilies of the valley, azaleas and rhododendrons was a large water tank, built high on stilts, which was removed soon afterwards.

It was easy to get to London in those days. There was an hourly bus service to Pulborough station, and the return fare to London was only ten shillings. There were just three stops on the fast line to Victoria – Horsham, Dorking and Sutton – but Beeching and the expansion of Gatwick Airport sadly put an end to that comfortable journey. The station was beautifully maintained, with real fires in the waiting rooms and immaculate flower beds. A weekly cattle market was held just beside it.

In those days I knew every car (and dog) in the neighbourhood. Females could walk the lanes safely at night, the only fright being from ghostly swooping barn owls or bats. The roads were excellent – well surfaced, with little traffic and courteous drivers. We drove at a leisurely pace along the West Sussex lanes, enjoying the peaceful downland countryside. The corn was still being harvested in stooks, and farmworkers layered the hedgerows painstakingly by hand. They all wore corduroy trousers which were strapped tightly below the knees to prevent rats from gaining access inside the trouser legs!

I have fond memories of the Storrington to Amberley road where I learned to drive and could safely practise a hill start. I would not dare to, there, nowadays!'

EAST GRINSTEAD IN THE 1920s

'I was born in London, but came to East Grinstead in 1926. My father, a photographer, had bought a business here. Most of his work was done in the studio but he would go to people's houses, sometimes several miles away. He rode a push bike with his wooden tripod strapped to the cross bar, and his camera on the carrier. We lived in a "modern" three bedroom semi for which my father paid £800. Mr Broad, the farmer, delivered milk, dipping a copper measure into the churns on the back of his pony and trap. Mr Elphick delivered paraffin for the oil stove used to heat the landing, and the Rippingill oil stove my mother used instead of the coal range. Mr Ledword delivered bread and cakes in a covered hand-pushed baker's cart.

I attended the old fashioned elementary school. It was about a mile from my home and we did the trip four times a day; no school dinners then. The infants were in one building with the lavatories in a block in the corner of the playground, the one with the lock being teacher's. Our teacher Miss Day, a kindly little person, taught us well. She had her own form of punishment. Too noisy, you spent ten minutes in the corner with a rattle; too much talking, and you wore a large "tongue" round your neck for the rest of the session.

Walking home from school we would stop at Stennings timber yard, to watch the tree trunks being unloaded from the carts drawn by up to four shire horses. Sometimes the men would be sawing up the trunks into planks, with large saws. Nearby was a small forge, where we would see the horses being shod. At the top of our road was a pottery – nothing very fancy, mainly flower pots of different sizes. The workshop was in the basement, and the three Foster brothers lived in the house looked after by their sister. We were allowed to stand and watch the pots being made provided we did not talk.

Thursday was market day. The cattle and sheep would be walked into the market in Cantalupe Road where they would be put in covered pens. Sometimes you could see their heads looking over the wall as you walked past.

In those days East Grinstead was connected by rail north to London and south to Brighton via Lewes while another line ran west to east from Three Bridges to Tunbridge Wells. The only line left is the London one.'

SIDLESHAM AND THE LAND SETTLEMENT

'In the 1930s Sidlesham (twelve miles in circumference) was sparsely populated and was mostly farming land.

In the north of England and Wales the coal miners were out of work and their families were desperate, so farmland was purchased by the Ministry of Agriculture to provide smallholdings for these men. Three farms were bought in Sidlesham and on these 40 houses were built with approximately four acres of land each. The men came from areas in Durham, Northumberland and Wales. They lived in large huts for a year, which were later used for social and office purposes. During this time they were trained in pig and chicken rearing, greenhouse produce and soft fruit growing. At the end of that twelve months their families started arriving to begin living in their new homes.

The village all-age (five to 14 years) council school, though adequate for some 130 local children, had to be extended to serve some 300 to 350 children. Thus the first glass-fronted classrooms were built, mains water supply was brought three-quarters of a mile instead of pumped water from wells and flush toilets were installed. More pupils meant more teachers were needed, central heating was put in and the playing field was extended. The provision of school dinners brought an inspection visit from the Minister of Education. In the classrooms, North and South were brought together with a variety of different dialects.

The County Committee of the WIs were at the forefront in making the newcomers feel welcome by arranging talks and craft sessions. A

25

'North & South' social by the Sidlesham WI was an hilarious evening still remembered. Children and grandchildren still make Sussex their home and no longer is the village inbred.

Over the years horticulture and agriculture have had many changes and no longer is there pig and chicken rearing or soft fruit growing but a concentration on greenhouse crops sprang up.

Inter-marriage took place, and after the Second World War returning servicemen with gratuities took over some of the holdings, bringing many new talents, but still keeping Sidlesham a green belt in the middle of the Manhood Peninsula.'

DOWN THE STREET

Walk down any village street and you would probably find that mainstay of village life, the post office and general stores. These shops had a wonderful smell all their own and were the heart of the community where gossip and assistance were to be found as well as food and drink. A little further on might be the local pub, with the village policeman keeping an eye on things. If it was market day locally, of course, cattle and sheep would throng the roads and lanes. And every village had its characters, fondly remembered, and its customs, such as 'rough music'! Sadly, in the 1920s and 1930s, you would also have come across the 'roaders', trudging from one workhouse to another for a bed for the night.

THE VILLAGE PUB

'Visiting my grandparents in the 1930s was quite an adventure. Once a month, on a Sunday, when there was a full moon so that we could see to walk home (no street lights), we set off early in the afternoon and walked for about a mile and a half to the top of the hill where we caught a bus to Milland church. Sometimes it failed to come along so we then had to walk for about half an hour.

The church was hidden in the trees, as was the small old church also in the churchyard. We walked to the gate in the fence, through a small copse then down the flight of stone steps to The Hollow, a lane with high banks leading to the road. On the way Father would point out birds' nests, squirrels, small mice and other wildlife, it was a game to see who spotted them first. At the end of the lane there was the loud thump, thump of the ram which pumped water up to the big house; no mains water here.

It was a short walk to The Volunteer Arms, a big rambling place. The kitchen was dark. Wooden shutters covered the window at night and the room was lit by a hanging oil lamp. The black coal range was used for cooking, especially the delicious scones my grandmother made for our tea, spread with tasty farm butter. In the centre was a white scrubbed table, at the side a dark dresser which held crockery, white with a gold band. The chairs were all wooden, some had a thin cushion on them.

The beer was kept in barrels in the cellar leading down steps from the kitchen, and was brought up, a glass at a time, to the bar through a stable half-door in the kitchen. If there were not too many customers, Grandfather would sit in the kitchen until he heard a shout of, "Giles, another 'un please", then off he went down the steps.

The bar was a long room, floor and tables scrubbed white. Customers sat on forms or on a few chairs by the fire. Another room entered through a door in the porch was called the smoking room. This was used by ladies, usually strangers, as it "was not done" for a lady to drink in the bar. This room was small and had high-backed seats like pews. A door led into the kitchen and drinks were usually served that way.

The house had two flights of stairs, one by the front door which was hardly ever used, and the other led from the kitchen and had a twist in the middle just before the top which was the club room, used occasionally for meetings. The bedrooms led from this room. Underneath the kitchen stairs was the larder and from the other side a door led into the scullery which had a large sink and a brick copper. The bowl in the sink had a handle so that water could be dipped from the copper. The floor was brick. There was also a mangle, buckets and other utensils for washing. When the farmer watered his animals the water in the tap dwindled to a trickle and sometimes stopped altogether. The lavatory was a wooden shed in the garden; buckets under the wooden bench seat were emptied through a door at the back.'

THE VILLAGE SHOP

'It is said that my great grandfather was quite a wealthy man who had his own carriage and pair, and owned a grocery business in Worthing, but was a gambler and lost it in a game of cards.

My grandfather came to Findon about 1873 and started his grocery and general store in a small shop in The Square. He eventually moved to one of a pair of cottages nearby, with his shop adjoining. The front parlour of the house was turned into the post office. The public telephone box was inside the office and large enough for a person to be seated when phoning. Over the years the grocery shop has been considerably enlarged, and when the cottage was taken in it was found that the walls were of wattle, daub and horsehair.

My father took over the business in the early 1900s. No goods were packaged as they are today. Sugar was in hessian sacks and had to be weighed and put into different coloured bags, or pokes, eg yellow bags for demerara. Dried fruit, haricot and butter beans, split peas and lentils, rice and tapioca were also loose and had to be weighed out. Tea came in large chests made of plywood. The only machine was the cash register. All the bacon rashers were cut by hand, the rind being removed by a swift stroke of the knife. Biscuits were kept in tins with glass-topped lids, and broken biscuits could be bought for a few pence. Spices were always sold whole and gave the shop that particularly lovely smell. There were no refrigerators of course, but a large cellar which ran under the house was used for storing bacon and cheese.

Ginger beer was sold in stone bottles and fizzy lemonade was in glass bottles with a glass marble in the top, which you had to push down with your thumb to "open" the bottle.

There were chairs at the counters for the customers to use when selecting their requirements or giving their orders, to be delivered by errand boys on their weighty bicycles with the high-fronted baskets. Sawdust was spread on the floor, which was swept up and replaced with fresh every night from the local sawmill.

Treacle was kept in casks and customers brought their own jamjars to be filled. One day the carrier arrived after the shop had closed for lunch; he tried to offload the cask on his own, but it slipped, rolled across the road, hit the wall opposite and broke. The children returning to school after lunch had a high time walking in the treacle and dipping their fingers, and copious amounts of sand, sawdust and straw had to be used to clear it.

Two men, besides my father, served behind the counters, and one woman. One man drove the van – a very early Ford – to get orders from such outlying places as Myrtlegrove, and then delivering them. One other woman was in the desk as book-keeper.

There was a carrier's cart which plied between the villages, and later a motor van. Parcels from Worthing were brought by the Southdown bus and left at the shop for collection. Bookings for the bus were made in the shop, and morning newspapers were also sold there till after the Second World War.'

Emily Mant at the door of her Post Office Stores in Birdham in about 1900. Shops like this were at the heart of every village, open all hours for goods, gossip and advice.

'On leaving school in the 1940s I started my first job at our local village shop in Slindon, as a trainee book-keeper, starting work at 8.30 am until 5.30 pm with a half day on a Saturday, and no Sunday opening. I soon found, however, that I was expected to do certain other work such as serving customers from behind the counter and also assembling orders to be delivered the following day by a van driver. Looking back I recall the way different commodities were packaged, for instance granulated, demerara and soft brown sugar came in one cwt and two cwt sacks and had to be weighed on the shop scales, first put in special sugar bags and then tied with string, this being one of the first jobs to learn. The Grocer's Knot was one thing I never mastered, as I always seemed to get it back to front!

Most other items that were sold had to be weighed from bulk – flour, rice, sago, tapioca, all kinds of beans and peas. Dried fruit all came in bulk and was weighed according to the customer's requirements. I remember clearly during the summer months being stung many times by wasps as the dried fruit was always kept in drawers and attracted them. The worst ones of the dried fruit range were the sticky dates and glacé cherries.

All bacon came in what was called "sides", which is half a pig, and was hung in a large safe to protect it from flies as there were no cold counters or refrigeration when I started work. All rashers and bacon joints were cut from the sides as needed and wrapped in greaseproof paper – in fact nothing was pre-packed. The main cheeses came in wooden crates and weighed 60 lbs. The cheese was covered in waxed muslin which had to be removed before the cheese could be cut with a special cheese wire to the weight the customer required. Butter came in 56 lb blocks in wooden boxes mainly from New Zealand. I remember the fernleaf emblem marked on all boxes. After removing butter from the wooden box it was placed on to a heavy slab of thick slate known as a butter block. Then the butter was cut with wooden butter pats and patted into weight and shape ready for sale. Pure lard came as did the butter but was cut with a special lard knife.

Biscuits were delivered to the shop in square tins all weighing ten to twelve pounds. The biscuits were all loose and had to be weighed and bagged in half pounds and pounds. Tins were charged at two shillings each and had to be returned to the manufacturer when empty. Sweets were mainly loose and were stored in tall glass jars, all having to be weighed. There were a few selections of bars of chocolates, dairy milk, nut chocolate and Mars bars but nothing on today's standards. All types of spices, namely pepper, mixed herbs, cloves etc were weighed in a special "cone" which was made out of greaseproof paper. Items like candles were sold loose by the dozen in two sizes and were a big seller as was paraffin oil. All this seems a far cry from my original book-keeping but I still had to return to this as the need arose, which was often.

Although the war had finished in late 1945, food rationing still carried on for a considerable time, so this meant another of my tasks was to count the food coupons ready to be sent monthly to the local food office in Chichester.'

'I came to Loxwood in 1911 with my parents and sister, and we ran the local general stores. Bread was made by an employed baker in the old fashioned bread oven, using faggots for heating. He came after leaving school at 14 and stayed until he was about 70. In those days bread sold at twopence a loaf and penny lardy rolls were 13 for a shilling. Delivery of groceries in the surrounding villages was by horse and cart, later replaced by a delivery van.

Once a customer came in for carbide for his cycle lamp. As it was kept in a safe place at the rear of the shop, Dad shouted for a light, meaning a torch. Unfortunately, at the age of seven I took matches and unbeknown to Dad, struck one. The result was a big explosion. Dad was injured in the face, but his glasses saved his sight, and I lost my eyebrows – I am happy to say they grew again!'

'In her day Wivelsfield's postmistress, Connie, as she was known by one and all, was a veritable institution. Her father was the church verger and a room in the verger's cottage served as a sub post office and shop. The original post box in the cottage wall is still in use. No other post office could ever have had such a delightful "mistress" nor, I am sure, such a fascinating array of goods for sale. There were sweets and stationery, Brasso, biscuits, buttons, darning wool, shoe polish and, in season, Easter eggs, tops, marbles, hoops, skipping ropes and fireworks.

Connie was never in a hurry and nothing was too much trouble – she devoted great care and attention to serving even her youngest customers, especially when they were faced with the impossible dilemma of whether to buy a ha'penny sherbet dab or ten aniseed balls.

A red-brick path through a little garden took one up to the door. Stooping through the doorway a veritable Aladdin's cave opened up before one's eyes. Ancient beams were only a few inches above one's head, everything had an enchanted look in the half-light which filtered through the window. This window also did service as "shop window" and was always piled high with specimens of Connie's choicest merchandise.

As well as the post office counter there was another containing all the farthing and halfpenny goodies. Monster bottles of humbugs, mini bottles of ink, jostled for the best positions on the shelves above, with books and dolls. Suspended from strategically placed hooks were cards of hair slides, tubes of glue, shoe laces, hooks & eyes, pencils and sharpeners and thimbles. Safety pins hung in glittering festoons. When Boat Race day came round Connie always had a delightful choice of "favours". In those days, in the weeks preceding the race, most people wore "their" crew's colour – buttonhole-sized pairs of oars, rosettes, wool dollies, etc in light or dark blue and much store was set on the result of the race.

From September to November there was yet another counter with the most exciting and, to some, vaguely alarming, selection of fireworks, ranging from a ha'penny to tuppence in price. Then we spent our weekly pennies on fireworks instead of sweets and constantly gloated over the growing hoard – surprisingly they still "went off" on the 5th.

On winter afternoons, when the frail light could no longer penetrate the secret places of the shop, an oil lamp was lit and hung from one of the beams. The flame flickered and leapt every time the shop door opened, casting fearsome shadows around the walls, but Connie's reassuring presence emerging from a door at the other end of the shop dispelled our worst imaginings.

Connie knew us all and shared in our joys and sorrows. Time, of course, pursued its relentless way; Connie's father died at a ripe old age, a new verger had to have the cottage and Connie moved away from the village shortly after the Second World War. Another "institution" passed into the history books.'

THE LOCAL BOBBY

'From 1924 to 1939 my brother was the local policeman at Sullington – a "Jack of all Trades" and he was on duty for 24 hours a day. However small the problem, he was always there. The telephone rang constantly (usually answered by his wife), messages taken and passed on. On one occasion I remember, a distraught wife called – she had just learned that her husband was seeing another woman, and she asked what should she do. Tongue in cheek, she was told to give him something to remember, so when the errant husband returned she did just that and hit him on the head with a frying pan and knocked him out. She telephoned the policeman again. What should she do, she enquired, she felt sure she had killed him. On examination however, there was no real damage done. The marriage mended and, as they say, they lived happily ever after.

Although the policeman had been on duty sometimes all night, he was often called out to investigate a robbery, or an accident (usually on a push bike). He also took messages to people who had no telephone, from relatives in hospital.

He also accompanied the local nurse or midwife when they were called out urgently during the night, very often to families living on the South Downs. Here again, the only transport available to him was a push bike. He was everybody's friend.'

'The policeman at Loxwood, Mr Boys, was well known. Any drunks and he would put them in a wheelbarrow and tip them over the Sussex border into Surrey.'

THE WORKHOUSE AND THE 'ROADERS'

'My earliest memories are of the late 1920s. One in particular made a great impression on me. Just down the road from us at Horsham was the workhouse. This was a place where poor people with no homes could get a bed for the night in return for an hour or two's work the next morning (usually in the vegetable gardens). One cold winter evening I remember my father brought a man and his wife and two little girls of about seven and eight to our house for a warm up and a cup of tea, while they waited for the workhouse to open at six o'clock. This poor little family had trudged many miles that day, the man looking for work. They were walking from one workhouse to the next, going all over the country. We were not at all rich but I felt like a millionaire compared to them.'

'Tramps were regular visitors at our house at Cuckfield, on their way for a night in the workhouse. They knew a kettle was kept on the kitchen range, so they would ask for hot water in their can, then for a "pinch of tea". If the tramps had any money they had to pay for their night's stay, so they wrapped cash in a rag and hid it before reporting to the workhouse. Hopefully they retrieved it the following day, but if they were ill or detained the money was sometimes found by others.'

'My father had to retire early from the Indian Army owing to illness, so we decided it would be fun to run a tea shop. We found just what we were looking for on the old A27 at Bosham – it was called The Nutshell.

During our time there in the 1940s we were visited by quite a lot of tramps who wanted hot water for their tea.

One of the first was an auburn-haired boy in his early twenties; he asked if he could do some gardening in return for a meal. Father said "Yes" so he got going. It turned out that he had been a Bevin Boy and had worked in the coal mines during the last two years of the war. The darkness and confined space had worried him so much that he decided he could never be shut in again and took to the roads. He had lunch with us and during the conversation it turned out that he had been at a very well known public school – a real gentleman of the road!

Another favourite of ours was an old man with a long white beard; he always wore black and carried his belongings in a little cart. He sat and drank his tea in the garden before moving on again. He visited us once a year and on the third visit he asked my mother if she would be kind enough to lend him ten shillings as he wanted to go over to the Isle of Wight to see his son. She gave it to him, never expecting to see it again. The spring came and with it came the old man who took a ten shilling note out of his pocket and said, "Thank you, ma'am, for lending it to me." Mother said that it was all right and he could keep it but he insisted that she had it back, saying that if she didn't want it would she please put it in a charity box, preferably one for children.

The third one was very unusual. I was coming along the A27 very late at night and happened to look down a lane on the other side of the road. About halfway down was a silver cylinder, pointed at both ends; it stood on four legs, and a blue light shone from halfway down, the whole thing shining in the moonlight. At this particular time UFOs were very much in the news. This must be one, I thought, or if it wasn't I felt it had no business to be there. I was almost home so when I got in I rang the police. They came in a flash – and I went back to see what happened. The policemen hummed and ha'd and scratched their heads, then crept down the lane – it turned out to be a tramp who lived in the contraption and pulled it around with him!'

MARKET DAY

' "M" stood for Monday and for Market Day for our village. Before daylight in winter, or seven in the morning in summer, the sound of herds of cattle and flocks of sheep being taken to Barnham market by the drovers made the roadside dwellers close all gates and block entrances, otherwise strange beasties would invade gardens! En route, the animals would have had a chance to drink from the last pond before market, some two miles away. The animals left plentiful evidence of their passing and the children walking to school had to beware, because there was punishment waiting for those who arrived with dirty boots.

On a personal note, one market day was exceptional. I was eleven years old in July 1932, when among my favourites, the calves, I saw a little bull calf tethered with three others in an iron-railed pen. I fell in love with the beautiful fringed eyes, and the white heart mark on his forehead. So I climbed into the pen and held on to his rope, and when the auctioneer took the bidding I bid one shilling for the calf. No one bid against me, and the auctioneer knocked it down to me! As there was plenty of spare milk at Grandma's dairy I was able to keep him all the summer holidays. Then I sold him and used the money for new school shoes.'

'The largest cattle market in the south was held every Monday at Barnham. Cattle from local farms were walked up the lanes and main road. Where the car park is now, in the station yard, there used to be cattle trucks from all over the South and the West Country. The cattle were then driven early Monday mornings across the road to pens in the market; and in spite of all the cattle and truck movement, and the people that poured into the village, by 6 pm there was never a bit of litter of any sort to be seen.'

CHARACTERS

'Two characters I remember well at Westbourne at the turn of the century. One was the lamplighter, who could be seen carrying a ladder over his shoulder at dusk. He filled, trimmed and lit each street lamp. Also, as the village had no newsagent, he would walk to the next village (about two and a half miles each way) and delivered the *Evening News* to almost every house in the district. Yet again he could be seen shaking a very loud bell and crying "Oh yez!" and giving out the latest messages and events.

The sexton, gravedigger and bellringer, Mr John Sims, was a burly genial man with a strong baritone voice. He gave a wonderful rendering on the bells of morning and evening hymns. He was in charge of the cemetery and would remark to anyone who passed when he was locking the gate, "Those that are in don't want to come out – those that are out don't want to get in!"

My neighbouring children had an "Uncle Ted" who was in the Royal Flying Corps, and one day he was going to fly over and wave to us. We waited expectantly at the appointed time and he flew over us, clearly visible in the open cockpit. He waved to us and we waved back, very excited. He was our hero for a long time. I wonder what he would have thought of Concorde!'

'My grandfather was occasionally called upon to help villagers write letters of a business nature. One day an old man came to see him and explained that he didn't want a letter written for him, he just needed a bit of help with his spelling.

He had recently been to a horse fair near Brighton and bought a carthorse but on getting it home and trying it in his waggon he found that the horse "would not gee" when he clicked his teeth at it. Could my grandfather please tell him how this was spelt?

Grandfather told many a tale. There was the story of the farmer's boy leading a cow on a halter and rope along the road to a neighbouring farm. The cow, suspicious of the journey, was being very recalcitrant and the boy was having a hard job to hold on to her. An elderly villager was leaning over his garden gate watching and called loudly to the boy, "If you caan 'old'er, doan you let 'er goo!" (Sound but difficult advice to follow.)

On another occasion Grandfather was coming home from Haywards Heath market and drew alongside a fellow named George from the village. He stopped and offered him a lift which was readily accepted as George was carrying a heavy sack over his shoulder. When he got into the cart he sat with the sack still on his shoulder so Grandfather said, "Put you sack down in the cart, George," to which George replied, "Ow naow Mr Baartlett, you'm kind enough to give me a ride, I'll carry me own taters!"

'One man at Loxwood would carry his boots to work so as to make them last longer.'

ROUGH MUSIC

'Rough music was performed for the last time in Camelsdale at the beginning of the First World War. This was a means of conveying to a person that the village considered that he or she had conducted themselves scandalously. Pots, pans and anything that made a noise would be banged by a crowd of villagers outside that person's home.'

'I came to West Hoathly in 1940 for the first time. Coming from Petworth, I thought what a lovely village West Hoathly was. I married in 1942 and returned to live with my mother in law at No 1, Melchbourne Villas.

One night in 1947 my brother in law and some of his mates came home and said a certain person had been moaning and telling them off because he said the boys were making too much noise outside his house. After his moaning at them for three nights, my mother in law

36

said, "Enough's enough – I'll put a stop to this moaner once and for all!". My mother went to the police with details of what she intended to do. They had no objection, but stated very firmly that it had to be carried out for three nights, at the same time each night.

She called a meeting and rallied all her supporters, and word soon got round that she was going to have a Rough Music "do". We started outside the village hall at 6.45 pm. Everyone had dustbin lids and sticks, bells, drums, trumpets, tin cans on strings, mouth organs, old saucepan lids, kettles – anything you could bang and make a noise with. I have *never* seen or heard anything like it. Mother in law led the band of musicians, as they were called, to the person's house. I think that on the two or three nights of the racket there could not have been any people staying at home, because in the end people came from Horsted Keynes, Turners Hill, Ardingly and some from Haywards Heath to join us. The third night there must have been between 200 and 300 backers.

I did smile to myself. After the Wednesday, Thursday and Friday nights' noise, the person who moaned was nowhere about to moan at the boys on Saturday night.'

CHURCH AND CHAPEL

Sunday was a special day, set apart from the working week. The vicar took an interest in the lives of his parishioners and attendance at church or chapel was expected, while children also went to Sunday school, sometimes twice during the day. This was not considered a hardship when the time for the annual Sunday school treat came around, a fondly remembered outing in the days when children rarely had a holiday outside their town or village.

EVERY SUNDAY WAS THE SAME

'I was sitting in my garden on Sunday morning when a coachload of children were held up at my gateway, delayed by a traffic jam, and I could tell they were on their way to the seaside. My thoughts went back to the Sundays my sisters, brother and I spent when we were children.

For us, every Sunday was the same. In our home, we prepared for

Sunday on Saturday, nothing was left to Sunday which could be done on Saturday. On Saturday mornings we did the vegetables. My brother cleaned our shoes for Sunday and also fetched the coal and wood in for lighting the fire, which my father did. On Saturday evening we had a bath and our long hair was brushed, plaited and tied with ribbons. Before that, we had to iron the ribbons as we never wore the same ones on Sunday as we had worn in the week. We also tacked clean collarettes on to our dresses. I always did this, as I was the eldest. In the summer my brother wore a sailor suit to Sunday school and also if we went out for a walk.

When at last Sunday arrived, after washing up the breakfast dishes we were dressed in our Sunday clothes, our hair was unplaited, brushed and tied in two bunches. When we were ready we were allowed to walk round the garden until it was time to go to Sunday school, which must have been at about ten o'clock. Sunday school was held in the weekday school. On our way we had to call for my aunt, who was a Sunday school teacher. She always made sure that we had not forgotten our prayer books and a collection for the church. I still have a prayer book which I was presented with by the vicar for good attendance at Sunday school.

After Sunday school we walked straight up to the church; we always managed to sit behind a pillar, giggling, we were so bored! We often dropped a book, making a loud clatter, and the ladies of the village would scowl at us; we were so afraid they would tell our father we would then try to behave.

We arrived home in time for lunch and had to put on pinafores to keep our dresses clean. After lunch in the spring and summer our father would take us for long walks in the countryside along the footpaths, which seemed miles, but we did enjoy those walks as father would tell us about the wildlife we saw, and told us the names of all the wild flowers. He would make us flowers from the pith from the bullrushes if we happened to come across a pond. On these walks we were never allowed to skip along or run about. We had to walk along very sedately because it was Sunday!

Sometimes, on these Sunday walks, we would call on a farmer friend, and I was always fascinated by some things he had in a small glass tank on a table by the window They were white and were called "holy bees", so that farmer informed us, because they never worked on Sundays! If we visited during the week they were going up and down in the tank but they never did on Sundays. Our friend told us that the liquid was "holy wine"; to this day I am still wondering what could have been the true explanation.'

'Sunday in our house at West Hoathly was very different from the rest of the week. We went to Sunday school, and our homework for the week was to learn the collect for the day and be ready to say it. The one I loved was in Advent which began, "Stir up, we beseech Thee, the wills of Thy faithful people". I would rush home to my mother and say, "Is everything ready for Christmas, for this is Stir up Sunday?" I hear it now at the 8 am service and it lifts my heart.

Then we all went to Evensong, walking a long way in the darkness in the winter. Sunday tea was grand – the best china and a lace-edged tablecloth, and lovely home-made bread, butter, jam and cakes. Sometimes we had a section of honey, still in the comb, such a different flavour and so thick, not like the runny stuff we buy now. We kept our own bees. We always had aunts and uncles to tea, smartly dressed in their Sunday best and very jolly. They stayed and went to church with us and then came back for a glass of home-made wine, a biscuit and music. We had a gramophone with a huge horn and lovely records. But as I got older things improved quickly and soon we were trying out the marvels of wireless – 2LO calling, and then hymns and an address. At first we had a crystal set and a "cat's whisker" (a bent wire which was used to find a good place on the crystal). We got a better set as time went on.'

THE VICAR TOOK AN INTEREST

'The vicar took a great interest in the children at the church school in North Mundham in the early 1900s. At Christmas he gave each child a warm jersey, red for girls and navy for boys. He also organised a sort of Thrift Club for the villagers for sixpence a week, and this helped to pay for boots, clothing and coal. The coal was brought up to Dell Quay by barge and farmers collected it by farm cart and delivered it to the villagers.'

'In 1909 the Young Woman's and Girls' Clubs were opened at Fernhurst for those over 14. Regular meetings were held on Thursdays from five to seven o'clock at the village hall, the weekly subscriptions being a penny and a halfpenny for the younger ones. The meetings were varied by fancy and plain needlework with music or reading, and a series of fireside talks on various subjects. The last half hour was devoted to drill and exercises.

In the winter of 1912–13 "good, hot soup" at a halfpenny a cup was sold to the schoolchildren three times a week. The number of tickets sold was 692 and the total cost £2 16s 2d.

The church also raised money for the unemployed after the First World War and found work for them draining the marsh at Kingsley Green.'

WE WERE EXPECTED TO GO TO CHURCH

'I was born in 1916 at Pallingham Cottages, Wisborough and Sunday was the high spot of the week when I was young. Sometimes my brother and I would cycle to Littlehampton, and other times in Sunday best we would walk with our mother to join the 45–50 people who packed the very tiny Bedham church where two services daily were conducted by the Fittleworth vicar. This was a great social occasion, a meeting always of the same people, and sometimes the vicar would offer us a lift home in his automobile (a very rare sight) – a treat my mother declined as being far too dangerous!'

'Church dominated Sundays at Boxgrove and Halnaker in the early 1900s. We went to services in the morning and evening and also attended Sunday school. While we were still at school the vicar, Rev Hill, died and all the children had to walk past his coffin to look at the body and pay their last respects. We always had to curtsey to the vicar and his wife if we met them in the street.

On Sunday mornings at Boxgrove after the First World War, the Duke and Mr Watkins, the two churchwardens, would arrive for morning service in bowler hats and we would pick a buttonhole for each of them and shyly present it. Matins was attended by all the local gentry but I enjoyed evensong most when the church was filled with villagers and the singing was loud and hearty. In winter the lamps were turned out one by one after the service by Fred Budd and Arthur Salisbury the sidesmen. I can still smell the smoke and feel the eerie darkness as we trooped out of the church and across the moonlit garden.'

'Although we lived near the sea front in Worthing our family attended Tarring church some two miles distant and on Sunday mornings we would all be expected to go to church as a family, properly attired for the occasion. My father was a sidesman and always sat at the back of the church, and in front of us would sit an "elderly" lady (probably at least in her thirties!) – she always seemed to wear a grey squirrel coat, be it winter or summer, and if I or my brothers or sisters attempted to sing any of the hymns, she would turn round upon us with a loud "Sssshh!". The sermons were long and uninteresting, but I and my friends who also attended the same church would listen intently to each word and play the game of going through the alphabet (ie listen for a word containing the letter "A", when you had heard this, carry on to "B" and so on). Upon reaching "K" it was the signal to turn over your prayer book in your hand and if, as we did on one memorable occasion, you went right through the alphabet to reach "Z", this was the signal to drop your prayer book with as loud a noise as possible.

At school we had our own chapel (a consecrated sanctuary at the east end of our gym) where we had some really uplifting services suitable for young people. Our chaplain had a very bad leg and it was considered a privilege to be chosen to help him up the sanctuary steps before and after the services. I well remember one occasion when several of our older and very fit girls "fainted" so they might get out of the service before time. Our headmistress was most considerate, telling them she was so sorry they were not well and as they were in such a weak state of health she felt it was unwise for them to do any sport for the rest of the term – as they were all girls in our lacrosse or hockey teams they really got their just desserts.'

MAKING MUSIC

'Birdham church has an air of tranquillity these days, but in the days when bequests to other churches were noted as two cows or three ewes, there was at the western end a gallery for the village musicians. Records show that the instruments were a cornet, a bass-viol and violin. There is an entertaining story of a violinist, an irascible old man, who on one occasion when a fiddle string broke, flung the luckless instrument from the gallery down to the body of the church shouting, "Goo down there and boide there!" I suspect this may have been the same character who would sometimes say in a very audible voice above the music, "That goos well." '

'My father was an organist from 17 years old. He played at a chapel in Worthing until he was called up in 1917 and went to France as a bandsman in the Queen's Regiment He was also a stretcher bearer, as were all bandsmen in those years. Having to remain after the Armistice was signed, he played the organ in a German village for services before returning to England.

To go to church was a normal thing to do for my sister and I. We had to take turns to go and "blow" the organ anyway – you had to watch a lead weight between two positions and if it fell below the line then Father had no power! We used to take our Tiger Tim comic to read, and once or twice got carried away.

During the war years girls and women were introduced into the choir at Balcombe church as the young men were called up. Servicemen stationed around came and sang in the choir while they were waiting to be sent abroad, and when on leave our village men would return to the choir.

When at East Grinstead my father founded the North Sussex

41

Choirs Festival, which was held on the nearest Saturday to St Swithun's Day. Many village choirs from the surrounding area came and rehearsed in the morning for the performance in the afternoon, and afterwards there would be tea for everyone in the village hall.'

'In the 1920s at Findon, I earned one shilling and sixpence a quarter for singing in the choir at matins and evening service. Ten years later boys were earning a penny each service and a penny for choir practice. If a boy behaved badly at practice, he was fined a penny.

In the 1920s I would spend my singing money on a penny glass of lemonade at a little cafe in the square, or a quarter of Nestle milk chocolate for threepence, a sherbet dab for a halfpenny, chocolate coconut a halfpenny a tube, or humbugs at a penny each.'

SUNDAY SCHOOL TREATS

'I was accepted by baptism into the life of Lancing Methodist church in February 1917. This took place at home as my father had been called to serve in the Army when I was a few days old.

My first memories of church are of playing with sovereigns my father had in a case attached to his watch chain and placed in the opposite waistcoat pocket. Another thing to keep me quiet was playing with the head of my mother's fox fur.

My first attendance at Sunday school was in the infants. I remember well the leader, Jimmy James, who was a Father Christmas-type figure who would tell us stories from the Bible in a way that we loved.

At five years we went into general Sunday school and together we would sing the first hymn, my favourites were *Onward Christian Soldiers, All things bright and beautiful* and at harvest, *We plough the fields and scatter.* We were now in the large hall, where dividing concertina-type shutters would be pulled down for our age-allotted classes. The register would be marked, and this was very important as marks would be added up and at Christmas, prizes would be given, the value of which was according to our attendance. After a bible story there would be questions to our teacher etc, then we would push up the shutters again and sing the closing hymn.

A highlight of the year would be the Sunday school Anniversary and a platform would be erected at the front of the church and we would sit facing the congregation. This was the only obligatory time for Sunday school children to go into church. A previously practised entertainment would be given.

Being of church-going parents I would attend Sunday school at ten o'clock, church at eleven o'clock with my parents, two o'clock

Lancing Methodist Sunday school children enjoying their annual treat in 1922. These outings were eagerly anticipated at a time when many children rarely travelled far from home.

Sunday school and at half past six church again. I recall quite young, going to church on wet and windy nights and singing *Rock of Ages* and being worried about those poor sailors on the rough sea.

A day looked forward to by all the Sunday school members was the yearly outing. We would save our pennies for weeks before, and when near the outing, numbers coming to Sunday school doubled. When the outing day came we would assemble at the station and how exciting it was when the train came in with compartments marked "Reserved". Our destination would usually be Hassocks or Burgess Hill. Hassocks was my favourite as I loved the tall tower (we would climb up and slide down on a mat). There were round-abouts, coconut shies etc. We would meet in a marquee for a very plain tea. Having got all the pupils together there would be races in an adjoining field and pennies would be given to the winners.'

'Sundays and our social life revolved around the local Methodist church. It was morning Sunday school, into morning service until the hymn before the sermon, and school again in the afternoon. Once I was in the choir at the age of twelve, it was evening service as well. Highlights of the year were Anniversaries when the three Non-conformist churches, Baptist, Congregational and Methodist, supported each other in turn. So there was always some rivalry as to which school put on the best show, and of course that ensured a full house for our efforts. I remember asking my grandfather to make my "best dress" in white and green when we performed *God's Garden*, and I was a lily of the field. It was many years later that I discovered that the lilies were scarlet poppies! We received our prizes (always books) on the anniversary evening; the better the attendance, the better the book. It is sad sometimes to see these much-loved prizes, often 60 or more years old, turning up in charity shops. During the war, the Sunday school Council tried to stop giving these prizes, but the older children turned out their own from earlier years, so that the little ones should not be disappointed.

Then we had two treats; a Christmas party with – oh joy! – no restrictions on the number of cakes we ate, though some of the tougher boys got more than their fair share, and the summer treat of a trip by charabanc to Hassocks or Littlehampton.'

GETTING ABOUT

It isn't so long since horses provided the main form of transport for work and for pleasure, or since the first cars were objects of wonder and affection for their eccentricities. Motor traffic also brought with it the tarmac road, ending the days of the dusty dirt roads for good. Buses brought a new freedom for country dwellers, and steam trains were part of everyone's lives.

WHEN HORSES DELIVERED THE GOODS

'I well remember the days when the horse was used to deliver our daily needs in Horsham. Cars were owned by only the wealthy few in the 1920s. I especially remember the old horse which brought our milk each morning with Alf the driver, who could be heard whistling streets away. Most days I would wait at my gate with knobs of sugar and a bucket of water if the weather was hot. The trouble was that one day I was not at home and the old horse would not budge from my gate. Another horse brought our coal and we would have two shillings and sixpence ready for a bag of the best Derby Brights.'

'In the 1920s I would rush home from school to watch the horses and waggons come out of the council stable yard in Market Road,

Chichester. The sight of them coming out in order for their working day was unforgettable. The horses were so big, shiny and bright and the clopping of their hooves and rattle of their brasses was most musical. One to eight, the numbers were on the side of the waggons. Most of the drivers wore caps and some had moustaches. We had our favourites; mine was number six, Mr Dibley. They all gave us a wave and told us to hurry home.'

FROM CARRIER TO BUS

'The horse-drawn carrier's van was the only passenger transport, four days a week, at Birdham in the early 1900s. If required, a card with his initials was put in a window facing the road for him to call. He left Birdham about 10 am and returned about 6 pm. He could carry about six people. He took orders for shopping of a great variety such as getting a joint of meat, cough mixture, or bringing out children's shoes on approval. The shopping was brought home under the passenger seats. He and all the other carriers stabled their horses at the Fountain Inn at Chichester.

The first bus was a converted war ambulance in 1919. It seated four passengers each side where the stretchers had been. This was followed by the Blue Sapphire buses which held about 20 passengers and had solid tyres. These were later taken over by the Southdown buses. Double decker buses with open tops were only allowed when the road bridge was built over the canal in place of the swingbridge in 1924.'

'I remember going to Worthing on an open-topped bus, with wooden seats and a kind of apron to protect passengers from the rain. If one was really lucky, it might be possible to sit next to the driver. The fare was tenpence return from Findon.'

'Journeys by bus in the summer months in open-top double decker buses were a delight, though one did have to watch out for overhanging branches – many a lady had her hat "toppled" if not careful. In the winter in cold or wet weather you unclipped the waterproof cover and laid it across your lap, but your top half was exposed to the elements and if the bottom deck of the bus was full you just had to sit it out.

The drivers and conductors were all very friendly; they would even stop en route for someone waving a letter and take it into Haywards Heath. One conductor, "Dusty" Miller, would collect a shopping list from our next door neighbour, do the shopping in his break time and deliver it on his journey to Balcombe in the afternoon!'

45

'In the early 1920s travelling from Funtington was very restricted. Only the large houses could boast they had a car, except one whose owner travelled by pony and trap and kept a groom. The ones who had a car had a chauffeur and were very much "looked up to" by the everyday labourer.

There were three ways to get to Chichester, the first being to walk all the way from Funtington. This could be a leisurely walk, there being no traffic on the road; in fact the road was little more than the width of Watery Lane. Secondly, you could walk to Bosham station, the short cut being through "Nineteen Acres" (the pathway through the churchyard) through the School Dell and Mount Noddy and Ratham to Bosham, and catch a train to Chichester station. Thirdly, you could travel with the carrier. Two names spring to mind – Mr Chuter and Mr Joyce. The carrier would call in if he saw a letter "C" on a piece of cardboard in the window. He would pick you up about 8.30 am but didn't come back home until 4.30 pm. For his journey he would charge a penny or twopence. Whilst you were about your

With a little ingenuity the whole family could travel by bicycle. With few cars on the roads, cycling was a cheap and enjoyable form of transport.

46

own business he would be shopping for other customers. You gave him the order and he would go into the appropriate shop and bring home the goods on "appro", returning the next day with those not wanted and the money. The drapers soon came to know their customers through the carrier.

This changed in 1928 when Mr Davys came to live in Funtington and set up a garage and taxi business which flourished. In 1931 the Southdown Bus started up a run from Chichester to Compton and this was well patronised, particularly as the last bus was about ten o'clock in the evening and we were able to visit the pictures and get the last bus home, a pleasure denied people living in the village until the arrival of the bus. By this time the road had been cleaned up and widened (half the width it is today) and the tree branches cut off.

If we wished to go to Portsmouth we cycled or walked to the station and put the cycle in the guard's van on the train, the return journey being taken the same way.

Not many people had holidays in those days, but if you were lucky and went to the chapel (which is now the Scout and Guide Headquarters) the minister and his wife who owned a furniture shop in Chichester (now Whitmore Jones) hired a Southdown Bus and took all the children who attended and their mothers to Bognor on a Thursday in August. They had to provide their own lunch, but they were also treated to a tea in the tea shop along the front. No wonder the attendance at the Congregational chapel rose steeply pre-August, as the C of E Sunday school children only had a "bun fight" in the vicarage paddock!'

ROAD IMPROVEMENT?

'Is it possible to imagine the busy A29 London to Bognor Regis road as an unmade village street? It was until the mid 1920s at Westergate, when it received a tarmacadamed surface. No longer was the mud or dust to be churned up by the baker with his bread van, the milkman with his two-wheeled float, the coalman with his cart, the brewer's and timber drays, and the many farm waggons and carts. But the horses still left lots of goodies for the roses, of course.

The vibration caused by the heavy steamroller lumbering to and fro to level the new hard surface, was soon followed by the vibration from the Foden steam waggons. These contractors' vehicles were manned by smutty-faced men who had to stop the vehicle at roadside ditches to suck up water to fill the boiler and enable steam power to be maintained. The steamrollers often drove along the road, levelling out surface problems or journeying to farms to provide the power to pull ploughs to and fro across large arable fields, the method used before the more general use of tractors. The pretty sight of primroses and celandines which coloured the banks of the open stream flowing along the street edge, was lost in the mid 1930s when much of the water course was covered by a footway to provide some safety because of increasing motor traffic.

In the summer strings of charabancs, often more than a dozen, carried seaside bound visitors from London through the village on their way to Bognor beach. We would wave and call to the smiling passengers as they trundled by. They often had to queue at the closed gates awaiting the passing of the steam trains travelling the mainline railway. At either approach to these gates the Red Cross Association laid out "Penny Sheets" into which it was hoped passers-by would throw a penny, which they did very often to support a good cause.'

THE FIRST CARS

'The vicar at Tangmere church had an old car, probably the only one in the village. The children used to play in the road and on one occasion he ran into a child but was driving so slowly no damage was done!'

'My father kept horses in the old barn at Tripp Hill and he had a waggonette which he used as a taxi. Later, he bought a car and ran a taxi service with it and sold petrol. After he died my mother carried on the business. At that time the petrol came in cans which were stored in a pit at the bottom of the garden. It was very heavy lifting them out and carrying them to the road. When I was old enough I had to help. One old pump had to be checked every half gallon – and in those days the cars needed oil and water as well when they stopped in. I think in the early days we were the only people selling petrol in the village.'

'Our family didn't own a motor car until 1935, when we had an Austin Seven which was called Annabel. Father taught himself to drive – why Mother allowed us to go with him when he was learning goodness knows. One day he drove a good few miles with the handbrake on; there was a dreadful smell and a deal of smoke and we had to wait while things "settled". Another time a wheel came off in Balcombe Forest and he really hadn't much knowledge of cars. It was bought for £12. In 1940 she was laid up in the rectory yard, propped up on bricks, and in 1943 someone offered my father £15 for her. He was delighted with the profit!

When Father was organist at Easebourne church he had a motorbike. He always said it was most important for him to know the routes and times of the bus company so that if he broke down there was a bus behind him to get him to the church on time. One Sunday soon after he departed from home he returned rather scratched and battered – the brakes had failed and he had gone through Farmer Turner's hedge of holly and hawthorn. Somewhere his plate with five teeth had dislodged and got lost and we were dispatched to locate it – and we did.'

'The first car I bought was a secondhand Morris Cowley 12hp in 1935. It had a dicky seat and my sisters, when they came for a ride with my mother, had to put on extra clothes and each had a hot water bottle! I paid £25 for it and to the best of my recollection sold it for £30.'

OUR RAILWAY

'We had steam trains in the 1920s of course, and the majority of freight was carried by goods trains. One very hot summer day in the 1920s, when I was about nine, a spark from a passing locomotive landed in the field adjacent to the railway line at Billingshurst, igniting the field of hay and causing a terrific fire. Some livestock was lost and there was damage to sheds and some houses. It necessitated evacuating people from nearby cottages. The fire was fought with water from our garden wells and from the brooks, and it resulted in our well becoming permanently dry.

At the station was a taxi service run by horse and cab. The same family owned the station shop, selling everything from candles and paraffin to tea and sugar. It was a very small, narrow shop and the owner, a small plump man who always wore a bowler hat and a once-white apron, was a real character of that age.'

'In the 1930s there was a special Cheap Day ticket for early closing day, and on a Wednesday from one o'clock you could go by train from Haslemere to Waterloo return for two shillings and sixpence.'

'The holidays were coming and that meant that the big trunk would be brought down from the attic. The tray part would be taken out and kept for the best clothes and everything else would somehow be got into the bottom. We all got excited!

When the trunk was at last ready, it was collected and taken to the railway station and we all went to see it off. The tickets had already been bought. The trunk was weighed, the tickets inspected and for the sum of two shillings the trunk would go off on its own. And it always got there, whatever the destination. It was all a lovely part of the holidays.'

'Not so long ago it was possible to travel from Grange Road Station to High Holborn without the necessity of rainwear. One left Crawley Down at 6.40 am, pausing at Rowfant, arriving at Three Bridges at 6.50 am, changing platforms (under cover) to the main line, catching the 6.44 am fast train to London Bridge, arriving at 7.45 am, then by Underground (the Northern Line) reaching one's destination by 8 am.

Grange Road Station was built in 1860 and changed little until it was demolished in 1967 under the Beeching Plan. It was a pretty little station situated in a quiet village. It had one platform, a signal box and a level crossing. It was decorated with flower beds and hanging baskets. As there was no mains electricity it was lit by Tilley lamps which hissed merrily. In cold weather the waiting room always had a blazing coal fire which reflected in the row of wellington boots left by the regular passengers until their return in the evening. The staff consisted of "Old Sid" and "Young Sid", who carried out the combined duties of stationmaster, booking clerk, porter, signalman and crossing operator. They were always cheerful and helpful – you could have your hair cut and your warts charmed. A season ticket ordered on a Friday night would be delivered during the weekend ready for Monday. Those few passengers catching the first train would be treated to a cup of tea with the driver before departing.

The train usually consisted of a rather antiquated steam engine (a 2-4-2 class) – one of three known affectionately as "Pip, Squeak and Wilfred" – usually hauling two ancient carriages. For a period the early morning train comprised several main line through-corridor coaches being warmed up before being attached to the 8.20 am London train. The fact that Mr Beeching travelled on this particular train may have had something to do with it.

A regular unit of rolling stock was a Director's Observation Car complete with a rear-facing bay window, carpets and free-standing armchairs.

The service provided in this rural backwater was remarkable. An alternative service was always available should the train fail to run. On one occasion, a mile of copper signalling wire had been mis-appropriated near Forest Row, rendering the line inoperative. However, a Rolls Royce taxi arrived to transport the four or five regulars to Three Bridges in style and on time.

The Three Bridges and Royal Tunbridge Wells line provided an hourly service operating a single line system with a brass baton or key carried by the driver. This allowed the signals to be cleared in one direction only. The line passed through some of the most beautiful parts of the Sussex Weald. However, under the Beeching Plan the line was declared uneconomic owing to insufficient passenger use and it was closed. Ironically, shortly after closure, the expansion of Crawley Down began and the population increased dramatically.

One summer's evening in 1967 the last passenger train left Grange Road Station in the presence of a large part of the village's population and those from the surrounding area, including the incumbents of The Royal Oak. In a moving ceremony the Copthorne Silver Band played *Auld Lang Syne* and the village bade farewell to Grange Road Station and the branch line.'

OPENING THE CROSSING GATES

'In the 1920s the railway went from East Grinstead to Three Bridges, through Crawley Down. There was a level crossing near Auchinleck Court.

At this time we had a very dedicated doctor who lived in Sandy Lane. Although there were never any trains at night, the crossing gates were always firmly closed. This was a bone of contention between Dr Foot, the stationmaster and the crossing keeper, as it involved a detour by the main road to get from one part of the village to the other. After many discussions, the doctor warned the stationmaster that if he ever had an urgent case on the far side of the railway he would have no hesitation in going through the gates. Eventually, on a stormy winter night a message came to the doctor that one of his patients was in labour in Sandhills Lane. The moment had come and he drove fast down Station Road and put his bull-nosed Morris car at the level crossing gates and crashed through them and off to his patient. A lovely baby was safely delivered and the crossing gates were never again closed at night.'

THE SELSEY TRAM

'The Hundred of Manhood and Selsey Tramway (1897–1935) was the only means of travel apart from horse-drawn vehicles between Selsey and Chichester until after the First World War.

In 1895 the idea for this railway was first put forward by Mr E Ivatts, who had organised the building of other small railways. The estimated cost was about £21,000. In 1896 at a meeting of the council in Chichester it was decided to go ahead with the scheme with certain modifications. Legal arrangements were looked after by the firm of solicitors Raper, Freeland and Tyacke. (This firm still flourishes in the village under the name of Raper & Co.) Almost 100 men were employed on the laying of the track and by the summer of 1897 the line was finished. It was opened on 27th August amid great excitement and high hopes of a prosperous future for Selsey. It was felt that the railway would certainly bring more visitors. The fare to Chichester was one shilling and twopence return. For the first journey the train consisted of three cars handsomely decorated in crimson and white. Villagers waved gaily as the train passed and at Sidlesham Mill (the foundations may still be seen) Mrs Steven, aged 86, waved too. A grand luncheon was given at Beacon House attended by all the notable persons in Selsey and Chichester.

This railway, throughout its useful life of 38 years, always had that quality which today would be described as "Emett-like". Firstly the track wandered haphazardly between the stations, secondly this extract from the 1917 timetable displays this quality: "This timetable is only intended to fix the times before which the trams will not start". The guard was also the ticket issuer and collector at first. At the peak of its prosperity 300 people were sometimes carried on one journey to Selsey during the holiday season.

The local farmers and fishermen found the goods service extremely useful but in about 1919 a bus service began to run between Selsey and Chichester and private motor cars began to be more common. This railway had only one fatal accident during its career. In September 1923 two coaches and the engine *Wembley* were de-railed and fireman H Barnes was killed.

The fortunes of the railway began rapidly to decay and in 1935 services were suspended "until further notice". In due course all the rolling stock was sold. As late as 1947 Sidlesham station could be seen almost in its original state but this too has been removed.'

'I remember going by train to Chichester in the early 1930s and boarding the Selsey Tram at Terminus Road. This was an extraordinary vehicle – a mixture of train/tram/bus which shook and rattled alarmingly and made a tremendous noise. The driver had to crank it up from time to time – I thought it was most exciting.'

HOUSE & HOME

THE HOUSES WE LIVED IN

Families were often much larger in the past than they are today and many small cottages were overcrowded as well as lacking the most basic of 'mod cons'. People did their best to make their homes comfortable, despite the restrictions of poverty and, after the war, shortage of furniture. Moving house was often a simple matter of loading possessions into a handcart and setting off for the new house. Even those moving onto new estates faced fairly primitive conditions, but at least they had the promise of a brighter future for their families.

WE WERE ALL POOR BUT DIDN'T KNOW IT

'I was born in 1916 in a small primitive cottage at Parbrook, Billingshurst. All the downstairs rooms had flagstone floors and were very damp. The only floor covering was coco-matting laid in strips, and peg rugs made by my mother from old clothes. These could be replaced when the damp penetrated and caused them to rot.

The rickety wooden stairs led to two bedrooms, one door opening between the two. Under the stairs was our coal store. The coalman used to shoot coal straight from the sack into it – imagine the dust!

We had an outside loo which we flushed by taking pails of water with us on each visit. There was a well in the garden, in which we used to keep butter, milk and meat. The provisions were placed in a bucket and lowered into the well by a chain.'

'I came to live in Flansham, which is a small hamlet about three miles from Bognor Regis, in 1919. The house we lived in had three bedrooms, a sitting room and a large kitchen where all our meals were eaten. There was a kitchen range to cook by, and a large scullery which had a larder and a copper for heating the water. We had no electricity or gas, but oil lamps and candles were used. There was no running water, we had a pump outside which sometimes froze in the winter. My parents or eldest brother had to bring in buckets of water for use indoors for everything. The toilet was also outdoors and this had to be emptied every week by my father, not a very pleasant job.

The furnishing of the house was quite good for those days, but it was linoleum (not carpets) on all the floors, and a rug here and there. These rugs were made of cut up discarded material worked into canvas or sacking. We only had one armchair and that was for my father's use, and if one of us was sitting in it we always had to get out when he came home.'

'I grew up in Steyning at the time of the First World War, when we were all poor but did not realise it as everyone we knew was in the same situation.

Many working people lived in small Victorian terraced houses, one room and kitchen downstairs, two bedrooms above. Where did they sleep the large families most had? No one had a bathroom and many houses had no water inside, but were supplied by an outside tap between each three or four houses, usually in a wooden case to hinder freezing up. Most houses fronted straight onto road or street with just a small back garden in which would be the toilet, flush or earth as might be.

Lighting would be by lamps and candles, heating by coal fire and cooking by kitchen range. More fortunate families lived in the older, detached or semi-detached cottages with large gardens, as we did. We also had gas lighting downstairs, though candles in bedrooms, and a gas stove for cooking because my father was an employee of the local gas works.

Water for washing day or baths was heated in a copper by a small fire underneath. Baths would be taken in a large zinc bath, in front of the fire if you were lucky. Much later we did have a bath heated by a solid fuel stove – but not a proper bathroom. I don't recall electricity in Steyning before the end of the First World War and the streets were lit by gas lamps.

The room we most used held a large table with leaves to let out, various wooden chairs, a larger one with arms for Father, a leather armchair by the fire and an old fashioned sofa with high back and sides along one wall, a piano against another wall and an umbrella stand in one corner. A built-in cupboard on either side of the fire held on one side china, cutlery and tablecloths, and on the other old books and periodicals, also our various board games.

In front of the fire would be a rag rug and a carpet of some sort on the floor. The table would be covered by a fringed table cloth when not in use for meals.

The sitting room proper, used on Sundays or for parties, had another sofa, several carpet chairs and chairs with upholstered seats and one armchair. A small table by the window held a plant, and there was a book case of better books, a corner cupboard which held special treasures and a built-in low polished cupboard on either side of the fire. In the bedrooms we did not have much but beds, a chair each and hanging space for clothes.'

'I was born in Sidlesham on 2nd October 1920, the fourth child in a family of six children, into the slump after the First World War. My father had served with the REs and returned to really hard times.

Our home in the early days was small – my father partitioned the bedrooms. The kitchen had a brick floor, clothes were boiled in a copper in the kitchen and food cooked on a coal fire range there, which had to be blackleaded, and the hearth and doorsteps whitened. A large mangle with wooden rollers also stood there, together with a scrubbed wooden kitchen table and windsor chairs A nursery guard stood round the fires. Lighting was by oil lamps downstairs and candles upstairs. Washstands with jugs and basins were in the bedrooms for a daily washing, and bath water was heated in the copper and tipped into a long tin bath. The garden was small, but later when I was twelve we moved to Fishbourne to a large house with large garden, and from here I cycled to the girls' High School in Chichester. This was also my first introduction to fish and chips; a mobile fish and chip van came on Friday nights and stood outside The Bull's Head and you could get fish and chips for threepence.

Our home had a round inlaid table and chairs in the living room, also a sofa and armchairs, a rocking chair and a sideboard. In spite of being a large family the lamps were never a danger, no horseplay was allowed in the house and we all knew we had to behave ourselves. Cards were often played and we were encouraged to read, and of course there was always the darning and mending to do, also all our dresses were made at home. Sheets were turned sides to middle and bolster slips and underslips made from old sheets. Tablecloths were damask and usually white and old ones cut for table napkins.

Most men worked locally – women only worked as a rule if they were single, mostly in domestic service or shops. My oldest sister was a librarian and in those days books cost twopence a week from local lending libraries. It was not considered nice for married women to work, but occasionally my mother would go to some big house and cook for a big dinner party – she was a wonderful cook.'

'My father was a carter and worked with shire horses before and after being gassed in the First World War, so as the years passed he became an invalid with chest problems. We lived in a cottage on a common in Lodsworth with two bedrooms and three downstairs rooms. There were eight children, five girls and three boys.

I remember we all had to help with the chores after school. Mother worked very hard. Her day started at 4 am helping to get a herd of cows in from the fields and hand milking about 30 cows. She was back in time to see us off to school then she would be off to cook lunch for a local farmer's family. Dad gave us children lunch, which we came home from school for as the school was about a mile away. Mum would then help in the fields harvesting, silage making or sugar beet pulling until it was time for us to walk home from school.

The cottage we lived in was cosy although it was only heated with a range in the scullery – blackleaded of course. There was also a sink with one wooden draining board. There was a walk-in larder where there were earthenware crocks – one with eggs in waterglass, another with pork in brine and usually a cured ham hanging from a hook in the ceiling. In another corner stood a copper for boiling water for baths, washing and cleaning, a hip bath hanging from a hook for use on Friday nights. The front parlour had a large scrub-topped table where we all sat for our meals.

There was a huge fireplace where we could sit on stools on the hearth and look straight up the chimney and see the stars. The doors had wooden latches, lifted up by a bootlace tied round the latch and through a hole to the other side of the door. One would pull the lace and it would lift the latch. I remember on a number of occasions I would pull the lace out so that my mother couldn't get in to punish me but she always won because I would need to get out for food before mother would give in. The "small house" was at the bottom of the garden, not very nice on a wet night and not at all easy trying to stop the wind from blowing the candle out on your way down the garden path.'

MAKING IT COMFORTABLE

'My father was the Head Gardener at Stonewick. He kept chickens and supplied the local grocer with eggs. He also bred rabbits for the table. We cured the skins and made little furry bedside mats to keep our bare feet from the cold lino which covered the floor.'

'In the bedrooms in the 1930s we had iron bedsteads and feather beds. The feathers were oven-baked and the pillows re-ticked annually, remembering to rub soap inside the ticking to stop the feathers coming through. In the kitchen the red brick flooring was scrubbed with another brick to "clean" it, and wooden floors were scrubbed daily.

There was a great shortage of furnishings for the newly married during the Second World War but should something like lino or rugs arrive in the local town shops, news would travel fast and villagers would be onto the bus to join the inevitable queue.

In 1947 rent for a newly built council house with three bedrooms was £1 1s 9d and this included an electric cooker and an electric copper and all your rates.'

'We moved into our house in Washington in 1948. We were allowed "units" to buy furniture, so only essential items were purchased and it was "utility" and was plain solid wood. The floor covering was lino and we bought balls of soft string which we boiled and dyed with vegetable dyes and made rugs using a rug needle and hessian. Our first stair carpet we knitted in rug wool on large wooden needles. Agricultural wages were very low so we were quite proud of our efforts to make our home comfortable.'

MOVING HOUSE

'I was born in Worthing in 1932. We rented the house and when I was about two we moved. My father borrowed a hand cart and for several days after work he loaded up our furniture and possessions and pushed the cart over Ham Bridge to our new home in Congreve Road. When moving day came I waited by the front gate for my mother to bring out my pushchair but when it came it was piled high with saucepans, trays and the kettle, with no room for me. I remember very well the rattling and clattering of the pans as I hung on to the pushchair with one hand and my teddy with the other, grizzling and complaining as we struggled over the railway bridge at Ladybell Road.'

'Sometimes we had to move due to Dad's work and this was quite an event. Everything in the house was packed and loaded up, but the outside effects were a problem. There was the dog and his kennel, tame rabbits in hutches, the cat with his paws well buttered "to make him settle in the new place", a canary in a cage, goldfish in a bowl slopping water over all the way, two hives of bees firmly shut in and very angry, six hens and a rooster, the chicken house and run, garden shed and frame, bags of logs and sacks of coal etc, and a "four and a half" of home-made wine.'

NEWTOWNERS

'The building of Crawley New Town had only just started when I moved there in 1952, my husband having obtained employment as Catering Manager for Crawley Development Corporation.

Our home would not have been considered a desirable residence from the outside. It reminded me of a "home" I had had a decade earlier in another Nissen hut on a remote searchlight site without electricity or piped water. However, this hut was light and cosy inside with electric cooker and water heaters in the bathroom and kitchen, in fact all the mod cons. It was situated in Tilgate Forest amid other huts which housed building workers, and was called Tilgate Hostel.

We stayed for five years, during which time our two sons were born. They seldom saw other children but apart from that it was an ideal place for them to enjoy their first years. The men there, deprived of normal family life, took a great interest in the boys and I never had any fears for their safety – even though it could get a little noisy on St Patrick's night!

It was a very short walk for us to visit the beautiful grounds of the "big house", part of which was still standing before it finally succumbed to dry rot. I always felt guilty slipping through the fence, as it was all very private property then, including Campbell's Lake, on which we were told Sir Malcolm Campbell had tried out his record breaking speedboat, Bluebird. My husband suggested that the whole area should be opened up as a recreational beauty spot for Newtowners but his idea was received with horror – this could never happen!

The area of Tilgate now crammed with houses, shops, churches, schools etc, was still farmland then and I used to push my pram along the lower road to show my little boys the pigs.'

'Friday 4th January 1963, we were ten days into what was to be the coldest, longest lasting, spell of winter weather for many years, and were about to move to the six year old terraced house in Crawley allocated to us by the New Towns Corporation because my husband was classified as a "key-worker" by his employers.

I was about two months into my second pregnancy and feeling decidedly queasy as I cleared thick snow from the path outside the flat where we had lived for the five years since our marriage, but to my grateful relief, when we arrived outside our house, just behind the removals van, we found that the two young boys from next door had already cleared the paths ready for us to move straight in.

With the aid of drawing-pins, curtains were soon put in place and furniture was being put into provisional positions, when it began to dawn on us that the coke for the Ideal boiler for heating water, and for the living room fire, was rather late in arriving as arranged. A quick phone call (twopence from the box across the road) confirmed our worst fears; the coalman had returned our fuel to the depot as he had been unable to get a reply on Thursday 3rd January. Fortunately, a very apologetic representative from the Gas Board soon arrived with a small paper sack of fuel for the living room fire (no baths that night), and that and a fan heater and very ancient electric fire kept the frost at bay for that first day and night.

Because of the severity of the weather that winter there were very frequent power cuts, solid fuel was all but rationed and even the (town) gas was often at half pressure, but even so I can vividly remember how glad I was, during the next few weeks, that I had chosen a gas cooker when we were first married, as I often sat wearing almost all the clothes I possessed with my feet in the open oven door trying to keep warm, until I had mastered the art of keeping that boiler ("Ideal" it was not) alight long enough to heat the water and the kitchen.

I soon found the local shopping parade, although not for some time the shortest route there, and still recall my embarrassment on one of my first visits to the greengrocer's when my 18 month old son seized a shiny apple from the display and took a bite, before I could stop him. Apples were selling in that terrible winter at the then unprecedented price of two shillings a pound and I could only rarely afford them.

I registered with a doctor, very necessary in my expanding state, and soon began to make some friends – the first at a Tupperware party. I think those parties saved many a newcomer from total isolation in those early days, and eventually in March the snow and ice began to melt and we were able to see the "garden" we had inherited. I almost wished the snow would return when I saw the piles of rubbish we had also inherited.'

HEAT, LIGHT AND WATER

With no electricity laid on, houses tended to be colder and darker than they are today, light coming from candles, gas mantles or oil lamps and heat from coal or wood fires. Water had to be drawn from the well or pumped up into tanks, and few indeed had the luxury of a separate bathroom or an inside toilet.

COLD AND DARK

'Our houses were cold and dark by today's standards. Only the big houses made their own electricity, so we had lamps and candles until mains electricity came to Rogate in the mid 1930s. Then there were kettles and irons and vacuum cleaners, and small portable electric fires. There were few – or no – refrigerators or washing machines until after the war in 1946. Freezers were unheard of.

Houses were warmed by open fires, and most had a kitchen range of some sort, run on coal for cooking. Many people, though, went wooding to help out the coal. Wooden boxes on pram wheels were pushed out in the afternoons. Cookers that ran continuously came in the 1930s, the first Aga looking much the same as today's. The very early ones heated about ten gallons of water which was drawn off for use from a tap, and refilled through a hole at the back. We had our first Rayburn in 1950 – coal fired.

My father installed a plumbed-in bath in 1912, and it was the first one seen in Rogate in a small house. Otherwise hip baths were used in bedrooms, or the copper was lit on Saturday nights for the weekly bath and hair-wash in long zinc baths, which hung up in the wash-house for the rest of the week.

Flush lavatories were uncommon, too – there was a bucket in a little house up the garden. This had to be emptied into a hole dug in the garden. Indoors there were chamber pots, for use not ornament – no bedroom was completely furnished without one. Indoor sanitation was looked on by some with grave suspicion. Things improved

William Rice, coal merchant, about to set out on his rounds in Felpham. The coalman was a regular caller when we relied on coal fires and kitchen ranges for heating and cooking.

when first mains water, and then drains, arrived in about 1947. Until then water was either pumped or drawn from a well in a bucket and rainwater butts helped out. Water was precious and not wasted, though it was free.'

'Many small houses in Chichester had a front room which was for "best" and was seldom used. A narrow hallway led to the living room, with the kitchen off it. There would be a shallow stone sink where everyone washed, in the absence of a bathroom, and running cold water only. A zinc bath would hang outside the back door and water was heated in a copper (where washing was boiled – and puddings!).

Some cottages had deep winding stairs and sometimes there would be a gap between the top stair and the bedroom floors, so one had to step carefully.

Heating was a coal fire, maybe with a back boiler for hot water in more recent houses. Paraffin heaters were common, causing much condensation and damp. Bedrooms were cold and damp, though a coal fire might be lit in case of illness. Candles were not uncommon in upstairs rooms.

Fleas were common, so one carried Keatings Powder when visiting, dusting it into one's shoes.'

'Home was a flint cottage with a roof of thatch and one grate to cook on and to heat the four rooms. Water came from a tap across the road, which meant carrying buckets up seven steps into the house.

There was no electricity, only a mantle lamp, one bracket lamp and candles. If we needed to go to the "little house" after dark, we would take the storm lantern. The house was cold, but how we enjoyed our feather beds and our hot bricks to take up with us on winter nights; this was just an ordinary brick put in the oven to heat, then wrapped around in a blanket and put into the bed, then we were snug all night. A white honeycomb cover with tassles covered the bed and a washstand with jug and basin stood in the bedroom, while the wooden box, mostly filled with blankets, was graced with an antimacassar, white and starched, and the floor, lino covered, had rag mats for warmth.'

'There were very few houses at Birdham, mainly farmhouses and farm cottages for workers. Many were overcrowded as the average number of children was about six. The houses were cold, with a coal fire in the living room, a coal kitchener for cooking and a Beatrice oil stove to heat the kettle early morning and evening when the fire was out. Both the kitchener and living room fireplace were blackleaded weekly and the hearthstone whitened daily when the ashes were removed. The kitchener had the soot round the oven removed weekly with flue brush and rake.

There were only a few bathrooms in the village, one in a big Victorian rectory and one in a large farmhouse managed by the owner of the watermill. The water was pumped up by windmills some distance from the houses.

Houses were never locked in the daytime and not always at night as there was no thieving despite the Depression.'

'I lived in a three-bedroomed end-of-terrace house in Shoreham-by-Sea. We had no electricity; heating was by coal fire, lighting and cooking by gas, except in my top-of-the-stairs bedroom which had neither fireplace nor lights. I went to bed by candlelight, right up to the day I married in 1947. I remember this being very handy after the war, when power cuts bedevilled our lives, and every house was in darkness except ours.

There were two main bedrooms with small fireplaces, only used if anybody was ill, a stone-floored unheated scullery, the living room and the front room. This was only used on special occasions and on Sunday. The fire was lit after Sunday morning service, and we spent winter Sunday afternoons feeling cold and uncomfortable.

There was no matching furniture; it was mostly pieces picked up secondhand as, during the Depression, Dad, by trade a grocer, had some time unemployed. Lino covered the floors, with a rug in front of the fireplace, and there was a hair-cord stair carpet. The curtains were changed according to season, thin in the summer and thick for the winter. When blackouts were needed during the war, Dad nailed lino over a frame which was hung on hooks before the light was put on.

We were lucky during the war that we had a gas-heated geyser but, though the bathroom was stone-floored, there was no heater. We managed our weekly bath in reasonable comfort, though during the winters of 1940 and 1946/7 the water often froze in the waste pipe and we could not drain the bath. During the war, we invited members of the forces in for a hot bath for a shilling to pay for the gas. I have many memories of pink and damp young men, steaming contentedly in our living room. The washbasin in the bathroom was never used to my knowledge, as it remained cracked throughout my childhood. We all washed in the scullery.'

WELLS AND PUMPS

'My father worked on the Goodwood estate, and then he worked for the council, looking after the village – clearing the ditches and looking after the verges and hedges, that sort of thing.

In the 1930s they dug a new well in Church Lane at Boxgrove because of the drought. Before that, Goodwood used to bring a big tank down on a horse-drawn cart and round into Church Lane for the villagers. The well was sunk by what was then the allotments. There was a gate into the well and it was fenced off. Anyone could use it. The men used to walk up with a yoke on their shoulders, with pails, when they came home from work. They'd draw their water and that had to last them until the next night. There were no sinks or bathrooms then. We didn't have one put in the house until 1960.'

'My husband was the village policeman at Trotton in the 1940s. When we arrived at our new house, we found that we had to pump up the water. My husband had to draw water from a well before he went to school when he was a boy, but he had thought that day was over.

The pump was in the corner of the kitchen. It had to be primed and took 15 to 20 minutes to fill the tank in the roof. The house was on high ground and the big water tank was in the valley. Water was pumped up into a middle pump by an electric motor. We then had to pump it into our tank. I say we, but it was too difficult for me to do. My husband did it nearly every day and when he was away on a course, another policeman from Midhurst had to come and do it. Often when the water got low in the big tank or froze in bad weather, it came through a copper colour. Instead of white clothes they were often cream. This went on for eight years.'

'In the 1950s we lived in a property at Windfallwood Common near Lurgashall with primitive sanitation, no mains water or electricity. Light was provided by a large motor called a New Pelaphone which charged up banks of 20 large wet batteries. We usually had the engine in action when we were entertaining, but I often had to attend to a breakdown when we had guests. The engine also operated the pump for lifting the well water into the roof tanks. The installation of a cesspit improved things considerably for us, and some years later mains water and electricity were laid on.'

WOOD FOR THE FIRE

'I can remember when Blunden's brought the coal down on a solid tyre lorry to Boxgrove in the 1930s. I was about eight. Coal was one shilling and elevenpence a hundredweight then, but people were only getting a pound or two a week, so we didn't buy much coal. We went out wooding.

Blunden's would buy the rights to clear one part of the wood of young chestnut trees, an acre or two. They chopped it all down and made fencing stakes, hurdles and what have you. Then all the rough stuff they used to cop out and bundle up into what they called faggots. You could buy them for threepence or fourpence each. They were about four feet long and we'd poke them under the copper to heat the water.'

'Log cutting was one of the most important tasks of the year, as wood was free and coal expensive to buy. The estate we lived on gave each of the men wood for their fires, a field row of potatoes, and manure from the stables for the cottage gardens.

On Saturday afternoons in autumn and early winter my Dad would have to saw the loads of timber into about eight inch lengths to fit into the kitchen range. The wood was a mixture of old fence posts and rails and branches from fallen trees. Dad would saw away using his sawing horse and I would pick up the logs as they fell, to stack them neatly in the wood shed from wall to wall and as high as I could reach.

But to me, the most exciting times were when after our tea, my Dad would wrap me up warmly, light the lamp and we would go out to the wood shed, in the dark.

Here, Dad would hang up the lamp and split the bigger logs using his axe on the chopping block which was a section of yew-wood trunk, pale pink where the axe cut into the top.

I would hurry backwards and forwards to stack the logs, trying to carry two at a time to save a journey. The happiness I felt, in the warm glow of the lamp, helping to keep the family warm through the winter. My Dad would sing to me, old country songs and stories of when he was a little boy.

Bedtime came too quickly, but first the walk up the garden path in the moonlight to look up at the stars and to listen to the owls hooting, then off to bed with a hot water bottle, a very happy little girl.'

TOM'S HOLE

'We came to West Sussex as newly weds in 1953. We moved into our first little home in the October, a delightful Tudor cottage at Warnham, two up and two down with a Tudor lean-to, six ft wide, running the length of the house. This comprised a little kitchen with an Ideal boiler, a bathroom at the end, and a WC which literally was a WC in the form of an Elsan. So our first action was to get planning permission for a proper flush lavatory with a cesspit.

That cesspit, believe it or not, was dug out by one Tom Skinner, with a shovel! Every Sunday people would take their afternoon walk out from the village and walk across the garden to look at Tom's hole. It took several weeks to complete, and as I remember this magnificent enterprise cost £260.'

THE DAILY ROUTINE

Every week the household routine ran along well defined lines, each day having its allotted tasks. With few labour saving appliances, women's work really was never done. Washday in particular has stayed in the memory, with its monotonous and weary round of soaking, washing, starching, blueing, mangling, drying and ironing -- how many prayers went up on a Sunday for a fine day tomorrow!

LIFE AT THE VICARAGE

'I was born at Boxgrove Vicarage on 4th July 1913, the elder child of Richard Wells, Vicar of Boxgrove 1911 to 1926.

Our vicarage was a pleasant brick and flint-built house with the main windows facing south and east over the large garden. At the back were the stables, coach house, harness room, apple house, pig sty and other outbuildings. Indoors was the hall, dining room, study, drawing room, servants' hall, pantry, kitchen etc, downstairs and on the first floor nursery, four bedrooms and two dressing rooms, boxroom and bathroom; with three or four servants' bedrooms on the top floor.

The household consisted of our nurse, housemaid, parlourmaid and cook with a daily gardener and garden boy. Each had their well-defined daily work. The cook would rise at 6.30 am and the other maids a little later. She would light the kitchen range. The housemaid would do the fires and the parlourmaid bring my parents early morning tea, and lay the breakfast. She would also bring up cans of hot water and place them covered by a towel in the bedroom washbasins. Breakfast at 8.30 and my father would say Matins in the church at 9.15. My mother and I would accompany him and say the responses sometimes. My mother would then have her daily discussion with the cook to plan the meals.

On Mondays the laundry was sorted and packed in a huge wicker hamper and wheeled on a special flat barrow by Arthur Salisbury, the gardener, across the "Wobble Gates" to Mrs Hammond who did our washing. Meanwhile the lamps were cleaned and the wicks trimmed on the "slab" inside the side door and the knives cleaned and sharpened by the garden boy, who had already polished the shoes in a shed across the back yard. The house was swept and polished (the living rooms before breakfast and the bedrooms and upstairs landing later). After lunch at 1 pm the maids changed into their afternoon dresses. These were black with frilly cap and apron, morning dresses being blue cotton with plain aprons and caps.

In the morning we did lessons in the dining room with Miss Willard, our governess, who bicycled up from Tangmere. She never removed her hat and veil and wore a high net collar. Our favourite lesson was drawing, at which she excelled. We learnt a long list of spelling words each day.

My father always wrote the next Sunday's sermons on a Monday morning, revised them later in the week and learnt them on a Saturday evening. He was a good gardener and handyman and had a carpenter's shop at the bottom of the garden. The vicarage had to be painted every five years outside and he did most of this himself. Every afternoon he would mount his bicycle and go visiting. Sometimes I would sit in front on a hard metal carrier and accompany him. He called all the men by their Christian names and took a great interest in their work and gardens and said that he was more often called upon to heal a sick pig than their souls! We did not have a car but my mother had a pony and cart and later gave us a donkey and smart brown and yellow cart (which she bought in Portsmouth and drove back herself). We drove out on most afternoons; Mabel Longland our nanny, driving and often one of the maids coming too. On Fridays in the winter we drove to Lavant House for a dancing class. It was often very cold and we had a carpet-covered tin carriage hot water bottle for our feet. Later we had bicycles.

We had no telephone and urgent news had to be telegraphed, and there was a sense of excitement and dread when the telegraph boy with his red bike and pillbox hat was seen at the door with an orange coloured envelope. If we wanted to use the telephone we would go up to the post office run by Ena Gardner at Halnaker. Our milk would be delivered by Mr King with his float drawn by the old white pony from Mr Watkins' farm at Warehead. Bread and groceries would be brought from Mrs Wheatley's at Halnaker crossroads. Mr Henly was the baker and we never knew whether his white face was caused by the hot atmosphere or was covered with flour. We would go up to Mrs Wheatley's with our Saturday pennies and buy sweets from the big jars, done up in a twist of blue paper. Meat was delivered from Chichester, and we fetched two pounds of butter every week from the Goodwood Dairy where we were welcomed by rosy cheeked Miss Miller the dairymaid and taken into the large cool dairy to see the collection of china animals and birds on the marble shelves where great pans of milk stood.'

MONDAY WAS ALWAYS WASHDAY

'Monday was always washing day whatever the weather. In fact I grew to learn which particular work had to be done in the house each day. I was born in a mill house in 1907, so grew up always in hearing of the water rushing out into the mill-pool.

On a Monday morning early the copper out in the scullery was filled with water and a whole faggot of brushwood was lit beneath. A little old woman came in three mornings a week to help the maid who lived in. I used to watch her pushing the long faggot of wood further under the copper as it burnt. Presently the water was bubbling, a shredded soap-bar was added, also (I think) some soda, and the wooden copper lid put back on. Baskets of clothes and sheets were brought out to the scullery and sorted into piles. Woollens and fine frocks did not go into the copper. There was a long wooden copper-stick to stir everything in and the lid was put on again.

Nearby was the iron mangle with a large wheel to turn the wooden rollers. As I grew big enough I was just able to turn the wheel for fun, but of course nothing was going through. When the serious business of sheets and clothes were to be mangled I was forbidden anywhere near. On fine days the basket of clothes was taken out to the garden and hung up to dry.

Monday was also the day for the drawing room to be turned out. Furniture was brushed, ornaments dusted and carefully laid on the seats and covered with dustsheets, curtains shaken and tied up from the floor. The ceiling and walls were brushed with the cobweb brush. Then the maid brought a bowl of damp tea leaves and sprinkled them all over the carpet, later to be brushed up with a stiff brush and dustpan. She worked on her knees, going carefully all over the floor. The fireplace had been cleaned and relaid before breakfast if this was winter time.

My mother always did all the cooking herself on the black kitchener. This stove was the first job for the maid to clean and relight on getting down at 6 am. Tea was taken up to the big bedroom at 7 am. Breakfast was always at 8 am. This was before the First World War.

Twice a week Father came down dressed in his city suit and by 8.45 the pony-trap was at the front door to take him to Midhurst station for the London train, where he used to attend the corn market in Mark Lane on Mondays and Fridays. Of course he also bought wheat from the local farms. I can remember watching him looking at a field of wheat with the farmer. He used to pick an ear of wheat, bite it, rub it in his hands, then shake hands with the farmer to buy the crop as it stood. Unless it was pouring with rain I was allowed to go in the trap for the ride to the station and my mother drove us home again. My brother and sisters had already left for school. They came home for midday dinner and Father too unless it was a day for London, or Chichester market.

I started going to school in the mornings when I was five. I could already read anything before school, owing to my two big sisters. In fact, Mother used to hide the *Daily Mirror* because she found me absorbed in it one day!'

'Cottages were mostly "two up and two down", sometimes with a landing large enough to accommodate a bed. The front door led straight in from the street and the back room or kitchen would contain a blackleaded grate, on which all the cooking was done and all the water heated. It might also contain the copper used for the weekly wash and for heating the bath water at weekends. Sometimes the copper would be in an outside wash-house, usually opposite the back door. There was no piped water in Pulborough until the 1930s so water was drawn from the wells. Kitchen sinks were either of shallow stone or made of cemented bricks. Washing was done in a galvanised bath in the kitchen and this was used in front of the kitchen fire on bath nights – Saturday. This meant that all the clean clothes were worn for the first time on Sunday and dirty clothes ready for the weekly wash which was done on Monday, whatever the weather. When I asked my mother why this was always done on a Monday she quoted, "Those who wash on Monday have all the week to dry". On fine days after two rinses and the "blue bath" for the white articles, clothes were hung out on the line in the garden. If the weather was wet then the kitchen was festooned with the washing and the children given the front room in which to play.

Ironing was done on Tuesday with flat irons heated in front of the kitchen fire. Three were needed so that ironing could be continuous. The ironed clothes would then be hung on a clothes horse on the fireguard to air, smaller garments would be hung on a piece of string under the mantlepiece. If no paraffin stove was in use the kitchen fire was rekindled with paper and small pieces of wood; one old man I knew always took home each day small pieces of wood which he called "kittle brackets".'

'Monday was washday. All water was drawn from a well and the whites were boiled in the copper. They were then rinsed, blued, starched and mangled. Some hot water was then used to wash the coloured items, and the rest to scrub up, soak greasy baking pans and clean the drains. Dinner was invariably cold meat with bubble and squeak. Pudding was plain boiled rice so that the water could be saved to use as starch.'

'First the copper had to be filled with hot water, then a fire was lit in a small grate under the copper; paper, wood and coal was used for this and sometimes it was a job to get the water really hot. The washing was put into a large zinc bath standing on a stool, with plenty of hot water, soda and Sunlight soap, and a scrubbing brush was used. Then all the whites were put into the copper and turned with a copper stick until they boiled, which could take a long time. After the boiling all the clothes would be taken out of the copper and rinsed twice and then blued with a blue bag in a third rinse. Next they would be put through a large mangle, and in about 1928–30 a wringer with rubber rollers made life much easier and not so hard on the clothes.'

'By the time the washing had been done the kitchen was full of steam and my mother red and perspiring from the sheer physical effort of it all. Then it was a quick dinner of cold meat and mashed potatoes followed by a Spotted Dick which had also been boiling in the copper. Once the clothes began to dry they were rolled up damp, or sprinkled with water if they were too dry and then rolled, and the ironing began.

The three flat irons were put on the kitchen range and used in rotation, my mother first spitting on them. If it hissed or sizzled the iron was hot enough for cottons or linen. If not, it was put back to get hotter or used for woollens and finer things. The hot irons and damp clothes generated more steam. The heat, steam and smell of soapy clothes created a very familiar and comforting atmosphere for a small child sitting in a corner and "keeping out of the way". This was in the 1930s and 1940s.'

FOOD AND DRINK

Food may have been plainer and less varied in the past, but how those meals of our childhood bring back memories. There were always the treats too, like fresh herrings straight from the fisherman, muffins from the muffin man, real toast -- and home-cured bacon from our own pig! Baking could be something of a hit and miss affair, but our mothers did wonders with the most basic of equipment.

DAILY FARE

'In the 1920s it was considered very important to have a good cooked breakfast, mainly eggs and bacon and fried bread. Sometimes porridge would be served in the winter. There was bread and marmalade to finish. I remember the excitement when we first had Force cereal especially saving the coupons for a stuffed "Sunny Jim".

Saturday we would have a joint – when it was beef, Yorkshire pudding would be served, when lamb, boiled suet pudding. I don't remember having pork except at Christmastime. Always there were plenty of vegetables as my father grew them. In summer strawberries, raspberries, apples and plums would form our dessert. All the fruit was home-grown and my mother made a lot of pastry for pies. Sunday we had tinned red salmon for breakfast (it was very cheap in those days) and then cold meat for lunch with lettuce and tomatoes when in season, home-made chutney and pickle. It was considered wrong to cook on Sundays. Monday was also cold meat and Tuesday the meat would be made, if beef, into cottage pie and if lamb a hot pot. Always we would have meat. Occasionally my father would wring the neck of a chicken (I hated this but worse was the smell when Mum removed its innards). Steak and kidney puddings would be boiled in a basin with a cotton cloth over.

For tea we had to eat a piece of plain bread and butter first before we were allowed jam, although my mother made the jam from home-grown fruit. My mother had weekly a large fruit cake that we started Sunday and there would also be rock cakes.

At night my father would be served bread and cheese and before I went to bed I'd be given a spoonful of cod liver oil and malt and a peppermint boiled sweet.

When eggs were plentiful Mum would put them in waterglass in stone crocks. Plums would be bottled and runner beans would be put down in salt.

It was a treat on Sunday to toast muffins and crumpets on long brass forks in front of the fire.

A cup of tea and a biscuit would be brought up to bed by my father on his rising. Tea would again have been served for breakfast, with Camp coffee or cocoa mid morning. We would enjoy ginger beer from a stone bottle. At 5 pm we had tea with our meal and cocoa before bed. In summer Mum would always have a jug of home-made lemonade available, the cut lemons being put in a jug with sugar and boiling water poured on.'

'Dinners were a midday meal and rarely deviated. Saturdays: roast beef and Yorkshire pudding, or lamb and baked suet pudding; no sweet, it was not considered necessary. No bird or pork either; pork was for Christmas only. Sunday: cold meat, church being important, but a steamed pudding was left over a low gas while we were out. Monday: cold meat, milk pudding, sometimes tapioca, very unpopular, or macaroni, much nicer. Monday being wash-day, it had to be an easy meal. Tuesday: shepherd's pie or pea soup if the meat had run out. Wednesday: corned beef and vegetables. Thursday: sausages or liver and bacon. Friday: fish, brought round fresh by the local fishermen who had been out all night in their boats. We had a pudding of some sort each day but these varied.

Tea was not very exciting and was strictly set out. One slice of bread and butter plain, one with paste and one with jam. No more and no less, or we did not get cake, which was made on Saturday and rationed to one piece each per day so that it lasted all week. My brother and I used to turn the plate round so that the largest slices were the nearest. The worst teas put before us were food which we had not eaten at dinner; it came up for breakfast next day as well if we still left it. So occasionally we went hungry to bed, though where possible my brother and I did quick swaps when my mother was not looking. We were often hungry, especially during the war, when I had free school dinners. These were very frugal and, whereas my friends had high-tea when they got home, I only had the bread-and-butter tea as "I had already had my dinner".

Christmas Day was a source of joy never experienced by today's children who normally eat well. We had sausage rolls for breakfast, why I do not know. Pork, apple sauce and sprouts for dinner, none of which I liked, but I tucked in happily to roast potatoes, parsnips and sausages, as for once we did not have to eat what was put in front of us. Then the pudding, which I really enjoyed, covered by hot custard. Tea included tinned fruit, a very special treat, mince pies and the cake, which Mother invariably burnt. It was the only time she used the oven over our fireplace instead of the gas stove. When I think of the hours I spent stoning raisins and cleaning currants! Still the puddings were good. Even during the war we managed a pudding and a cake by saving our rations.'

'In these days of fast and convenience foods, to remember the lovely home-made food of my childhood and early married life gives one's tummy a warm glow. Syrup pudding, spotted dick and custard, boiled rice with jam, fruit roly-poly to name a few. Mutton stew, bacon roll, corned beef hash.

A rare treat was a Sunday roast. When it was beef, the end result was very productive: minced it gave us shepherd's pie on Monday and rissoles on Tuesday, while the lovely basin of dripping with the thick brown jelly gave us two teatimes of luscious dripping toast. If Mum got to it first it was the stock for home-made soup. We grew all our own vegetables. Apple trees were Forge Russet and Pearmain, with a damson and Victoria plum. The hedgerows produced blackberries, giving us jam and jelly, rose hips, sloes for wine, chestnuts, hazel nuts and beech nuts. The taste of chestnuts roasted on a shovel over an open fire was unbelievable.

My grandmother's stone-flagged larder floor was full of huge wine crocks with every kind of wine imaginable – parsnip, potato, carrot, blackberry, elderberry, sloe, marigold, apple scrumpy and many more. One could get inebriated very cheaply! My Dad had the shooting rights on two local estates so we were lucky enough to get rabbits, hares, pheasants and partridges quite often. Dad supplied the local butcher with rabbits; he was paid fourpence each and they sold for sixpence. Our butcher had the meat hanging outside. No deep freezers or cold store, just slabs of ice delivered twice weekly. We all survived this apparent lack of hygiene.

This way of life continued until wartime rationing began and then we did have to tighten our belts. Surprising as it may seem, my family – there were four of us – managed quite well; in fact it did us good. We kept rabbits and chickens, so we had regular meat to supplement our one shilling and sixpence worth allowance. We always had eggs, so even without fat I could make sponges and swiss rolls. I missed the dried fruit and brown sugar, and trying to ice a Christmas cake with mock icing made from dried milk powder, using beetroot juice for colouring, was hilarious. I did manage to make an eatable omelette with dried eggs. We folk in the country were lucky because we had room to grow all our own fruit and vegetables. I missed rice very much though, also oranges and bananas. The wartime cook had to be very ingenious, but it was a challenge thinking up new ways to making a little go a long way. My family came through it well nourished and I still look back on Lord Woolton's cook book with nostalgia. I still have mine, also my ration books. Good old days? In many respects, yes.'

MUFFINS AND ICE CREAM

'During the winter months the muffin man visited Balcombe. He would walk through the village with a high-sided tray on his head, ringing a bell, and we would rush out to buy the muffins. I suppose he came by train from somewhere, but to this day I have never found anyone who knew who he was or where he came from. But his muffins were good!

We made our own ice cream. The Ice Man, as we called him, would call, driving an open lorry, and he would throw a sack over his shoulder and place a large block of ice on it for delivery to our house. It was my sister and I who had the job of breaking the ice up and putting it in the ice churn, where it was ground down by handle. Custard powder and other things were added and then for ever and ever, or so it seemed, it had to be turned by the handle until it was the right consistency. Anyway, Phyllis and I much preferred Mrs Malthouse's ices (she had a shop and tearoom in Mill Lane). Even our dog Gyp liked hers better! He would take himself off to visit her and she would give him a penny cornet. He would return with the pointed end sticking out of his mouth – obviously he had taken heed of what Mother had said to us: "I do not want you eating ice cream in the road!" '

HERRING-ALIVE-O

'It must have been in the early 1930s, when I was about eight years old, that I remember the Bognor fishermen with their handcart piled with herrings walking all the way to the council houses at Balls Hut, Fritwell, to sell their fish at 20 for a shilling, or if there was a real glut, 30 for a shilling.

Times were hard then, no work and precious little money, and we used to listen on a Saturday afternoon for the clang of the handbell and a shout of "Herring-alive-o!" and everyone would come running with their dishes. We were a family of seven, Mum, Dad and five children. There were fried herrings for tea that night, a large dishful were put into the oven to souse, and the rest were threaded onto strings and strung across a corner of the kitchen to dry into bloaters.'

TRUE TOAST

'The placing of a square of factory-wrapped and sliced bread under the hissing spluttering flame of the grill, revived memories of the making of toast in my childhood. It was then a pleasurable domestic chore which vanished long ago with the passing of the open fire and the kitchen range. Toast, then, was a delight.

That toast of long ago, we made from bread baked by the local baker, whose bakehouse was no more than the length of a cricket pitch distance from our house. The aroma of his daily bakings pervaded the whole district, and often I awoke to the smell of freshly baked bread. Hurriedly dressing I would scamper across the road to collect for breakfast those delectable loaves and rolls still hot from the oven, and whose fragrance filled the awakening street. Often the baker would allow us to "help" in the preparation and baking of a batch, and there was nothing nicer than those piping hot, shapeless lumps of dough we had moulded ourselves and placed with care with the aid of a peel in the oven to be baked with his crusty cottage loaves.

Toast was never part of a meal, but was regarded as a special treat on a winter's afternoon to compensate for the red noses, cold feet and hands of children unwilling to leave their outdoor games and pastimes. Sitting before a bright fire, on chair or stool, fork in hand, the bright live coals quickly restored warmth and colour to blue knees and chilled limbs. As soon as knees could bear the searing heat no longer, the first side would be toasted to perfection. With speed the bread was reversed, and the second side presented to the fire, until once again it forced one back with scorched skin but triumphant with the slice an unblemished golden brown.

Toast had to be eaten at once, not allowed to flag or become limp, before the pools of melting butter or dripping infiltrated its soft hot centre. Mother and aunts would cut their slices into slim, neat rectangles, to be nibbled in a genteel manner, but we children favoured the eating of the whole round held in the hand, palm uppermost, between thumb and second finger stretched to their limit across the width of the slice, and for its support, the third and little fingers curled beneath.

The disappearance of the open fire, and the invention of the electric toaster, led to the demise of this simple delight. Seated around the hearth in the dusk of a winter's afternoon, illuminated by the firelight, devouring rounds freshly made and spread with the jellied drippings of the Sunday roast, is a memory that drifts across the taste buds of my mind.'

SAMPHIRE AND SEA SPINACH

'In the early years of the century at Selsey, samphire shoots were picked on East Beach to be pickled in vinegar and eaten as a great delicacy. This is a kind of succulent plant which does not seem to be around anymore. Sea spinach was picked and eaten as a vegetable and this still grows among the shingle.'

HEDGEROW HARVEST

'In the autumn hazelnuts were shaken off the trees around Cuckfield, then stacked in their shells in a jamjar between layers of salt. With the lid on, they were buried in the garden until Christmas.

The hedgerow harvest produced crabapples and blackberries for jelly. Wine was made from produce from field or garden at no cost except for the sugar. A Sussex speciality was made from pea-shucks, also oak leaves, sloes, bullaces, cold tea and a bee wine. A local farmer provided mangels for wine so that when returning from market he could call in for a sample.'

'The sight of the first dandelion filled me with dismay. It was always the same – I was just beginning to enjoy the spring, had picked the first celandine, then the primroses and wild violets, and was looking forward to the bluebells, when appeared the first gaudy dandelion. I hurried up the path to the field named the Hop Garden. How I wished it was still full of hops, but no, I knew it, it was yellow with dandelions. Soon the baskets would be brought out and the two sacks, one to be knelt on and the other to be filled with dandelion heads from the baskets.

My mother was one of five sisters, all of whom drank dandelion wine. To them it had magical properties. It was food for colds, as good as quinine – which, in fact, it tasted like. If you had to spend hours ironing and goffering as the sisters did, your thirst was very great, and a glass – or, in the daytime, a cup – of dandelion wine revived you. It had the same effect as a couple of aspirin. You felt a new woman after drinking it.'

'Ginger-beer "plants" were popular and passed from one family to another. This required "feeding" daily with ginger and sugar and after about three weeks lemon juice and water would be added to make gallons of this healthful and refreshing drink.'

BAKING DAY

'I baked in a brick oven which was filled with bavins (faggots of brushwood) in bundles. When burnt out, the ashes were swept out (about a shovelful), then the oven was mopped out with water and bread and cakes put in. When the baking was done, beetroots or possibly bacon was put in saucepans to cook and afterwards the oven was lined with paper and clothes put in to air. My neighbour, who had seven children, baked all her own bread once a week, using yeast from the making of beer, at a cost of threepence, bavins being two bundles of three ha'pence.'

'We lived outside Midhurst and in the 1930s we were one of the last houses on the gas main. The pressure was sometimes very low indeed; I can remember my mother and a neighbour cooking their cakes in the same oven as if they had both used the oven at the same time the pressure would have been almost non-existent.'

KEEPING A PIG

'I was born in Charlton in 1899. Food was more wholesome in those days, I'm sure. Several of the local families had pigs – we bought them from the farms when they were tiny piglets, and we used to try to fatten them up and make them better than anyone else's. At pig-killing time the pigs were weighed and got ready and then the village pig-killer came round. The carcase was hung up in the outhouse and the pig-killer came again the next day and cut it up into joints. Whole sides were hung up to be smoked where there was a big chimney. We gave joints to our friends and neighbours because we knew they would look after us when it was their turn to kill their pig. The killer stayed to tea that day and we always had the pig's liver for tea.'

'After the Second World War food and petrol rationing was still extremely tight (resulting in only one car on average every 20 minutes in the middle part of the day along the A264!). One could register as a Pig Keeper and every six months would be allowed to keep half a pig to be cured at home. Nearly every litter of pigs has a runt, which was penned separately and sold for £1 or 30 shillings. We bought several and kept them in the greenhouse for warmth. They were very tiny and pushy and used to escape periodically. Once our gardener, bicycling to work from Copthorne Bank, met them at play in the yard of The Duke's Head. He called out to them, "Pigs, come!" and they trotted along behind his cycle, home again, looking very pink. One day they even visited the general shop next door, and were helping themselves to dog biscuits out of a bowl of loose ones on the floor. The shop's owners were remarkably relaxed about it and we soon had them rounded up again.'

SHOPPING AND CALLERS
TO THE DOOR

Regular callers to the door included the milkman, the baker and the butcher, as well as travelling salesmen. Shopping from home was quite normal, and many shops allowed you to have goods on approval, delivered and collected at their own expense. Tradesmen went to great lengths to capture new custom, even to visiting people *before* they had moved into the area!

SHOPPING BY CARRIER

'An important person in the early 1900s was the carrier. He owned a van and he came round Lower Beeding once or twice a week. If you needed any supplies from Horsham a flag was displayed outside the house as a signal for him to call for a list of requirements. These he purchased and delivered. What a welcome service that was.'

'There was no shop at North Mundham, and farm workers did not get paid till late Saturday evening when they walked into Chichester to get their shopping. During the week a carrier's cart would take passengers to Chichester, or he would fetch packages for the villagers for a small charge.'

EMILY

'In the early years of the century shopping presented quite a problem for the residents of the small village of Lurgashall but to some extent this was overcome by the energy of a middle-aged woman whose name was, it is believed, Emily. She wore breeches and carried a haversack. She would call at the various cottages and take "orders" for such small items as reels of cotton, tape, buttons and knicker elastic etc. She would then walk the six miles to Haslemere, make the necessary purchases and return to deliver the goods to her customers who would willingly pay her the few pence she charged. Whatever the weather she would carry out her self-imposed task.

In addition she would collect small quantities of lard from the "big house", Blackdown House – home of the Aldwyn family who were generous benefactors of Lurgashall church of St Laurence and who were one of the few families to be able to afford really large joints

The delivery van and the errand boy's heavy bicycle wait outside the Broadwater Cash Stores for the orders to be made up. Shops provided a competitive service and were happy to deliver, free, to our doors.

which provided a surplus of lard. Loaded with packets of this much sought after fat, Emily would deliver them to those of her customers who so desired it. How much she charged no one now living seems to recall but whatever remuneration she received was willingly paid by her grateful customers.'

COLLECTING THE DIVI

'A little flannel suit for my son in 1935 cost about five shillings in Marks and Spencers. These suits my friend and I usually bought out of our Co-op "divi". The children had to take lunch to school on "divi days" while we went to Brighton. After doing our shopping, we would daringly go into The King and Queen and have a three-penny glass of port and a twopenny Welsh rarebit. We felt we were really living it up!'

ON APPROVAL

'Most shops in Worthing were family owned in the 1920s and all the tradesmen knew their customers personally. The tradesmen gave a very good service in those days and you could have goods delivered on appro, so that you could decide in your own home what you would like to buy. Shoes or clothes, for instance, would be delivered to the house one day and collected back the next (usually by bike), and any purchases made would be charged to the customer's account.

Food shops were very different from today. All dry ingredients such as biscuits, butter, cheese etc, would be weighed and put into paper bags, and even eggs went into a bag. After purchases had been made the shop assistant would put all the different prices onto one of the bags – usually the sugar bag – and add up all the prices in his head. If you wished, an order could be taken into the shop or sometimes assistants would call for orders at the back door of the house, and the order would be delivered next day. It was the same procedure for the butcher.'

TRAVELLING SALESMEN

'When the carrier's cart was the only form of public transport, country people relied a good deal on travelling salesmen for their needs. Some could be very persistent in purveying their wares and they received short shrift from my grandfather. On one occasion a man selling sewing machines was being particularly pestiferous! Grandmother already had one machine and so did not want another, but the salesman was insisting she try one of his machines and had dumped it in the doorway. It was at this point that my grandfather arrived home. He soon sized up the situation and, since the salesman would not remove his machine, Grandpa picked it up, carried it across the yard and threw it into the duck pond. He then went back, picked up the salesman and deposited him in the pond too. The salesman departed covered in duckweed and did not return!

I remember one little man, Mr Piper, who trudged round the villages carrying two huge portmanteaux. He was so short, no more than four foot, and his cases were so large that they barely cleared the ground. He and his sister had a small haberdasher's shop in Haywards Heath – she looked after the shop and he "did the rounds". The things he sold only cost a penny or two each and I cannot imagine how he managed to make a living but he was the happiest and most cheerful little man I have ever known.'

THE BUTCHER, THE BAKER AND THE MILKMAN

'Prior to the First World War milk was delivered at Wivelsfield by taking a churn of milk to the customers in a horse-drawn float and

Before the days of bottles and cartons, the milkman delivered straight from the churn. T. Bartlett had a round at Wivelsfield before the First World War.

serving it straight into each customer's jug by means of special milk ladles – half pint, one pint and two pint. The ladles were cylindrical with a long upright handle and a reverse hook at the top with which to hang them on the churn.'

'The butcher, the baker and the milkman all came to the door in horse-drawn vans at Worthing. We always went out to stroke the horse's nose and the baker would let me give his horse his nosebag of oats in the middle of the morning. We had to be quick to rush out with a bucket and shovel to get any manure left on the road before anyone else, for my father to put in the old bath behind the green-house to use as liquid feed for his tomatoes and chrysanthemums. Worthing had the finest greenhouses in the South, and the flavour of Worthing tomatoes was the best. There was no question of salad all the year round then, and we all longed for the first tomatoes and let-tuce of the season.

The baker called every morning and he would bring the loaves to the back door in a large bread basket for Mother to choose what she wanted. In the 1920s the milkman called twice a day – very early in the morning before breakfast, then again during the morning. The milk was supplied at this time from a milk churn, the milk being put straight into a jug. Later, in the late 1920s to early 1930s, milk started to be delivered in bottles. At Christmas, the milkman always left a present of a carton of cream.'

'My mother and I arrived at Lancing station from Ealing in July 1933. We started our walk to Sompting, about one and a half to two miles, each carrying necessities for the day in case the removal men had lost their way! A van pulled up and my mother recognised the driver – a rep who had called on her in London to obtain her custom with the local dairy. He offered to take us to our new home and said that he had left samples of milk, butter and cream for us.'

'My maternal grandparents ran the bakery in Bosham. A covered cart was pushed by a young lad for the twice daily bread delivery and sometimes I was sent off to deliver special orders. After my grandfather died, my parents helped my grandmother with the business but unfortunately my father knew little about breadmaking (he had always worked on the railways) and was not very successful. He got into trouble with the authorities for adding mashed potato to the dough to make the bread whiter, and the family had to sell the business.

On Sundays, people brought their joints to be cooked in the bakery ovens. It cost a penny. The joints came with the peeled potatoes around the meat and large dollops of dripping on top. If the joint was brought before eleven o'clock it was ready for collection soon after noon – possibly to be collected on the way home from church.'

WHAT WE WORE

New clothes were a rare treat for many families in the past, and children were more likely to live in hand-me-downs and 'turned' clothes and to keep their best for Sunday. Styles of dress have changed enormously, particularly for women, since the beginning of the century.

WEARING THIN

'The children I knew were dressed very simply during the years

1912–18 and during the period of the First World War clothes became scarce and expensive so economy was practical and patriotic.

My brothers and I wore woollen jerseys, the boys with corduroy shorts, I with pleated skirts. The jerseys were high necked, buttoning across the shoulders, mine on the left and my brothers' on the right.

When "wearing thin" set in on the fronts and elbows, the garments were turned back to front to spread the wear. My brothers were wild with indignation because their buttons were now on "the girls' side", apparently insulting their masculinity. My sister and I didn't much like the change but we did not protest; I think it was seen by our brothers as some kind of "promotion" for us.

Protest continued until the "proper way" was achieved, to be resumed when turnabout time came again. I am quite sure that my brothers would have preferred darned or even patched fronts and elbows to those hated girls'-side buttons.'

'A great deal of mending was done at home in the 1920s. Household linen was carefully repaired, sometimes by darning. Sheets were turned sides to middle. Adult garments were sometimes unpicked and cut down to make clothes for children. A coat might be unpicked, the material turned and restitched together to make a coat that looked like new, so it was said. Little was wasted. Heavy material not suitable for other purposes was cut into strips and made into rag rugs. A special hook was made for this purpose. Some people were very artistic and blended colours to good effect.'

HOW WE'VE CHANGED

'New born babies had a flannel bandage to keep the cord dressing in situ, next a woollen vest, and then a linen bandage three or four inches wide was wound round a few times to support the baby's back. Next a thick towelling nappy was applied. This was followed by a long flannel petticoat with another towelling napkin put under the baby to keep the petticoat dry. A long white embroidered gown was put on for daytime with a white shawl, and a plainer cotton gown used at night. Bibs were always worn. After a few weeks the baby was "tucked". Short attire consisted of two petticoats – one flannel and one flannelette; the skirt of the petticoat had three tucks and was gathered into a cotton bodice which had a draw tape round the neck and waist. A short dress was usually white for the first few weeks and often smocked at yoke and wrists. Hand knitted garments came in fashion after the First World War and babies had woollen dresses and woollen pram sets with leggings, jacket and bonnet.

Schoolwear for girls consisted of woollen vest, stays, and flannelette drawers with gathers into bands with buttonholes to attach to stays. Liberty bodices came later. They wore flannel and flannelette petticoats, lined serge dresses with long sleeves and cuffs, black ribbed stockings, lace-up boots, and a white pinafore was always worn, either plain linen or a frilly cotton one with lace insertions – all were starched. Later on came blouses, tunics and blazers. For headwear girls wore tam-o-shanters and later on felt hats were worn in winter and panamas for summer. Berets arrived in the Second World War.

Young boys wore girls' clothes until they were "britched" when they were toilet trained. When school age they wore knickerbockers with ribbed black stockings and lace up boots, until short knickers came in fashion worn with coloured socks with fancy turndown tops. Shoes replaced boots at a later date. Long trousers were worn after leaving school. Rubber boots and mackintoshes appeared and much later plastic macs, jerkins and anoraks. Flat caps were worn until berets came in fashion.

There was less change in men's wear, but soft collars took the place of stiff ones. Trouser leg width varied frequently and turn-ups to trousers disappeared. Hats changed from flat caps to trilbies and bowlers.

Great changes in ladies' wear have occurred in my lifetime. At the turn of the century they wore woollen vests with camisoles, with whale-boned corsets laced up at the back with hooks and eyes at the front, followed by a chemise or waist petticoat to the ground. A skirt was ground length, often embroidered with braid, which was matched with a long fitted jacket. Blouses were high necked and with long fitted sleeves, often trimmed with lace or frills. Hats had wide brims and perched high on the head, lined with sateen with a draw string, secured by hat pins and often embroidered with masses of artificial flowers and fruit. Black stockings and lace-up boots or shoes. Older women wore little black bonnets adorned with flowers and a net which covered the face. Black stockings and elasticated boots and a cape or shawl completed the apparel.

Fashions changed in the 1920s. Corselettes followed corsets and later suspender belts with bras. Rayon replaced cotton. There were shorter skirts and jackets, and more variety in colours and materials. Hats became smaller and pulled down. Light stockings became available, and more variety and colour in shoes. Blouses were varied and many were short sleeved. Dresses were three-quarter length and had loose fitting sleeves.

84

Everybody had Sunday clothes and everyday clothes. Clean clothes were put on every Sunday and best top clothes. These were worn to church and later for walks.'

FROM BIRTH TO DEATH

We were far more likely to be born, to be ill and to die, in our own homes than in the local hospital. Every family had their own tried and trusted home cures -- some of them sounding worse than the ailment they were meant to treat! Many a child had their tonsils removed on the scrubbed kitchen table, and the doctor and the District Nurse were familiar and trusted figures in the town and village. It is as well to recall also, however, that illnesses we now rarely encounter, such as TB, scarlet fever and diphtheria, were once commonplace and deadly.

HOME CURES

'In the early 1930s, when a grandchild had a cough, my grandfather would pick from the downs the leaves of a wild plant called mouse-ear (of the chickweed family). He would then make a thick syrup for us to drink. But when a child had whooping cough, the leaves would be picked from a cemetery as these were much larger and stronger.'

'Our health was generally taken care of by our parents, using many home-made country remedies. I remember a salve for healing cracks and splits on hands that my father used to make by boiling herbs. When the potion had hardened it was rolled out into sausage shapes in clean white rag. When it was required the salve was gently warmed over a flame and then applied to the hands.'

'Adders collect in great numbers during the spring. On two occasions in the Fittleworth area, I have seen a heap as big as a bushel skip, on a bank. While I stood watching, more adders were making their way to the heap. Although I saw this around 70 years ago, their habits must still be the same today, though their numbers have declined.

My father caught adders in March, taking fat from two places behind the head of the adder. The fat was rendered down into oil, the oil being very valuable for cuts. On one occasion a neighbour had a thorn in his eye, but the oil applied took it cleanly out.'

'A gipsy remedy for a wart in Cuckfield was to heat washing soda with a flame from a match or candle. When the soda melted, the liquid was put on the wart. Other old treatments included using a dock leaf for a nettle sting, a blue bag (from the laundry) for a wasp sting. Eat sorrel for nettle rash.'

'On my mother's side, when her grandmother was married at Bognor, a plant was thrown into her wedding carriage with the words of advice to look after it. It has been grown in the family ever since as a medicinal plant; the back of the leaf as a poultice, the front for healing. Many years ago Morton Swinburne, then editor of the *Bognor Post*, wrote to the Kew Zoological Gardens enquiring into its origin and was told it was Cretan Spikenard from the island of Crete, and was in the balm used in biblical times.'

'My grandparents lived on a farm in Sussex and between 1912 and 1921 I frequently stayed with them. As a town-dwelling child, I was fascinated by every aspect of rural life, particularly my grandmother's activities. She had a herb garden which produced most of the materials for a number of simples, comforts etc. I recall that my frequent (and perhaps not quite honest) sore throats were soothed by her blackcurrant cordial. She made raspberry and blackberry too, and sloe gin and a great deal of wine.

I loved to help her with the preparations, especially with the balms and salves. Plantain leaves were pounded (often by me) and mixed with clarified lard to produce a lovely green salve; white sulphur balm was a splendid yellow – sulphur seemed to be much used in horticulture in those days. Quassia chips (twopennyworth from the chemist on market day) were used to make a hairwash guaranteed to keep hair "clean" in more than one sense. Cold cream was made from lard with eau-de-cologne worked in, and sometimes eau-de-cologne mint was pounded and added. This was considered very good for the complexion, which was protected, even in the country, from the sun by shady hats or sunbonnets. This was the only cosmetic that I knew of.

My grandmother seemed to be accepted as a wise woman (no murmur of "witch") and her cures were in great demand and much esteemed.'

OPERATIONS AT HOME

'I can vaguely recall having my tonsils out when I was six years old in 1922. White-coated people brought something like a trestle table into our bedroom at home in Chichester. I was put on it and a mask put over my face. I must have objected and made a lot of fuss because I kicked the doctor and he fell over. He was prone to swearing and was very annoyed, so I heard about it for many years after, but I recovered with the help of a nurse.'

THE DOCTOR AND THE DISTRICT NURSE

'Henfield is full of ancient twittens. Other counties have their gunnels and slickets, but in Sussex they must be twittens – narrow foot passages generally with high walls or fences, providing short cuts between boundaries. Sometimes they are used by ponies, as they must have been for years, finding an easy route to the common or the stable. In 1981 a new twitten was made by Elm Lodge, a double-fronted early Victorian house. This was very properly given an old name – Caudle Street – because a century before, Elm Lodge had been occupied by one of a line of doctors, Adolphus Caudle.

In September 1950 Broadbridge WI were instrumental in opening the first Baby Clinic in the village, a tremendous boost for the better care of local infants. Nurse Gardner was the school nurse and Health Visitor for many years.

87

It was recalled by his descendants that Dr Caudle fitted a speaking tube from his front door to his bedside through which to receive any urgent messages, and each night his horse in the stable behind the house was left saddled and bridled ready for a possible nocturnal call. The good doctor also rode to hounds.'

'Dr Clement Chaplin came to Angmering in 1905 and his surgery was a wooden structure built in the garden of his house in the High Street. The waiting room had hard benches, no heating, and his bicycle stood in the corner. He would never allow anyone to clean the surgery so it was festooned with cobwebs on the ceiling. He made up his own medicines in a little cubby-hole by the side and held two surgeries every day and one on Sunday.

He would also extract teeth. His daughter Prudence said that he attended to her lying on the dining room table!

Dr Chaplin ran a club to cover payment for treatment and some of the men paid into Friendly Societies. Patent medicines like Iron Jelloids and Kruschen Salts were bought at the grocer's but everyone had their own remedies. My aunt took hot water for indigestion, Father had a boiled onion for a cold and we rubbed our chilblains with a raw onion. When I fell in the playground and broke my arm Dr Chaplin set it and told my father to send the bill to the school authorities – and they paid it. When I had to have a tooth filled mother hired the horse and cab from The Lamb and took me to Littlehampton.

One day Dr Chaplin called on a lady when she had slipped to the "loo" and as she had left chops frying on the stove he obligingly turned them for her. She complained that she couldn't keep her boys in bed with measles so he suggested throwing tin-tacks on the floor.

One summer Mr Harris brought his fair to the ground behind Chappy's garden – I never hear *Valencia* without recalling it and still have a vase my sweetheart won at hoopla. However, the doctor objected and since no one dared disagree it came no more. When a meeting was held in the school – now the library – to discuss street lighting he vetoed this too as he wanted to keep Angmering a village.

His wife, a formidable lady who had been a matron in a London hospital, was an excellent needlewoman and held craft classes. She could never understand why I "gave them a miss" but if she had seen my embroidery she would have done. She always won the needlework competition at WI but this didn't go down well so the committee made her the judge! She once made a patchwork quilt and lined it with woollen squares cut from underclothing. It was raffled in aid of WI funds and Mrs Wells, who won it, said that she went to bed under the doctor's pants!

Dr Chaplin died in the 1940s and it was said that if only he had taken more holidays or rest days he would have been with us longer. The surgery is no longer there but we think of him when we pass his house called "Chaplins".'

'As the daughter of a country doctor between the wars, I feel privileged to have known a wonderfully dedicated, tolerant and patient breed of men.

There were many occasions when my father was called out in the middle of the night. On our front door there were two bells and the one marked Night Bell rang above the door of my parents' bedroom. Doctors would often stay all night with patients perhaps who were suffering from pneumonia and approaching the "crisis" (no antibiotics in those days), and all the family would be grateful for the involvement he felt with them.

Doctors were consulted on many aspects of their patients' lives, and with a twinkle in his eye my father would tell of one well to do lady he attended who sought his advice on buying her house cow – or on the style of corset she should wear.

My father loved riding horses, for exercise and for fun. We rode every morning from seven o'clock to eight, often taking in an early morning call on patients who lived in outlying cottages, or calling at the cottage hospital, where I would hold his horse while he visited the wards and had a chat with Matron on the night's events.

A simple story was told to me of the events following the death of an infant at a farm in Lurgashall parish. Two ladies were carrying the little coffin to the churchyard when towards them came a motorbike. The rider stopped and stood, cap in hand, while the sad little cortége passed by. Things moved more slowly in those days.'

'Before 1917, if a nurse was needed in Pulborough she came from the Wisborough Green Nurses' Home. After the home closed in 1917, Pulborough & District Nursing Association was formed with Mrs Tomkins as Secretary/Treasurer, a position she held until 1946. To be sure the nurse would be available, people paid a subscription to the Association. These subscriptions were levied under four headings – Labourers; Artisans, Gentlemen's Outdoor Servants and Small Farmers; Tradespeople; and Gentry. The District Nurse's duties covered general nursing, midwife and health visitor in homes, health visitor in schools ("Nitty Nora"), and she was present at clinics, both in school and the village.'

'When I came to Findon in September 1935 a nursing association was in existence and had been for a number of years run by a very efficient voluntary committee. If you belonged to that association you paid an annual subscription of four shillings and sixpence a year and this entitled you to all nursing services. If you required midwifery you paid an extra £2 for a first baby and £1 10s for subsequent ones. We nurses visited mostly for a fortnight and mothers never got up for ten days, the only rest some mothers had until the next confinement. We never had any trouble with deliveries; though weather and social conditions made things difficult sometimes.

I remember going to a confinement high up on the downs, putting my car around the back of the house. All was well early in the morning when it was time to send for the doctor, so I lent my car to the husband; the doctor arrived, the baby was born. I packed up and went to get the car: no car in sight. I went back to the house and said, "Where is the car?" All looked astonished. What had happened was the brakes had not been put on securely, the car went rocking down into the road below, through a hedge and down again in to a farm yard, the car still upright. This is not the end of the story. I had in the back seat of the car a box of classical gramophone records belonging to a gentleman friend; they now looked like liquorice allsorts – end of romance!

For me the procuring of a gas and air machine was the highlight of the 1940s. It made a wonderful contribution for the relief of pain for the home confinement of mothers – a real landmark, as was the prescribing of antibiotics and all the immunisation for diphtheria, whooping cough, measles, polio and scarlet fever. The new National Health Service was just starting to make headway.

Terminal illnesses were a great problem; no hospices in those days, but care for them we did, sometimes three visits a day and always a late evening visit. Heroin and morphia were our main standby. Families were more available to give help in those days and, what's more, willing to do so; no problem of the one child only to take over the burden of caring for the elderly.

When I came in 1935 the school had about 90 pupils. The yearly school medical inspection was always a source of worry to me: lots of children had warts. I remember the doctor saying to me, "Get rid of the warts by my next visit". This was done and on the next visit he congratulated me on the success of the treatment. However, I didn't inform him that I sent the children down to a lady in the village who was a very successful wart charmer; I rested on my laurels!

The head inspections were another source of worry. At the beginning of each term I descended on the school and sorted the children out. I hated the job as much as the children did. I believe this practice has now been given up.'

THE SLATE CLUB

'West Chiltington in 1910 had a Slate Club, run by the village landlord, to which each member paid one shilling per week, out of about twelve shillings wages. If a member was sick he was paid ten shillings per week, and any surplus money left in the Club was shared out just before Christmas. My mother was widowed very young, with four small children, and she was given four shillings a week from the rector. This money came from a collection made by two good ladies from the wealthy of the village and given to the parson to distribute.'

'My father was a grocer who worked in various national stores, eg International and Home & Colonial. He went round Shoreham on his bike to private houses taking orders which were then made up in the shop. He was often wet through when he came home for his midday dinner and caught chills, but he did not stop off work unless the chill turned to pleurisy. He used to get the boys in the shop who caught cold to bag up flour, saying that the amount of sneezing this caused got rid of the germs. What it did to the flour was not considered; this was in the 1930s. He paid money into a Slate Club for sick benefit, and we were panel patients in a doctor's practice. When off sick, beneficiaries were checked on, and had to be indoors by dusk in the winter and six o'clock in the summer. If you were fit to be out, you were fit to work.'

TB AND THE FEVER

'My sister Joan was born in 1919. She loved swimming and was a member of Worthing Swimming Club which was based at Heene Road Baths, now demolished. When she was 16 she developed tuberculosis and was sent to Aldingbourne House, near Chichester, which was then a hospital for chest diseases. My father and mother would take us to see her every Sunday, and I remember sitting with her on the beautiful wrought iron balconies which surrounded the house and which can still be seen from the A27 today. Unfortunately, there was no cure for TB then and she died at the end of 1936 at the age of 17. I was four at the time and I can remember her coffin being put on the hearse at the front gate.'

'In the 1940s, just before I started school at Billingshurst at the age of five years, I contracted tuberculosis in my glands. There were no drugs available and I can remember the doctor telling my mother that because of the war it was not possible to send me to Switzerland. So he sent me to Chichester instead, where there was one ward for ordinary patients and the rest for soldiers. When they needed all the spaces for service casualties, we were taken by train to Coventry. My parents were not told where we had gone and they tell me it was weeks before they found me. When they did my father came to fetch me and the train he was in was bombed (this was just before the Coventry bombing).

I had one operation while I was at Coventry, and in those days you were taken into the operating room before you had been put to sleep. I can remember lying on the table with doctors around me when the siren went and everyone fled. I am sure it was just for a few seconds but I can assure you it felt like a lifetime.

When I got home the doctor found me a place in a hospital at Alton. My parents were allowed to visit once a month during the summer, but not at all in the winter, and could only come to the end of the bed. I had a lot of operations and sent about two and a half years in bed, but I am one of the lucky ones – I went home.

In Horsham there were two camp schools for children with health problems, one for Sussex children and the other for children from London

I often think back to the frightened and lonely little girl I was. I saw a lot of people die of the illness I had. My bad dream was that they would think I was dead when I was only asleep.'

'When my husband was five in 1932 he contracted scarlet fever and remembers being wrapped in a blanket, carried from the house on a hard board and put in the horse-drawn ambulance for the journey to the isolation hospital in Spitalfields Lane, Chichester. Visitors were not allowed but messages could be left at the gatehouse and passed on later.

In 1936 a brown ambulance replaced the horse and was used until the end of the war when it was given to the St John's Ambulance Brigade, who ran the ambulance service in those days. Paid staff operated during the day but for the rest of the time the service relied heavily on volunteers. This meant being available from 5 pm to 9 am every night, all day Saturday and Sunday. Volunteers were also used for the London runs, which were fairly frequent, paid staff not being used if it meant them returning to base after 5 pm.'

EVERYTHING THAT WAS GOING

'At Findon school in the late 1930s I believe we were the only one-parent family. Compared with today's statistics we were rare. Even the meaning was different as my mother was a widow at 28 years old in 1933 with two small children. Help was more help-yourself than State given. Her pension was ten shillings for herself, five shillings for the first child and three shillings for the second child – this never increased. So families were the only other help. We lived with our grandparents who could only help with childcare, not finance. From the day after my father's funeral my mother took any work that came along, night or day; from taking in laundry, housework, early morning cleaning at the local public house and washing milk bottles at the farm dairy, to laying out the dead in the parish. A relative would knock on our door at any time for her services. Bereavement for a family often meant new shoes for my brother or myself, if they could afford the ten shillings fee themselves.

There was no bathroom, flush toilet or water on tap in our house and gas lights only on the ground floor. I don't think any of these factors were responsible for my falling for every yearly epidemic that came along, as I was really well fed and cared for. Starting with chickenpox at 18 months, I followed on with mumps, german measles, diphtheria, measles, whooping cough and ending with scarlet fever on my tenth birthday in 1939. I was very lucky to miss polio in summer 1938. This caused the death of my nine year old school friend; I remember going to the shop with my mother to buy flowers for her funeral. I chose gladioli as her name was Gladys. As her father worked as gardener at Muntham Court she was buried in their private cemetery at Muntham Clump, near Tolmare Findon. For the rest of that summer's school holidays we were confined to our back yard and forced to gargle and sniff salt water up our noses every day in the hope of prevention. Our treatment when we caught whooping cough was to be taken round the village wherever the workmen were tarring the roads to breathe in the fumes.

Another weekly ritual after our bath in front of the fire was a dose of syrup of figs. My grandmother thought we should be clean inside and out. I rebelled so often that my mother gave in to me, but got the bottle out each week so Granny never knew. I can't remember if she ever made a comment about the bottle lasting so long. I loved wearing my cotton wool jacket next to my skin when I had pneumonia; as I regained health it was taken off not at one time but bits were pulled away daily until none remained.

My mother tried her best to keep us healthy, from doses of cod liver oil and malt to wearing what was called an iodine locket round my neck on a thin piece of string. This was a round of bakelite (early plastic) material with small holes in it, which smelt of iodine. My favourite medicine from my Granny was for what she called "the runs" – a spoonful of raw arrowroot powder mixed with port and sugar. When the cold on my chest needed the tallow spread on a piece of brown paper treatment, I was not too keen to go to school as the smell lingered. I preferred the smell of camphorated oil. Our family had remedies for most ailments of the time. So when people remarked how pale my brother often looked, Mum cured that by touching his cheeks with the rouge puff before taking him out. Comments then were on how well he looked.

Having diphtheria at the age of five I was taken up to Swandean isolation hospital for an eight week stay. My mother had been ill for some time before but was not diagnosed until I had the symptoms. My brother was carrying the germs in his nose, so to stop the doctor putting swabs up his nose he put a bead up his nose, which did him no good at all. While I was in hospital my Gran and Grandad would walk from Findon to visit me on Sunday afternoons. By standing outside the window near my bed, they brought me eggs and sweets from my mother which she could ill afford. Even so these were shared in the ward so we only had half a boiled egg each and one sweet a day after our afternoon rest. When I was fit enough to return home I cried as I didn't want to leave my new home.

When I had scarlet fever I was then taken to the isolation hospital at Portslade. There one poor man was in a ward all on his own so on non-visiting days when we were recovering we pushed younger patients around the grounds in a big old pram. My Mum kept in touch by sending me Mabel Lucie Attwell postcards two or three times each of the five weeks I was in hospital. I can't remember ever being homesick, but only enjoying my time. I guess it was a sort of holiday which I didn't have normally. I felt more privileged than hard done by as most of my school friends had never been to hospital like me.

Everyday tumbles meant cut knees. This my Gran said was only gravel rash. To heal the cuts she would pick a cut leaf from a plant in the garden, wash it and place it over the wound, securing it with a strip of clean old sheet. One side of the leaf was for healing, the other for inflammation. If by chance the cut turned septic then the good old poultice was applied, which wasn't so nice when it dried crispy or stuck to the wound.

In spite of all our childhood setbacks I think we turned out to be pretty healthy adults.'

A CHEMIST IN THE 1920s

'My father, George Steggles, was a chemist in Petworth for some 40 years until his death in 1930 but the time that I know most about is the 1920s when I was a schoolgirl. His work then was very different to that of a chemist of today. Then by far the greater part of medication was in liquid form, for which a prescription was written out (not printed as today) by the doctor which had then to be dispensed by my father from the various drugs (kept in glass stoppered bottles all labelled in Latin, green or blue glass for the dangerous drugs and plain glass for the others) ranged on shelves along two sides of the shop. There were few, if any, proprietary brands of drugs in those days and sometimes my father had to make up pills using something rather like a butterpat to cut the mixture into small cubes which he would then roll into a ball with his hands. He also dispensed many preparations for use on horses and other farm animals.

On certain days each week carriers would come into Petworth from outlying villages, generally in horse-drawn carts, but latterly one more enterprising than the others came in a motor van. They would bring lists of requirements given them by the villagers which would be left with my father to get together while the carriers went to other shops on similar missions. When the goods were collected and paid for by the carrier he was allowed a small discount on the price and, with this and the fee paid to him by the villager, he made his living.

Except for very large items very few articles purchased in the shop were handed over without being wrapped in white paper of a suitable size (from a stock which had previously been cut into a number of different sizes) and sealed at each end with red sealing wax, a small spirit lamp always being kept lit to melt the wax. There was no question of popping things into bags!

My father had one of the first telephones in Petworth, his number being 12, and frequently orders would be received by phone from the larger houses. A schoolboy was employed for two hours daily, after school, to deliver these orders to places in the town. This could involve wheeling, on a small truck, anything up to a crate of twelve syphons of soda, or mineral, water to any of the houses.

Many people looked upon my father as a substitute doctor and he produced many medicines for children's illnesses charging no more than a few pence. He was, too, often called upon to produce a suitable "draught" for gentlemen who had imbibed too freely the previous evening!

The shop opened daily at 8 am and on Saturdays did not close until 8 pm. It was closed Wednesday afternoons and Sundays, but, living on the premises, callers frequently came out of opening hours and, since more patients were nursed at home then, doctors would telephone at any time during the night for a cylinder of oxygen or other items required by their patient and then send someone to collect them.'

BIRTH AT HOME

'Before the 1960s, when much engineering was done to improve the flow of the river Adur, the Henfield floods were an inspiring sight each winter. With a few days of rain the river filled and began to overflow its low banks, covering the adjoining fields with several feet of water.

A friend told me that as a child in the First World War, living above the flood level, she remembered the anxiety among the grown ups when the floodwater surrounded the carter's cottage and made the farm lane impassable.

In the cottage, the carter's wife was awaiting the arrival of her first baby, and neither Doctor's little car nor Nurse's bicycle could possibly get through the flood. My friend was proud to be stationed at a farmhouse window to report the agreed signal – a white towel from the frantic mother to indicate labour had started.

The towel fluttered, the farmer leaped into his cart. Up in Henfield the doctor in his fishing waders and the nurse in her galoshes were collected and the horse made easy work of splashing through the flood.

The baby arrived safely and everyone was pleased. Soon after, the cottage was pulled down and no trace remains, and the Adur very rarely floods. Rather dully, really.'

'When my sister was born at Ashurst a lady from the village, almost a Sarah Gamp character, was on call to bring babies into the world, and also see folks out. With my sister's birth imminent, she was heard to declare she needed a "little of God help me", meaning a tipple of gin, so to keep her happy they obliged. That was in 1920.'

'Social attitudes were very different in my childhood in the 1930s. When my father's cousin was found to be expecting an illegitimate baby, the entire family were horrified and shamed. My great aunt, the headmistress of Roffey school, was absolutely aghast, her place in local society "ruined". My grandmother declared she "would never be able to walk up the main Roffey street again!".'

'When my first baby was born at Sidlesham in the ate 1930s, I was pretty green (no sex education). You made your own sanitary towels, the waterproof for the bed was the back of an old mackintosh and around the bed, on the floor, were spread old newspapers. The baby had a florin, wrapped in cottonwool, placed on her navel and bound with a binder, which she wore for weeks.'

MARRIAGE CUSTOMS

'There was an age old tradition that when a bride of good reputation was married in Bosham church, a salute was fired from a gun on Quay Meadow. The new Mrs Layzell, nee Martin, was the last bride to receive such an honour in the 1880s.'

'On St Valentine's Day 1899 my grandparents Frances and William Mant were married. The following Good Friday, "the only day the Devil is not on earth", a small loaf was baked for them at Birdham Stores, at that time owned by my great aunt Emily.

Superstition has it that this loaf must never be destroyed or bad luck will follow and the marriage will be unhappy. I still have the loaf and although rock hard, it has never mildewed.'

DEATH IN THE FAMILY

'The corpse was always kept at home in my youth in the 1920s and the coffin was delivered when made. It remained at home until the

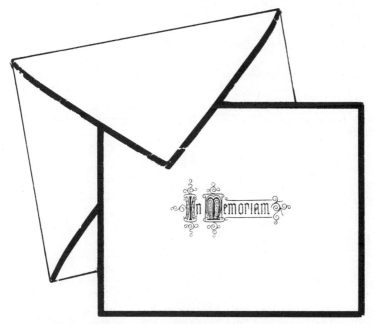

There must have been thousands of mourning cards such as this sent just after the First World War, when influenza claimed so many lives.

97

day of the funeral, when the funeral directors would call to screw the lid down.

The funeral would start from home with the coffin placed upon a bier pulled by the pall bearers and followed by the family and mourners to the church.'

'When I was a boy in Findon and someone died in the village, the Death Knell was rung four times between eight in the morning and midday. The bell was tolled three times for a man, and twice for a woman. If a person died too late to have the bells on the day of their death it would be tolled the next morning. This custom seems to have been discontinued many years ago.'

'At the turn of the century when the only form of immunisation against childhood illnesses was smallpox vaccination, an epidemic of diphtheria struck the village school of Wivelsfield. Of my grandparents' ten children, seven caught the disease. My grandmother nursed the first three to go down with the illness but when four more were taken ill she was unable to look after them herself. So four children were taken, with others from the village, to be nursed in isolation – in a marquee adjoining the churchyard. It was July so perhaps it was not quite as awful as it sounds.

Sadly, although the three nursed by my grandmother recovered, all four who were taken away died in the space of six days. My grandparents' farmhouse was in the centre of the village and almost opposite the wheelwright. He was also the local undertaker and my poor grandmother had to endure the sight and sound of her children's coffins being made. This tragedy was a truly sad blow to such a happy family.'

CHILDHOOD & SCHOOLDAYS

A VICTORIAN CHILDHOOD

London strung with lights for Queen Victoria's Diamond Jubilee in 1897, the circus coming to Worthing in the 1880s, childhood memories of Victorian dinner parties and horse-drawn bathing machines on the beach -- these reminiscences were written in the early 1950s, by those who had grown up in the Victorian era.

DRESSING FOR DINNER

'In retrospect early childhood is wrapped in a sense of warmth and security. The love of parents (tempered with a certain Victorian severity), the familiarity of the nurseries, a devoted nurse, and the lack of change, were all mine. Little things stand out with startling clarity.

These were the days of pinafores. Every possible type was worn by children. For best wear they were made of fine muslin, tucked and trimmed with rows of fine lace, satin bows tying them at the shoulders.

Our nurse, Lizzie, came from Norfolk, and as a great treat I was allowed one night to have by my bed the glass of water which contained her false teeth.

On Sundays my sister and I wore coats of white cloth, the small shoulder capes edged with a band of beaver, close-fitting bonnets edged with the same fur, with little muffs to match hung on cords. How well I remember the painful snap of elastic under the chin as Lizzie put on these bonnets.

I once peeped into my mother's wardrobe and saw six sunshades, each more lovely than the other, some with silk fringes, others with an edging of tiny silk roses, the linings made of tucked chiffon. They leant gently against the cascade of fluffy petticoats made of broderie anglaise threaded with black velvet ribbon, others of taffetas, with rows of frills which made an enchanting rustling sound when worn.

Her dressing table had a daily attraction for me, crowded with little silver pots, brushes and combs with cherubs' heads in beaten silver, and a little china ring-holder in the shape of a sprouting branch on which the rings were hung. Booklets of Papier Poudre, each sheet lightly impregnated with powder, and a mild form of lipstick called Lypsyl, very greasy, without much colour, but smelling sweetly.

A young cousin came to stay for a dance and I was allowed to

100

watch her dressing. Frilly drawers were quickly hidden by a silk petticoat, a camisole threaded with pale blue ribbon was slipped on, and a dressing jacket of pink silk, while from a drawer she produced a strange object, rather like a long sausage over which she brushed the front of her hair. This artificiality was technically known as a "rat". Then she put on her evening dress, with a ruched and tucked bodice of chiffon cut discreetly low, the skirt long, wide, and frilled, in which she looked enchanting. The final touch was perfume sprayed from a small cut-glass container. She took with her elbow-length white kid gloves and a delicate lace fan.

I loved to watch the table being laid for a dinner-party. A cloud of chiffon was ruched in the centre of the table, and a silver horror called an épergne placed in the centre with stiff flowers in the little vases attached to the centre column. Then little fussy silver baskets filled with chocolates were arranged on the chiffon. On the sideboard was placed a silver shell on a square base which was later filled with boiling water in which a silver spoon with a handle of enormous length was put, so that it would be really hot for the succulent gravy from the joint or birds.

After a dinner party we could hear from our nursery quarters the sound of the piano and songs and duets from male and soprano voices. If we ventured out to the landing a pale blue wisp of smoke would rise gently from the rich cigars smoked by the men guests.

A lovely sight was to watch the lamplighter stringing the town with a necklace of tiny diamonds as with his wand he passed from one gas lamp to the other .On Sundays we listened for the bell of the muffin man, with his basket of hot muffins carefully covered with a green baize cloth. All signs of a gentler and more leisurely age.

I remember having lunch with my grandfather whose big square beard smelt faintly of peppermint. A vast joint was placed in front of him. With a long and dangerously sharp carving knife he would cut off the shoulder from a fore-quarter of lamb, squeeze the juice of half a lemon on the saddle, place a large piece of butter on it and then press the shoulder down on the spot for a few seconds. The uncut shoulder was always carried away by the parlourmaid for another occasion.

The summer holidays at the seaside were full of excitement. Lizzie would take us to the hired bathing machines, drawn by patient horses to the water's edge. The machines contained a strip of wet carpet, a narrow bench to sit on, and a small piece of cracked mirror on the wall.

Grown ups and children wore long loose bathing dresses with rubber caps drawn into elastic and everyone held on to a rope in shallow water, bobbing up and down with wild shrieks of fear mixed with joy. Few people could swim in those days. For lunch we sometimes had my favourite sweet, a Charlotte russe, moulded sponge fingers with whipped cream in the centre.

Back home the first early morning sound came from underground, the energetic pulling-out of the dampers in the huge kitchen range so that the water would be hot to fill the shining brass cans with red flannel covers which were carried to the bedrooms many floors up.

And the last little sound was the humming of the black iron kettle on the hob of the night-nursery fire, so that Lizzie could make herself innumerable cups of strong tea, and then Mother bending over us to say goodnight.'

THE CIRCUS COMES TO TOWN

'I was born in February 1876 at Salvington near Worthing, within a stone's throw of John Selden's cottage. I well remember the great snowstorm of 1881. It came in the night and when we got up in the morning snow was piled up as high as the hedges, and when the thaw set in it was like rivers everywhere.

When I was five I started school at West Tarring. We had moved nearer there then but were still in Salvington. The school was held then in a very old building that was Thomas à Becket's palace, adjoining the fig gardens in which he was supposed to have planted the first fig tree that was brought to England. My grandmother lived quite near and my sister and me always used to go and see her before and after school. We often went into the fig gardens and asked for a halfpenny bargain, and used to get a dozen or more specked figs, apples and pears.

I always went to Sunday school twice on Sunday. We looked forward to the school treat in the summer. We used to meet at the school then march to the church for a short service, then to the meadow where we had tea in a marquee and races and scrambles and swings. It was real jolly.

Then there was the grand time in 1887 at Queen Victoria's Golden Jubilee. Everyone had dinner after parading round the village with the brass band and the fife and drum band. Most villages had their own band in those days.

One thing we always looked forward to was when Sangers Circus came to Worthing from their last stop at Littlehampton and had to pass our house. The ponies and elephants and camels use to walk all that way. We always got up early that morning and waited for them with apples and they seemed to remember from year to year. Then Mother would take us to Worthing to see them parade round the town and a grand sight it was, and we finished the day paddling in the sea.

When I left school at the age of eleven I started sewing for the neighbours and in the summer fruit picking in the gardens my father had charge of. I don't think anyone could have had a happier childhood.'

THE FAIRY LIGHTS OF LONDON

'It was the summer of 1897, the year of Queen Victoria's Diamond Jubilee. I was a very little girl but the event is still clear in my mind.

After some childish ailment I was sent on a visit to a favourite aunt, who had a farm in Essex. On the great day of the Jubilee we talked of nothing else. I had seen the Queen once and it seemed remarkable to me that this old lady had been reigning for such a vast number of years. I remember we had a very special tea, and some children of my own age came to join in our celebrations.

The following Sunday my father came to take me home. He told me how they had hired a phaeton (a roomy sort of vehicle for a family) and had driven round London after dark to see the illuminations – a somewhat prosaic word for what we termed "fairy lights". This weighed heavily upon me, for although I had enjoyed myself, nothing could make up for not seeing London decorated and alight at night. I retired to the orchard to cry! Did my father sense what had happened to me? I think he did.

The next day we journeyed to Liverpool Street, and arrived there in the summer twilight. I can look back and see myself in a white sailor blouse and pleated navy skirt, long black stockings and buttoned boots, and of course a large straw sailor hat. Instead of the usual "growler" to take us across London, my father hailed a hansom cab and away we went. Young people now have never seen this marvellous vehicle. You faced the breeze, the driver sat high up at the back and there was a most intriguing little door in the roof, through which you gave the driver his directions. The cab had rubber tyres and ran swiftly and softly along behind what we used to call a "spanking" horse.

We travelled in that summer dusk from East to West and every moment was precious. The scarlet poles and festoons of paper flowers and hundreds of fairy lights – such a sight I had never seen. I remember the magic drive up the Mall and the cabby stopping to let me have my first sight of Buckingham Palace. Then it was time to make for the station and our journey home. That evening stands out as one of the most vivid memories of my childhood.'

A DIGNIFIED PACE

'Life for Victorian children passed at the dignified pace of the family barouche. No motor cars or aeroplanes, radios or telephone bells to ruffle the calm of our nursery existence. Nanny in starched white dress and apron with a white cap with streamers in charge of two little girls in pinafores – red and white check for the morning, white with embroidery frills in the afternoon. What an immense amount of washing and polishing must have been done. There were rows of copper and brass cans in the housemaids' cupboard – brass bedsteads and fenders. The only "labour saving" device I remember was a speaking tube that led from the landing to the kitchen and that was generally used to tell the underhousemaid to stagger up the back stairs with a three gallon can of bath water or a heavy coal scuttle.

In those days we all dressed up in our best clothes on Sunday to go to church. My father always wore a morning coat and top hat and I recall my mother in her sealskin jacket, chinchilla muff hanging from her neck by a bead chain and a chinchilla tippet to match. Top hats and frock coats were the accepted uniform of the family doctor and the horror of a visit to the dentist was heightened by the vision of his long black beard and frock coat, with silk facings liberally bespattered with traces of his breakfast egg.

We were always enthralled to watch mother dressing for an evening party. Her dresses were laced up the back and pulled tighter and tighter by the maid till you wondered how she could breathe. Then the hairdresser (with frock coat and waxed moustache) curled her "Alexandra" fringe with tongs which were heated on a spirit lamp. He would whirl them round and round to cool them and then test them on a piece of tissue paper, producing a subdued smell of scorching. The final effect was positively regal.

If the party was at home we could watch through the bannisters the assembled company walking arm in arm into the dining room. As we slept over the drawing room we were later lulled to sleep by the music which struck up as soon as the gentlemen emerged from the enjoyment of their port and cigars.

Every summer we went off to stay with our grandmother, a most exciting journey involving two changes. After changing at Swindon (where we always bought a packet of Banbury cakes and six bananas), sandwiches, tasting strongly of eau de cologne, were produced from Mother's dressing case and were washed down with milk from a large medicine bottle. Arrived at the little wayside station we were met by the brougham (which smelt of moth balls) drawn by a pair of bay horses called Hercules and Eliza.

I think my grandmother's drawing room must have been a perfect example of Victorian taste. It was crowded with heavy furniture and the fireplace and piano were draped in velvet. Against the wall was something called a chiffonier, with a marble top, bearing a pink alabaster clock in a glass case flanked by two vases to match. In the middle of the room was a most peculiar object which accommodated three persons sitting back to back known, oddly enough, as the "sociable".

Family prayers in the morning in the dining room made a great impression. The butler, the pantry boy and the maids all trooped in and sat on a row of chairs against the wall. As part of the ritual, at a certain moment, my uncle George (who read the prayers) glanced at the clock, rose from his knees and blew out the flame under the silver egg boiler on the breakfast table. Then he knelt down again to pray for "Our Gracious Queen Victoria, Albert Edward Prince of Wales, the Princess of Wales and all the Royal Family".

We were very happy there playing with cousins whose parents were abroad. It was there that we learned to bicycle, going down to the gardener's cottage and back supported by our devoted and perspiring friend Russell the butler. This hero captained the village cricket team and played endless games of croquet with Uncle George on a perfect lawn, mown and rolled by a fat pony wearing leather boots.

My recollection of butlers is that they were invariably benevolent and entertaining as opposed to gardeners and coachmen who were apt to be brusque and uncooperative. My husband had a butler friend, Jack Chave, who used to amuse him for hours in the pantry playing tunes on a penny whistle – through his nose. Between cadenzas he refreshed himself by polishing the silver and taking an occasional sip of the old and tawny.

Paying calls was an exacting social duty and ladies would drive up and leave cards on a silver tray in the hall. On one occasion a stately dowager came bowling down the drive in her victoria holding over her head a pink lace parasol. When she alighted at the front door it became apparent that a swarm of bees had settled on the top of her parasol. She merely handed the buzzing mass to the butler and walked on into the house, "mistress of herself though China fall".

After the excitement of the Diamond Jubilee and the beginning of the Boer War I well remember the gloom that descended on the country when the old Queen died. Everyone wore black and even we children had dark grey coats with black braid. How jealous we were of a little girl who had a crepe bow in her hat! The Queen's passing put an end to a period. The aspidistras and india rubber plants were flung on the rubbish heap and the drawing room took on a new look with shiny chintz covers and quantities of silver photograph frames. We went off to school and nanny went to a new family in Berkshire. Our Victorian childhood was over.'

GROWING UP

In the first half of the 20th century, even those who lived in Sussex towns had an almost rural upbringing. The countryside was always within reach, and children knew the names of wild flowers and birds and where to find them. It was a time of freedom for children, when they could wander the roads and countryside without fear and parents were happy to wave them goodbye for the day without a second thought.

THE BUTLER'S SON

'In 1909, when I was three years old, my father changed his job from being butler to Mr Majendie of Hedingham Castle to become butler to a Mrs Joad, of Patching, near Worthing. It must have been a tremendous upheaval to transport personal belongings, furniture, and three children – I had a younger brother and sister. Not that I remember much about it, except standing under a wooden railway station canopy, watching the rain pouring down. However, the London, Brighton and South Coast Railway safely delivered us to Angmering station. From there we rode in the "station fly" – an ancient one-horse carriage – the three miles to our new home. We lived there for the next seven years.

"The House" was just across the village street, a rambling building with extensive lawns, gardens, greenhouses and stables. Mrs Joad, an elderly, invalid widow, was rarely to be seen, but she was presumably well looked after by a lady's maid, cook, kitchenmaid, head housemaid and housemaid, to say nothing of my father and Henry, the footman. The outside was looked after by a squad of gardeners under Mr Hack, a dapper little man in bowler hat and black suit. Part of the establishment were two horses and a carriage, cared for by a coachman and groom, Mr Kingsmill and Mr Page.

We children were objects of curiosity to the female members of the staff and spent a good deal of time over at "The House". We preferred the kitchen to the housemaid's room, as Mrs Gladys (all cooks of her station, whether married or single, were known as "Mrs") used to whip her own fresh cream and we were allowed to lick the basin. She was courted, in true *Comic Cuts* tradition, by a local policeman, and became Mrs Murrell.

Charlie Stamford was the local blacksmith, and must have been a good-natured chap, although he looked very fierce with a bushy moustache. We used to like to get in the forge and "help" him by blowing the manual bellows. He used to make us hoops from quarter inch iron rod, and "skidders" to drive them with. The skidders, being merely hooks of iron fitted to a wooden handle, soon wore through. If we resorted to sticks to thump the hoops along, the hoops also gave up the ghost and fractured. Charlie would then heat up the ends and hammer them together. I don't remember paying him for these services, but perhaps our father made it right with him. He made my father an iron bar to swan-neck down over the back wheel of his bicycle, with a ring at the top through which the saddle pillar was passed. The bottom end was screwed to a wooden box about one ft by three ft. A board was fixed from back to front of this box, which was mounted on two wheels. We three children then sat astride the board, and we had a three-passenger cycle trailer. My mother aptly said she wondered we didn't all break our necks.

The animal members of Mrs Joad's staff were Winkle, a donkey who was supposed to pull her about the roads in a little carriage, although I never saw this sight; a pony to pull the lawn mower, who incidentally wore leather boots while so doing; Jubilee, a cob, whose duties seemed to consist solely of mowing a grass paddock for hay; and, of course, her two handsome carriage horses.

The aforesaid Winkle spent his days in the paddock at the top of the village street, and was led down by a halter to his stable for the night. One day I persuaded Mr Page, the groom, to let me go and lead Winkle home. Up the street I went carrying the halter, opened the five-barred gate and offered the halter to Winkle. He looked at it as if he had never seen it before, pushed through the gate and trotted off down the road. I was terrified and tore off after him, thinking he wouldn't stop until he came to the sea. Of course, when he came to the little door into the stable yard, he calmly walked up the step and round to his box, with me panting after him. I can't remember Mr Page saying anything, but perhaps he knew Winkle had more sense than I had!

Organised amusement for small children was very rare. We went once to some "marionettes" at Angmering, which was a kind of puppet show. My father took us to a film show in Worthing, of which all I can recall was a scene showing a man having a brick thrown at him, knocking his teeth out, which he spat out as he ran away! A concert was held at the school, at which the children played a Kazoo band and sang. The only other performer I remember was a man swinging axes, Indian club fashion. He gave a nervous glance at the big oil lamp suspended over the stage before he started, but unfortunately did not hit it. A Kazoo, by the way, is a small woodwind instrument which produced a noise like a comb and tissue paper.

As we progressed in school, we formed the inevitable little gang, wandering about the village on our usually harmless exploits. We sometimes went up on the Downs, making houses from the blocks of chalk lying in the two disused chalk pits. They were never finished because we couldn't manage to build the roof! There was also a kind of folly up there, a huge square red-brick structure known as the "clock-tower". There was no clock in it, but the circular spaces left at the top could still be seen. The views from the Downs were marvellous: the coast stretching from Worthing almost to the Isle of Wight; the woods across Findon valley; and the fertile farms shelving down to the sea. All this, of course, completely wasted on us! The occasional car would creep along the road in the valley, in dry weather

The summer brought long days on the beach – and weren't we covered! This happy little group pose by the sea at Clympinge in the 1920s.

raising a plume of white chalk dust which settled on the hedges. A charabanc, under whose high back a venturesome cyclist could cling, would also sometimes be seen. A round balloon would occasionally sail along the skyline, and very rarely an aeroplane would appear. One made a landing towards Arundel once, and we made a mad rush on our cycles to see it.

Two racehorse training stables nestled in folds in the Downs, Hazelgrove and Mitchelgrove. The lads would exercise the horses on the Downs. Plovers would nest on the hills and we enjoyed the eggs, with their lovely pearly "whites" when boiled. We were instructed by my father not to take them if four were in the nest with the pointed ends inwards, as they would have been "set on". The stable lads reckoned they could find the eggs more easily, since their viewpoint was higher! Another delicacy was the moorhen's egg, which had to be removed from the nest, usually built some feet from the edge of its pond, by means of a spoon tied to the end of a clothes prop.

As motor cars became more numerous we took up the hobby of collecting registration numbers, which we entered in a little stiff-covered notebook. Imagine trying that today! We lived not far from Goodwood racecourse, and at Goodwood racing weeks the main road was quite busy. Some of us would stand at the bottom of the village road and watch. My father told us to notice which passengers had cheerful faces, which meant they had had a good day, and cheer them. They sometimes responded by throwing pennies to us.

We had no trouble in filling in our Saturdays and holidays, so long as we could get out. If we could not, we worried our mother with "What can we do now?". In this respect one of our aunts came to our rescue with a box of books, and I spent many hours enjoying Capt Marryat, G.A. Henty and other authors of boys' books. My brother and I thought it a good idea to save a little time on our leisure mornings to go to bed in our day clothes. This did not work as when my mother looked in when she went to bed, to our surprise she yanked us out and made us put our proper nightclothes on.

Clothes and boots must have been a problem to our parents. My father used to repair our boots, soling, heeling and patching them. We wore clothes on their last legs for Saturdays and holidays, better ones for school, and the newest ones for Sundays. We wore cloth caps, known as "gubbies", winter and summer. They were very useful when bird-nesting for catching eggs dropped by another boy up in a tree, and for carrying home the eggs in the peaks. Sometimes we would forget they were there, when we would literally have egg on our faces! Our hair was cut by my father, until my mother decided we deserved a more professional touch, when we were promoted to Charlie Stamford, the blacksmith. Charlie said cutting my brother's hair was like cutting sticks. We wore shorts all the year round, and in the cold weather the legs would get wet and chafe the backs of our legs. No one wore "long-uns" until they were 14 and left school. One of our mates sported a straw boater which had the bow at the back as opposed to the left side. This, he informed us, was the latest fashion.

My brother found an interesting pastime in church one Sunday. It was the custom to fit circular rubber heels to boots by means of a central screw to save wear on the leather heel, the idea being to rotate the heel to spread the wear. When Mr Brown, who sat in the pew in front of us, knelt for prayers, his upturned heels were within my brother's reach, so he amused himself by turning the rubber heels as fast as he could. Mr Brown said after the service that he had felt a "strange sensation" in his feet.

An important milestone in the life of the village was the day Mrs Joad bought a motorcar, a big Fiat saloon. Mr Kingsmill, the coachman, either refused the job of chauffeur or was deemed too old, so Mr Page the groom was taught to drive. It was amusing to hear him, when washing the car, making the same purring noise to keep the dust away from his nostrils, as when he was brushing down the horses. However, Mr Page was later supplanted by a younger man, Mr Catt, peaked cap, breeches, shiny leggings and all. He took Mr Page's house next door, and Mr Page moved down the street. We never took to Mr Catt. I think the feeling was mutual, because he was not always out of earshot when we made meowing noises.

When quite young, we were sometimes privileged to go and play with Miss Tonins over at "The House". She was a young relative of Mrs Joad's. We could not help wondering why she spoke in such a funny way. We did not realise that rich people sent their children to expensive schools to acquire this peculiar accent!

During two summer holidays two little sisters from London spent some time in our village. While we boys scarcely realised the local girls existed, it is a strange phenomenon that most of us fluttered round these two girls like mesmerised moths round a candle! It reminds me of the taboos imposed on primitive young men not to associate with maidens of their own neighbourhood, but to seek mates from other tribes. On the other hand, being precocious little Londoners, perhaps the girls simply preferred playing with boys!

As my brother and I matured, (I was then nine years old), we would get a Saturday job of pheasant driving. We were placed at the end of a wood to prevent the birds running away from the beaters and avoiding the guns. Paper and matches in pockets, firewood gathered, we each made as big a bonfire as we could. Although we were a good distance from each other, we could communicate by shouting and the occasional sprint to one another's post. At midday an old man would come trudging round with our lunches – a bottle of stone ginger beer and two sandwiches, one of meat and one of cheese, the bread being cut at least half an inch thick, right across a large loaf. This was very welcome. By late afternoon we would be collected by the beaters on the last drive, and joined them to the finishing point. There we were paid our shilling each and trotted home, very pleased with our day's work.'

A FARMHOUSE CHILDHOOD

'My grandfather retired to Birdham in the 1920s, to a thatched whitewashed farmhouse, keeping a few fields as an interest and here I spent most of my school holidays. Great were those days of eternal summer with few houses fronting the roads but with lanes leading back to the farms and here we children helped with the harvests, riding on top of the haycarts and joining in with the carter when he shouted "Stand-ard" to the horses. At the time of cutting the corn and as the square in the middle of the field became smaller, we helpers would stand with sticks poised to race the rabbits, which we never seemed to catch.

We indulged in the teenage activities of the time – learning to smoke in the barns, sliding down the hayricks, riding our bicycles without lights whilst keeping a wary eye for the appearance of the village bobby, PC Slaughter. We had the children from the shop, the schoolhouse and the farm as our playmates.

And now we come to the ditches – full of frogs, water, tadpoles and curling ferns. What greater delight then, armed with a stout pole, anchored firmly in the mud if you were lucky, soaring, soaring high over the ditches. I don't remember if we learned the art of poling from the Scouts who camped each year in one of my grandfather's fields but later I was inspired to keep a tent in the same field for the whole summer and from school would cycle down each Friday. Cycling along he Birdham Straight was soon accomplished, pedalling furiously from one telegraph pole to the next and then freewheeling to the next. Needless to say, there was little traffic.'

ON A COUNTRY ESTATE

'When I was a schoolgirl in the time between the two world wars, work was very scarce and a job precious. My father was a chauffeur in private service. We lived in a cottage on a large country estate and whatever life was like for adults, their long hours for little pay and always the trapped feeling of being in a tied cottage, life for me was marvellous. Beautiful surroundings, woods, fields, even the big garden when the lady of the house was away on one of her many cruises. There were only two children on the estate, the gamekeeper's daughter and myself, since our brothers had left school and no longer classed as children. We had wonderful times with very few conventional toys but our imaginations had palaces at the root of a large beech, a sailing ship was a bendy birch, and Robin Hood and Lorna Doone were in every meadow.

The estate was way out in the country in the heart of St Leonards Forest with only neighbouring rich estates adjoining, but a bus went twice a week to Horsham. It was always crowded. Wednesday was market day; sometimes if my father had an errand in Horsham or Crawley he would take us in one of the cars but this was a rare treat. Another treat was Cricket Week, when the large estates provided teas for the County cricket at Horsham. The maids from the "big house" accompanied my father with a huge wicker hamper, and if there was room I would tag along. We spent a whole day in the glorious sunshine; it was often the only holiday we had. Our lady employed eight indoor servants, three gardeners, two game-keepers, three woodsmen and a chauffeur. It was a way of life that disappeared after the Second World War.'

'I was born in 1904 at Halnaker on the Goodwood estate. We lived with my grandfather who was a shepherd on the estate. His wage was 18 shillings a week. I remember at Christmas the Tenants' Party, and on Boxing Day the Hunt used to parade round the village, giving bags of fruit and nuts to the children. I was told a housemaid at Goodwood House was paid five shillings a week and two shillings beer money and two shillings washing money. The beer and washing money they gave to their mothers. Fourteen year old girls were provided with cotton dresses and hessian aprons; they did not get wages but were well fed and looked after, which was a great help as wages were small in those days.

We moved into Chichester when I was nearly seven as Mother wanted us to have better schooling and she could get more work to support us. It seemed so busy a place to we younger people after the quiet of the country. There was always music in the streets, and Saturday nights there were hot roasted potatoes, and costers' barrows with fruit, fish, winkles and other shellfish, all on sale until quite late at night. The displays in the shops at Christmas were marvellous. The shopkeepers took pride in their shops and the displays drew a lot of people into the town. We often spent Sunday afternoons window shopping. I remember the Home & Colonial shop once made a picture with all dried fruits of Arundel

Castle, the windows being "lit up" with red and yellow glacé cherries cut up.

Goodwood Race Week was another treat for we children as the town was filled with out of work actresses and actors who entertained us in the streets. To us it seemed like Fairyland. Also we got the chance of some pocket money as the racegoers would throw out handfuls of coppers, especially if they had backed some winners.'

'I think I remember most vividly the lovely spring weather when we saw the banks covered with primroses, and the warm summers when we would hurry home from school to take our tea out in the hayfield. We would walk up to the farm behind the full waggons and ride back again in the empty ones, all horse-drawn of course, and on the last run we rode two together on the backs of the spare horses.

During school holidays my sister and I and the boy from the farm on the estate where we lived would spend whole mornings in the Forest, finding sundew and sometimes gentians. At other times we would climb the rocks at Stone Hill. The highlight of the summer holiday was a day trip to Brighton, usually spent with friends. I remember my mother always made egg and cucumber sandwiches on these occasions!

We lived in the lodge, at the side of which was an old shrubbery. This we regarded as our little estate and we set it out with paths and little gardens and anything that was thrown away from the big garden where my father was head gardener, we retrieved and planted in ours. We even made a little lawn about six feet square, which we trimmed with scissors! The three of us worked there on Saturday mornings. I can't remember when we grew out of this, but I suppose we gradually found other interests.'

WILD FLOWERS FOR PICKING

'Moving from a town street to the Mid-Sussex Weald when I was ten, I revelled in the freedom of the countryside, and when I think back to that time, the early 1930s, I am instantly transported into a green lane with mossy banks teeming with primroses, dog violets and lady's smock, which we called "Milkmaids" – the earthy scent of moss mingling with the perfume of the primroses drifts from the memory, and is vividly real.

We carried small tight balls of wool in our pockets, and each handful of primroses, edged with leaves, was neatly tied into a bunch and tucked into a basket – or tied to a hazel stick, swinging upside down,as we triumphantly carried them home to be placed in shallow bowls on the windowsill – or delivered to grannies or aunts (hoping for twopence to spend on sweets!).

Woodlands too were a delight, carpeted with windflowers (we thought it a nicer name than "wooden enemies"!); there were clumps of primroses and dog mercury amongst the coppiced hazel where the sun came through, herb robert, and then a little later the bluebells – we didn't pick many of those, fragrant as they were in the woods, they didn't last indoors and soon began to smell unpleasant. We abhorred the weekend cyclists who went home in the evenings with large bunches tied to the carriers of their bikes, spilling along the road as they went . . . poor bluebells!

It is strange to think that then, wild flowers were for picking – and there was such a profusion that they just wouldn't be missed.

Sadly nowadays children have to be told, "Don't pick the flowers. . ." '

'In the days when wild flowers grew in abundance, I went out with the Brownies, and later the Girl Guides, on a Good Friday to pick wild daffodils and primroses to decorate the church for Easter. At Whitsun we would set off again to pick cowslips and bluebells and the fresh greenery. Come autumn, we were out picking "old man's beard" and berries. These outings became picnics and often involved a short bus or train ride which in those days was something to get excited about. Other wild flower and berrypicking outings were to gather them for my father to make wine. These trips were often combined with a special treat of visiting a farmhouse which provided "teas".'

TROUBLE FOLLOWED US ABOUT

'I was born in 1942 and I had two brothers, one five years older than me and the other ten years older. We were brought up on farms as my father was a groom. Going to the other farms to play with the other children, my brothers always had to take me which they were not too keen on.

Visiting the next farm, which was a dairy farm, we would walk through the sheds where a bull was kept in a pen. We would rattle a stick on the bars of the pen. This particular day we did this and carried on walking and there was an almighty crash. Someone had not secured the gate properly and the bull broke out and charged. All the boys being older than me could run much faster and leapt on top of a tractor in the yard, but I only just managed to reach it, with the boys grabbing me by the back of my clothes and pulling me to safety just in time. Trouble always seemed to follow us.

114

The lane outside our house was on a slight hill and very bumpy. My two brothers used to get great pleasure out of putting me in an old pram (I think I must have been about six years old), running so far down the lane, letting go and then trying to catch the pram before it got to the bottom. One day they did not manage to catch it up and it overturned with me underneath. I still have the scars on my knees today.

My mother bought me new sandals and Robin, the younger of my two brothers, said we would go for a walk. I wore my new sandals, with a promise I would not ruin them! He decided we would go down and sit on the river bank. Unfortunately, the field before the river was boggy and needless to say, my new sandals filled up with water and mud "No problem," said Robin, "We'll wash them in the river." We then had to sit on the river bank waiting for them to dry in the sunshine. Of course, they were ruined.

The field in front of our house was surrounded by the most wonderful row of huge fir trees. We decided we would carve the bark on the trees. We got into a lot of trouble for that.

In my teens, my friend and I had to cycle about a mile to catch the bus to school in Steyning. On our way home we had to pass an orchard with gates at either end. We used to cycle in one gate, collect apples and pears in our cycle baskets and ride out the other end. The fruit always tasted much better than bought!'

RABBITING AND MOLECATCHING

'At the turn of the century my grandfather had a dairy farm in the middle of Wivelsfield and as soon as his five sons were old enough to handle farm implements they had to do their share of the work with no thought of being paid. My father was second eldest and the ringleader of the five brothers. When he was nine and his elder brother, Thomas, was ten, they used to earn a few pennies by snaring rabbits around the farm and selling them at threepence each. They used to go round the fields in the evenings setting snares and check them very early the next morning. One morning they saw someone in the misty distance crouching over one of their snares. My father told Thomas to stay where he was and that he would go and punch the man on the head, run back to Thomas and Thomas was to trip the man up as he came running after him. All went as planned. The man duly got his head punched, my father turned tail and ran back to Thomas, who simply stood laughing his head off. The man was running full pelt in the opposite direction.'

'Springtime was when I accompanied my Dad out into the fields molecatching. Dad's special tools were a sharp pointed stick, traps, two ft high marking sticks and a pair of small bladed spade and forks.

We would set out after our midday dinner to the fields to find the traps, all of them "marked" with a stick. If they were sprung my Dad would remove the dead mole, clean the tunnel of loose soil with the tiny spade and fork, reset the trap, replace the turves around the trap so no daylight could enter the tunnel to warn the mole, push in a marking stick and go on to the next trap.

We would tramp the meadows together for two hours every afternoon during the molecatching season with me running on ahead to point out the marking sticks. If a trap was sprung, I would have to wait very quietly while another was set or moved to new ground.

A tally was kept of the moles caught and the number reached 300 some years. This was before I started school, from five years on I never had the opportunity to go molecatching again.

Many years later I asked my Dad why molecatching was so important. He told me that it was to prevent the valuable Arab horses on the estate from breaking their legs by trapping their hooves in mole hills! I wonder if it was really because Her Ladyship didn't want her green meadows marred by piles of brown soil.'

GAMES AND CHORES

Childish pleasures were simple and inexpensive in the days of hoops, tops and skipping ropes. Games seemed to have their own seasons and came round with comforting regularity, the rules known by every child. The road was the favourite playground, in those days shared with very little traffic. Many children also had chores to do, to earn a little pocket money to spend at the village sweet shop.

IN THE MIDDLE OF THE ROAD

'When I was young the sun shone all through the summer holidays, six weeks non-stop. You will say, "Of course it did not", but I know it did, because all our time was spent in the hayfield and on the hay-waggon. Then came harvest and after that we gathered blackberries and nuts. We had our meals in the fields and nothing ever tasted so good.

We played all sorts of games, mostly in the middle of the road, for there was no traffic to bother about. Games seemed to come in seasons and at regular times of the year: hopscotch, then hoops (iron ones made by the blacksmith for the boys and wooden ones for the girls). We whipped tops too, sometimes breaking someone's window when a top flew through the air, and always marbles at Eastertime. A paperchase was good fun, and hide and seek. I used to go to the sweetshop with a farthing and had several sweets to choose from.

I had a very happy childhood. It seems to me everybody made music years ago: in the village band, or just a tin whistle, a Jew's harp or a mouth organ, and everybody sang. Nowadays everybody listens – quite a different thing.'

'In late winter children collected clay and rolled it into small balls. They were dried on a sunny window ledge, coloured and used as marbles on Good Friday. Other games had their seasons – skipping, hoops, ball games, hopscotch, "faggies" (cigarette cards which were collected and swapped). Fathers made wooden spinning tops and used elder wood for whistles and peashooters. Clay pipes blew bubbles from soapy water.'

ROUND GAMES AND INDOOR GAMES

'In formal sessions in the playground as a change from drill (we had no school hall or gymnasium) we played round games such as Oats and Beans and Barley Grow, Here We Go Round The Mulberry Bush, Poor Sally Sits A-Weeping etc. In our playtime we played tag, which we called "He", skipping on a long rope as All In Together, or Salt, Mustard, Vinegar, Pepper, jumping over a rope held taut between two people; hopscotch, ball bouncing or throwing a ball up against a wall and catching it again to a number of action rhymes.

On the way home we rolled hoops or bounced balls while boys played marbles in the gutter or whipped tops.

In the lane and fields after school on summer evenings we played Hide and Seek, Off Ground Touch where you could not be caught if your feet were off the ground, rounders, or Hot Rice, a round ball game.

On winter evenings we had board games – Halma, Ludo, draughts and others, while with cards we played Old Maid, Donkey With

Tails, Pelmanism, Happy Families etc. We knew a number of paper and pencil games too, such as Consequences, Word and Question etc, and we might play these at small parties at home, or Dumb Crambo, Charades, Hunt the Thimble, How Green You Are – the list was endless it seemed.'

THE GAME OF FOG

'I have not heard of anyone playing fog since we played in the 1930s in the Chichester area. In some ways it is a cross between cricket and bowls.

The wicket is two saucer-shaped hollows about six inches in diameter cut into the "turf" about six to eight yards apart. The bats are two staves about three feet long cut from a convenient hedge or bush. The ball is a fogstick about six inches long and half an inch thick cut from the hedge. The players – at least four: two batters, two bowler/wicketkeepers, and any fielders you can find.

The bowler lobs the fogstick underhand to land in, partly in or partly over the far hole, thus bowling the batter out. The batter attempts to hit the fogstick and score runs as in cricket. The batter is out if bowled, stumped, caught, run out or successfully fogged ie run out after a fog. The batter is in his ground and cannot be stumped if one end of his bat is in the hole.

The fogstick is lobbed from whichever end it happens to be so one batter may receive many more lobs than the other.

If the bowler lobs the fogstick to land near the hole, either of the bowlers may shout fog and then nominate one, two or three as the number of spans of the fogstick needed to reach the hole. This is then measured by spanning the fogstick and if correct a fog ensues. The two bowlers withdraw and return with the fogstick concealed about the person of one of them. They crouch over their holes ready for stumping.

The two batters maintain their own ground by leaving their bats in their holes and, without personal contact, separately and/or together examine the appearance of the bowlers to decide which of them has the concealed fogstick. After conference and taking up their bats, with much bluff and counter bluff, they must attempt a run without being stumped or run out.

The bowlers, of course, must try to resist the bluff and counter bluff. When at last the run is attempted, they must produce the hidden fogstick and stump or run out the batter who has left his ground, or both.

The winner is the player who scores most runs.'

MUD CAKES AND GUG NUNES

'My overwhelming memory of my early very happy years was the great freedom enjoyed by my sister and me. We could walk or bicycle unaccompanied in perfect safety all round Halnaker and the surrounding countryside, looking for birds' nests and wild flowers or just exploring. We climbed trees and made fires in the garden on which we baked potatoes, and then ate the very charred results. Another pastime was to make cakes out of mud and "ice" them with ground chalk, finally decorating them with flowers before presenting them to my mother for her tea parties.

We didn't have many friends because we were rather isolated, and we would have loved to have joined the Brownies or something similar, but were never bored and started our own "societies". One society we did join, however, was Gug Nunes. We wore a smart blue enamel badge with rabbits' ears on it, and we had a song and a special sign to make when we met another Gug Nune. It was started by the *Daily Mirror*, which had a strip cartoon about three animals called Pip, Squeak and Wilfred, and we had to promise to be kind to animals.'

GIRL GUIDES

'The village Guide Captain at Wivelsfield was Ruth Hodgson and her sister Winifred ran the Brownies. If ever there were saints on earth, those two must have been among them! Between the wars the only holiday most village children had was the annual camp – this was a joint event between all the Companies in the district. The cost for one week including travelling was 17 shillings and sixpence and in Wivelsfield a local benefactress subsidised each Guide by donating the first ten shillings, while the girls had the whole year in which to save up the remaining money. As a result the Wivelsfield Guides had an almost 100% camping record. Our meetings were held in the church room or, in the summer when the weather was fine, in the vicarage garden. The church room was still lit by oil lamps which were suspended from the ceiling. To put them out one had to climb steps and, having turned down the wick, blow up through a hole in the centre of the base. In the winter those living in the centre of the village "saw home" those who lived on the outskirts. There were no roadside footpaths or street lights in those days.

Ruth Hodgson had a passion for figs. In the early 1930s there was a fig tree leaning over the vicarage wall into the churchyard so, when the fruits were fully ripe, it was not unusual for the Guides to bring gifts of lovely juicy figs to their Captain. She never knew where they had come from!'

COLLECTING CAR NUMBERS

'In the early 1920s at the start of the school summer holidays, we would meet our friend at the top of Westgate, called the Bottleneck because the road narrowed, armed with a notebook and pencil bought from our spare pocket money, to collect car numbers (and, if we were clever enough, the make of cars) on their way to Goodwood races. There was great rivalry at the end of the session to see who had the most. On the Friday afternoon we would gather with grown ups and wait patiently to see the King and his household pass through en route for Cowes Week.'

EARNING POCKET MONEY

'In about 1918, I carried milk from the nearby farm to a house up the hill on my way to school at Cuckfield. For this I earned ninepence a week. Sixpence of this went to a Shoe Club at school, which was paid out twice a year for winter and summer shoes. The remaining threepence was my pocket money.'

'As there was no mains water to the cottages at Ferring, boys would earn threepence a time pocket money pumping up water from the wells in the gardens to tanks inside. But what a long way that threepence would go.'

'Around the year 1920, our main mode of transport was by bicycle. I was ten years old then and was entrusted by my mother and father to go on errands. Most folks in Camelsdale at that time would know Mr Oliver of Olivers Mill, just below the ponds. My father sent me to him with some communication in a sealed letter. After handing this to him I was just about to mount my bicycle when he called me back and popped into my hand a whole half-crown! I was so astonished, I do hope I remembered to say "Thank you". What a happy little girl cycled back home. I remember thinking what a rich man he must be, and that I was the luckiest girl in the world.

Another errand of quite a different nature was to a little elderly widow called Mrs Nash, who lived in a tiny cottage since pulled down, to know if we could help her in any way such as shopping, chopping wood or going on an errand. The one I remember most was being sent to her doctor. She had written on a piece of paper, "Mrs Nash desires a tonic", and she got it too!'

'Threepence for pocket money went quite a long way. Favourite sweets were fairy whispers (for girls), sherbet dabs, aniseed balls, chocolate almonds at eight for a penny, and gob-stoppers. Most of these items were sold from the "halfpenny tray" in the 1920s, though several things only cost a farthing.

Lemonade was sold in bottles with a stopper like a marble, and ginger beer in stone bottles with a special spring stopper.'

THE BEST YEARS OF OUR LIVES?

Slates to write on, the aroma of wet clothes drying on the guard in front of the stove, long walks to school and no school dinners -- schooldays changed very little in the first half of the 20th century. Village schools continued to cope with all ages and standards of children and were a world away from the more modern town schools which some might be lucky enough to attend.

SCHOOLING BEFORE THE FIRST WORLD WAR

'The church school at North Mundham catered for pupils within a radius of two to three miles and the children had to walk from outlying hamlets across fields, taking sandwiches and a bottle of cold tea for their lunch. The classrooms were heated by pot-bellied coke fires, and on wet days the coarse woollen stockings were draped around the guard to dry. Boys and girls both wore lace up boots, and the girls wore lace-trimmed pinafores and, underneath, a garment they chanted a ditty about:

"Open like a barn door, shut up like a trap,
You can guess a thousand things, until you think of that."

Answer: lace-edged knee-length knickers, with an opening down the back to facilitate normal functions and avoid them dragging on the floor of the dirt closets.

There were no scholarships or high school, but the quality of the education was excellent. With few books and only slates to write on, very few children were illiterate. The teachers relied on the three Rs, children memorising tables and poetry, and with strict discipline and respect they were taught right from wrong.'

'I was born in Charlton in 1899 but I went to school in Singleton. I had the cane once because I didn't get my lessons right. When the girls got bigger they used to have cookery and laundry lessons. The infants school had a cottage attached to it and on Friday mornings two girls were told to go ahead and get the fire going so that the other eight or so of us could come there at ten o'clock and have the lessons. Then the girls had to go back after dinner and clear up and clean everything and leave it all ready for the next week.'

'I attended Boxgrove school when I was five, until I was 14. The teacher, Miss Brown, was very strict and we did not dare speak. However, there were two treats a year for the village children. At Christmas the Duke and Duchess of Richmond provided a tree and a little present for each child. We sang songs and were given a silver sixpence (which was taken home to mother, of course). In the summer we all had a trip to the beach at Bognor in the carrier's cart. When the weather was fine we were allowed to play in the lanes – there was little, if any, traffic then and the roads were rough cobbles or dirt tracks.'

'I started school in 1913 at Duncton. It was a church school next to the parish church. It was not very big, consisting of two rooms, infants and older scholars. There was a lobby to hang our coats. School commenced at 9 am with the calling of the register, then a hymn, prayer and teaching from the Bible. We learned the three Rs, also history, geography, needlework for girls, drawing, and for a time gardening for the boys. Our playground was close to the road. There was not much traffic in those days and we used to play in the road, hopscotch and skipping. The boys spun their tops and played marbles. We had drill outside when it was fine and played rounders. On Friday afternoons we would go into Burton Park nearby where we played stoolball and netball. The boys played cricket.

On the edge of the playground was a flagpole. On Empire Day the Union Jack was hoisted and we all stood round and sang patriotic songs – *Rule Britannia* was my favourite. Then we had a half-day holiday. Being a church school we attended the service at church on Ascension Day, another half holiday. We ended our summer term at the end of July by going on an outing, usually to Bognor.

In 1914, while on holiday, the First World War started. When we went back to school teacher said, "Of course, you all know what has happened since you were away." Our hands shot up and we cried in one voice, "Please Miss, we have got a war". When it ended in 1918 school was closed as there was a bad epidemic of influenza known as Spanish Flu. We had our Peace celebrations in July 1919. It was a lovely day: we all went to church, then off to Burton Park for our celebrations. Andrew Smith, the fair man, came with the round-abouts, etc. We had a whale of a time. Each child received a beaker with a picture of King George V and Queen Mary on it.'

'We had to walk about three miles to school at Cuckfield. It was a church school and we learnt the three Rs and religion. On Saints' days we had to go to church. We had no school dinners, we took sandwiches, and in the winter we had a hot Oxo drink for which we paid a penny a day. The headmaster had a magic lantern which he had slides for, though the only pictures I can remember were of camels. The lantern was always going out and we had to wait until he lit the candle again.'

WHAT WE WORE

'Until 1918 girls at Cuckfield wore black stockings and button boots, white pinafores during the week and fancy ones on Sunday. Underneath a dress there was a vest, cotton camisole, liberty bodice, navy blue knickers and petticoats (in winter one flannel and one white). There was no school uniform. After 1918 pinafores were not so fashionable, so I used to remove mine on the way to school, put it in my dinner bag, then replace it within sight of home. My mother soon twigged! As socks became fashionable, the black stockings were rolled down below the knees.'

'Do you remember liberty bodices? On my first day at school in 1916 I was dressed with a vest, combinations, liberty bodice, drawers, flannel and calico petticoat, dress, pinafore, black wool stockings with garters, button up boots, coat and tammy gloves or mittens.

My first impression of school was of forms as seats with writing ledge. There was a pulpit-looking desk in the middle of the room, the teacher had to step up into it, and a cane was placed across the top. The teacher was a very short lady dressed entirely in black, with a skirt almost to the floor. She had her hair, which was grey, dressed into a bun on top of her head. Most children were terrified of her.

To get back to the liberty bodice. It had buttons to which the drawers were attached. The drawers let down front and back and one button had to hold two buttonholes, but one awful day one side of my drawers became unbuttoned so the drawers were hanging down. I just cried and cried for one did not mention such things in those days. Now I now what the saying "droopy drawers" means.'

'I was in my very early teens, attending a day and boarding school

123

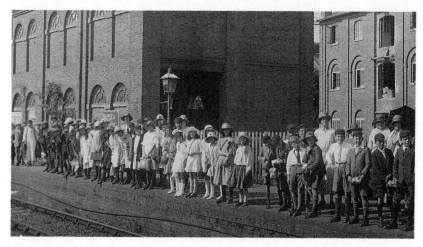

Schoolchildren wait on the platform for the train to take them to the Wembley Exhibition in June 1924, a thrilling and rare outing for many of them.

on the Sussex coast. The school exists no more and shall be nameless.

I had school dinners along with some of the day girls and I remember one very special one. The pudding was sago and for some reason known only to the cook it was served up in large, pale, glutinous lumps. I tried hard, but I could not swallow those lumps.

The mistress supervising the meal came over and looked at my plate. "Annette," she said, "You haven't eaten your pudding. You will sit there until you finish it. Even if it takes all afternoon. Food must not be wasted."

I tried, truly I tried. It was no good. The large pale lumps sat there, looking at me and I looked at them.

Authority in the shape of the mistress was called from the dining room and I saw my chance. I could get rid of the glutinous mess, but where? How? The other plates and dishes had all been cleared away.

What could I do? I was desperate. Then I thought of my big, roomy bloomers with the tight elastic round the legs. Still no sign of the mistress. In seconds I had spooned the sticky mess up the legs of my bloomers.

Authority returned and came over to inspect my plate.

"There," she said, "good girl. You've eaten it. It wasn't so bad, was it?"

Little did she know!'

'I attended Roffey All Saints church school in the 1930s. I wore liberty bodices, with rubber buttons, navy blue interlock knickers with a pocket for my hankie, woollen stockings (in winter) held up by suspenders attached to the liberty bodice, and a navy pleated gym-slip with a kind of plaited cord tie-belt.'

'Mother kept us home from school in the 1940s, because we had no wellington boots to wear and we lived down over the common from the school at Lodsworth. Mother had heard that other children had been supplied with wellies by the County, so in protest kept us at home. I remember it was a foul day and we were all watching from the window and sure enough, who should arrive but the dreaded Attendance Officer, a city gent in grey suit, suede shoes and carrying an umbrella, picking his way through the mud. To our great amusement, he slipped in the mud and fell. He was not amused. Mother told him we would go to school when we were issued with wellies like the children in the village and next day our wellingtons arrived. I guess he didn't want to visit the Hill family again.'

LEARNING THE HARD WAY

'I went to school at West Hoathly in the 1920s. The headmaster was a Welshman with a beard and a fierce temper, fiercer still when he wore his brown boots – why, we never knew, but it was a fact. He caned the boys unmercifully and appeared to hate the girls. As it was a church school we never had any new books and everything was worn out. All the same, he kept our noses down and turned out some good scholars. Others learned nothing at all and could neither read nor write when they left. School began and ended with prayers and a hymn, and in winter this was sung in darkness as the master would not light the oil lamps which hung from the ceiling.

The boys played truant regularly and the Attendance Officer was kept busy checking on all boys who seemed to have earache, belly-ache and every other ache, especially when the farmers had the threshing machine in, drawn by a traction engine belching out black smoke and puffing up the hill. The Attendance Officer was always called the Nuisance Inspector and I wonder now who was a nui-sance to whom. He had a difficult job, for some of the mothers were worse than the children.

Large families lived in small cottages and were nearly always badly fed and dirty. Some boys had great, heavy boots on thin legs with ankles chafed and sore where the tops of hard leather rubbed them. Many a time we who had a lunch tin of sandwiches and cake would find it eaten when we went for it, for others were too hungry to resist the temptation and would ask to go out during class and then rifle someone's lunch bag.'

'If there is one period of my life that comes to mind quite clearly, it has to be school days. Of the time spent during the mid-1920s and 1930s at the village school. I have memories which are interesting, if not always happy.

The building was erected in 1887 for the princely sum of £800 which was donated by the Reverend Edward Tufnell, the then new vicar of Felpham. The site, given by the Duke of Richmond, had an elevated position and the building, of flint and brick, looked quite imposing and was referred to as Felpham C of E school. The windows were at a high level so pupils would not be distracted. One small room was for infants, and a larger rectangular area for Standards Two to Seven.

The number of children never exceeded much more than a hundred, who came from the village and surrounding areas, a fact that seems incredible considering today's population. The large room was divided by a curtain, and during the winter an open coke fire at each end was cleared, and lit each morning early by the schoolmaster's wife. During extremely cold weather it was not unusual to find the inkwells frozen solid, and we were allowed to wear mittens.

The "Lord and Master" who ruled this little domain reminded us often that he had been a Sergeant-Major, and he certainly looked, and acted, the part. First lesson each morning was Scripture which "Sir" would take. It began well, adhering to the subject, but soon he would digress and we would be enthralled with tales of exploits in the First World War and other exciting stories. I remember wishing it would go on all morning because the next lesson was Mental Arithmetic – not an easy exercise for me. There was every chance that Sir would fly into one of his rages, the carefully waxed moustache would droop, and I, or another unfortunate, would be propelled none too gently up to the blackboard to correct our silly mistakes.

Many other instances of an unorthodox nature occurred, eg there was no PE, it was called "Drill", and took place in the playground. On a still day, the commands in a stentorian voice could be heard down through the village! If Sir was in a good mood, I was detailed to play the piano – and the pupils were *marched* into school to the strains of his favourite tune, Colonel Bogey!

However, there was one bright and eagerly awaited spot of happiness during the days leading up to Christmas, when a few tatty paper chains were strung up between the gas-mantle lights, and the "favourites" were allowed to warm themselves around the fires with the teachers. Everything seemed to be shining. Shiny new "Blackie" story books – prizes for good conduct, and attendance. A shiny new shilling each, donated by a village personage, *and* a shiny orange from the local coal-man who was a Governor of the school.

What more could we want?'

WORTHING HIGH SCHOOL 1920

'Worthing County High School was started in the 1880s in Bedford Row. The first headmistress was a Miss Melville Greene. When she retired, Miss Coast took over, and was there when the school moved to South Farm Road, and still reigned there when I left in 1930. Four other members of the Bedford Row staff – who had taught my aunt there, also taught me at South Farm Road.

The High school had a Junior House in Shelley Road, in the building which is now the Normanton Nursing Home. Three storeys high, it seemed enormous to me when I went there from the small school I first attended in Church Walk – where four classes were taught in a large conservatory.

Each June, Junior House was entertained at Thakeham to a picnic in the hayfield. In 1921, when I was due to start at Junior House in September, I was also taken on this picnic. So the bus which had collected the pupils from Shelley Road came to the south end of Park Avenue, where we then lived, to pick me up. However, when the bus stopped it was very full, and my cousin was near the front, but a kind lady sitting just inside the door took me onto her knee. When we reached the Findon Road, also then quite rural, she pointed to a horse and cart we were just passing and said, "Look at that big cartful of turnips". Unfortunately, the farm-reared child, having looked, said scornfully, "They're not turnips – they're mangel-wurzels!" When we arrived, my cousin rushed up to me and said, "Do you know what you've done?" "No – what?" "You've contradicted the headmistress!" I was scared stiff, but I heard no more till many years later when I attended her retirement party. Making her farewell speech, she looked at me, grinned, and said, "I was only once contradicted by a pre-school child – and unfortunately, she was right!"

We went from Junior House up to the main school at eleven plus, having passed a small test. Pupils from other prep schools also came then, and the scholarship intake. This, present pupils find very difficult to understand, they can't imagine some people having to pay fees and some not.

One of the Bedford Row maths teachers was, at that point, teaching us to divide and multiply decimals. She had a bright idea for making it simple. "To multiply, move the point to the door, to divide, move it to the window." Clear as day, we all did well. Until the next year, when we moved over to the main building – and the door and the window changed places. The serious mathematicians were all right, the rest of us floundered.

I can identify all the staff who taught me. Most of them stayed there for their entire working lives. A number of them had been engaged, but their fiancés had been killed in the war. Others were among what the newspapers so sensitively called "the surplus women" – left over, because potential husbands had been killed before they even met. Add to that, that any job was forfeit on marriage – it was not until just before I left that we had a music mistress who was a war widow, with two small sons. We found it *very* strange to say "Mrs" instead of "Miss".

We were extremely well taught by methods well in advance of the times, with mock elections, debates on topical subjects, and a very "green" outlook from Miss Coast, who exhorted us every holiday: "And be sure, if you picnic, to take your litter home with you – do *not* push it down a rabbit hole and think that will do."

Another thing I've found fascinates the pupils of the present-day mixed school is the way the boys' and girls' High Schools were kept apart. You might not ride to school with one of the boys – even if he were your cousin or next door neighbour. "What did you *do*, then?" enquired one young lady. "Rode one in front of the other, and turned round and shouted" I told her. "Far more conspicuous – and a danger to traffic!" The sixth formers were allowed to invite the sixth form boys to an annual dance – but they were eighteen . . . and well supervised.'

CHICHESTER SCHOOLDAYS 1920

'During the First World War the Recreation Ground at Chichester was ploughed up and planted with corn. I well remember the east–west path through the middle, iron swing gates at either end and sharp pointed railings bordering New Park Road. The other three sides were bordered by hedges and as we lived in the cul-de-sac to the north, our hedge was always riddled with gaps made by children getting through to play in the park. Beyond to the east were allotments, a few houses in Melbourne and Adelaide Roads and then the water meadows stretching as far as Westhampnett. This then was the background in which I played and from which I went to school.

My mother did not believe in early formal education and I did not attend school until I was six and then I went to the Bishop Otter College Practising School. This was a separate stone and flint building within the college precincts which had been opened in 1874 with accommodation for 203 pupils. Later a report credited the school with very good standards in literature, domestic economy, grammar and needlework but geography was only fair and maths failed to get a mention.

When I went there in 1920 there were 188 pupils each paying sixpence to eightpence a week. The headmistress was Miss Chignell (a past student of the college) and my teacher (untrained and from a local well-known family) was known as Susie Sunshine.

As a demonstration school it was always humming with activities, some of which would not be out of place today. I have many happy memories of class picnics at Fordwater (where Pennicott's coal carts still trundled through the ford), pond dipping in a pond just above the college, and gardening with college staff and students. Every May we collected wild flowers to send to a poor school in London – Hilda Road Infants' School in Canning Town, and wild flowers at any time were sent to another school in Clerkenwell. The spring outside and the stream running down College Lane to the pond at Dell Hole were a daily source of pleasure, as walking to and from school became a time of building dams, sailing boats and getting wet. Incidentally the spring still bubbles up under a grating at the entrance to the college car park. Cows grazed over the hedge in Oaklands Park.

Names have changed – we had "drill" in the college hall, "lavatories" were outside and were the only safe haven from chasing boys, classes were called "standards" and art was "drawing". Older pupils went to the Girls' High School for cooking, which seems a long way to walk, cook and walk back. There was also a self-supporting violin class. In records of the day there was much talk of illness, influenza, bad colds and chills, sometimes resulting in school closures and always reduced attendances on wet days. We had summer and winter timetables, finishing at 3.25 pm in winter to enable children to walk home before dark (children had no transport in cars or buses). Activities included visits to Shippams' factory, the waterworks, parents' afternoons, breaking-up concerts and in 1921 the whole school watched the eclipse of the sun. The school had special holidays for blackberrying, Empire Day (after marching in the Priory Park), Sloe Fair, where water squirters were much in evidence, and Alexandra Day Sports, as well as holidays for good attendance. Each year choirs were sent to the West Sussex Choral Competition in Worthing and were then treated to tea by the Managers. Incidentally all the Managers' meetings began with prayers and the school attended chapel in the college and the cathedral Lady Chapel. A local doctor was the school doctor and there were annual dental and medical inspections. A photograph of my class shows us all wearing black stockings and boots.

In 1922 the Practising School faced closure as there were many more schools in the area willing to take students and the college needed more accommodation.

If this picture seems very rosy I have had to remind myself that in childhood all summers were sunny and in later years I have often excused any unorthodox things I may have done by putting it down to being practised upon when young.

When I transferred to the Central Girls' School in Chapel Street the headmistress was Miss Warden, a petite, small-waisted, bloused and long skirted lady with a bun and strict manner. I don't think I was a very good pupil and when Miss Warden retired she came to live with us as a temporary guest. Imagine my horror!

The playground was grossly overcrowded but there was a netball court – with a drain in the middle. We still marched to Priory Park for Empire Day but discipline, religion and study were the watchwords. Out of school activities I remember best: this was the time of hoops, marbles, skipping, fag cards, spinning tops and conkers. Our small cul-de-sac was quite safe for children and we were often still enjoying these games when Mr Proudly the lamplighter arrived on his bicycle. Activities ceased immediately and we watched with bated breath to see if he could light the lamp and turn his bicycle round without putting his feet on the ground.

The schools broke up for Race Week which was always exciting and I was allowed to watch the traffic but not to join in when children shouted, "Copper gents throw out your pence". We walked to Goodwood and back, picnicking on the Trundle and sticking pins in the race cards to choose a winner. One year resting in Goodwood Park, Queen Mary and the Head Gardener walked across to the gardens and said, "Good morning". No security guards – not another person in sight.

School holidays meant days away and staying in the country, but life was still exciting and about Christmas 1924 a Mrs Brown took twelve schoolgirls in hand and the Twelve Chichester Mascots were born. We performed three scenes at the Corn Exchange, a dance routine, a patriotic flag and dance display and a grand finale where we were dressed in nightgowns and Father Christmas came down the chimney.

Sad endings are often happy beginnings and I moved on to the local High School. This involved cycling to school and on market days starting early as one was often behind a flock of sheep. We wore green gymslips and green summer dresses, white panamas and black velour hats and black stockings. Uniform and materials came from Mr Penny's shop in North Street where one was always greeted at the door and escorted to the appropriate counter. There were only about 300 pupils in the 1920s and under Miss Barton and then Miss

Matson the school was a very happy place. Nicknames were much in evidence; Jumbo, Polly, Buggy and Crawlers were staff whilst friends were Seed, Bud, Charlie and Shush. The curriculum was quite liberal – we played cricket among other sports, learned about other religions, current affairs and enjoyed holidays abroad. My most embarrassing moment came when as a prefect I was given charge of the Lower III who proceeded to let out dozens of newts. Pandemonium ensued, just as the head walked by and looked through the glass windows.'

VILLAGE SCHOOLS

'For many children in the 1920s our school day started with the adventure of an early morning journey by foot over a distance of two miles or more. In winter there were muddy footpaths and floods to be negotiated, the pupils carrying packed lunches, to be eaten later whilst sitting on coats in the playground on dry days, or in the cloakroom when wet. The children had to beware the hazards the daily cattle left in their wake, as they were taken to and from pasture! Wet boots and clothes were dried as much as possible, draped around the pot-bellied coke stove in the classroom. In the winter our infants' teacher would dose needy, undernourished children with cod liver oil and malt, dispensed by a large lead-coloured spoon from a large jar, one spoonful per child, the spoon used going from one mouth to the next, straight into and out of the jar, no hesitation; we all survived. School discipline meant no talking in class and punishment by cane. It was the age of ink wells and pen nibs, with all the fun and problems those create. Playground activities included fag-cards and marbles, skipping ropes and later the new fashion, the yo-yo.

1934 was a very lucky year for our school, when a wonderful headmaster was appointed who transformed our lives. Apart from the three Rs, he introduced the radio programmes, organised games with team strips, music and art were encouraged, while biology was taught through pollination, pruning, grafting, food preservation and bottling. The boys enjoyed working at real woodwork benches, but the girls had to travel to Bognor on the bus for domestic science lessons. Old books were rebound and sets of magazines bound. To give confidence to senior pupils, he taught them to write business letters for the school, and allowed them to use his typewriter for this purpose. Organised games for the boys were cricket and football, for the girls it was stoolball and netball. Social events produced by the school were popular in the parish, these were May Day with the Queen, country dancing and the maypole. At Christmas a carol con-

Infants school children of East Street, Littlehampton, perform in their percussion band on Empire Day in the 1920s. The half-day holiday was eagerly looked forward to.

cert with some sketches and entertainment always filled the village hall. For an all-age school, leaving age 14 years, we received as broad an education as was possible.'

'Sixty years ago Washington village seemed to be a much more relaxed and pleasant spot in which to dwell; this of course was before the motor car became such a dominant feature of our every-day life.

Our school day began at 9 am, with the ringing of the school bell at 8.55 am. The school always started and finished with the singing of a hymn, (bearing in mind that this was a C of E School).

At about a quarter to eleven we had a break, at which time we were given a hot drink by the head teacher's wife. This was so in my early days at school but later on, the whole school was supplied with fresh milk each morning. The supplier was our local dairy farmer and on reflection, it seems remarkable that this small farmer supplied not only the village school, but also the greater part of the parish, bearing in mind the primitive conditions he worked under.

Our dinner break lasted from twelve until 1.30, thus giving time for those that chose to have a hot meal at home. Others remained at school and ate their sandwiches.

The day ended at four for senior children and 3.30 for the infants. It seems a far cry from the village school of today. We more or less all needed to walk to and from school, there was very little worry over the problem of cars at the bottom of the school lane.

Friday afternoon was usually confined to sport. In the winter months the boys would play soccer on the recreation ground, when conditions allowed, and the girls netball. During the summer boys would play cricket and the girls stoolball.'

'At harvest time at Sidlesham between the wars, fathers went to the local District Stores (which sold everything from a packet of pins to a tailored suit) to buy wellington boots for themselves and their children from their harvest money. These would be worn from the September term and by the January snow they would be in holes and only plimsolls were available. Some mothers still sewed the small children into their underwear for the winter but this soon ceased with the coming of the school doctor. The dentist also came, to perform his skills in a caravan in the playground, and the nurse to examine heads for lice.'

PAYING FOR THE PRIVILEGE

'In April 1919 I was five years old and started at the Miss Mowles' little village school. This privilege cost my mother one shilling a week – a great privilege, yes, because the school was just one room and took only 20 pupils.

No books to write on, no pens, you each had a peg on which hung your slate and above it your slate pencil and chalk. We learned to write our name and age, do multiplication tables, and sang songs and a morning hymn to Miss Mowle on the piano. In the afternoon the second Miss Mowle taught us how to knit and do embroidery, even the boys did this. We had maps of the world on the wall and whatever the current news of the day, it was marked with a little flag. Remember, we had no TV or radio, only newspapers, so the world beyond our village was a closed book to us.

We had no playground so we played in the street, there being no traffic except the occasional horse and cart. No school milk or dinners, and the toilet facilities were in Miss Mowle's house next to the school. A weekly treat was a nature walk, when we named birds and picked wild flowers, which we pressed in big heavy books piled on the floor.

An annual treat was dancing round the maypole on May Day, also the Good Friday sports with three-legged, egg and spoon, and sack races.

This idyllic life continued for us little ones until we were eight years old, when we had to go to Pound Hill or Worth School. The village children who were not lucky enough to go to the Miss Mowles were already there. We all mixed in very well, and now we had domestic science for the girls and woodwork and gardening for the boys.

The school was a mile walk so it was not possible to go home to dinner. We roasted one of our Dad's potatoes under the big Canadian stoves in every classroom, if we were early enough. If not, we walked to the little shop run by Miss Rapley and she would do you a large cup of Oxo for one penny with a hunk of bread. We sat in a shed next to the shop on long wooden forms, and on a cold day this was sheer bliss!'

'Childhood days at Balcombe in the 1930s were idyllic, except for school! I was very timid, quite the opposite of my sister Phyllis, who would march into my classroom as soon as she heard my wail, look Miss Archer straight in the eye and say, "If you make my sister cry again I shall tell our mother" – I was sent into the corner for punishment and she got lines after school!

I was quite often late in the mornings. My lisle stockings caused me a deal of trouble. I had such thin legs they never stayed up, and hence I had to keep stopping to hitch them up. Phyllis would begin to drag me by the hand and then I'd fall and have to go back home and start again. One morning Miss Chaplin, our headmistress, once again found me missing at roll call and I was summoned into her study later in the day. "Late again, Sylvia," she said. Where I found the courage to answer, "Better late than never," I don't know, but it was shortlived as very quickly she replied, "Better never late!" From that time I became punctual for school and later for work.

Gym consisted of exercises with wooden dumbbells, indoors in winter and outdoors in summer. We had to remove our gymslips and were then resplendent in liberty bodices and knickers. We couldn't understand why the boys didn't have to remove their trousers. I remember my mother purchasing "a good reduction" in knickers at Mr Gilbey's shop at Balcombe; everything would have been alright but for the fact they were ginger, and no one else had ginger knickers but me.

We did have separate desks with lift-up lids but we sat on long forms. There were only two classes, Junior to nine years old and Senior to 14, then it was on to the grammar school at Haywards Heath. It has been a constant source of amusement to my children over the years that "Mother was educated for 30 shillings a term."

The retirement of Miss Chaplin meant the school was sold and we

134

had a headmaster for the first time in 1935, who was appalled at the lack of knowledge and did his best to raise the standard – but he didn't remain more than two years and the school closed. At 13 I should have gone to Haywards Heath to school but I decided I'd had enough. The Education Department didn't seem to worry about me and my mother was pleased to have my help in the shop so my schooldays were over.'

EXAMS AND EVACUEES

'My brother and I were first sent to the Catholic school as the nearest but when I startled my Sunday school teacher by crossing myself when I saw a picture of the Nativity, we were removed and sent to Ham Road School where, under the strict but benevolent eye of Miss Ball, we began our secular education. Ham Road School was an old brick and flint building, still in existence. The outside toilets consisted of a board with a hole in it, and the classrooms were heated by open fires. In the winter, if you were good, you sat near the fire, the naughty children at the back. I suffered severely with chilblains on my hands. Miss Ball had a heavy hand on the tops of our legs when we were naughty, but I learned to know her when I grew up and was very fond of her.

The school was moved to Victoria Road, and from there I took a scholarship at the age of ten, but I did not take this up until the following year. That year was the most boring I can remember. Being in the top class for two years meant that the lessons were a repeat of the previous year's, even the class readers. I re-sat the scholarship exam when I was eleven. My award was a generous one, for in those days West Sussex awarded on a sliding scale. The higher the marks you got the greater the benefits you received. Perhaps this is why I waited, for, as well as a free education, I received free rail travel to Worthing and free dinners. When I was 15 my mother applied for and was given a grant towards my uniform.

I started High School in 1939, and for some time we shared our school with London evacuees on a half-time basis. Then it was our turn and the school was sent to Newark-on-Trent. We went in schools, not families, unless specially requested, and my brother went to Rossington.

By the time I was ready to take my School Certificate examination, I was back in Worthing and we were being pestered by buzz-bombs. If an alert sounded in the middle of an exam, we all filed down to the shelters, on our honour not to say a word or the exam would prove ineligible and have to be retaken. To our credit, we kept absolute silence, and I remember during one alert I worked out in my head the plot of my creative composition. So I passed my School Certificate with exemption from matriculation, left school and started work the following week.'

'I remember walking from New Pound to Wisborough Green infants' school in School Lane in 1932 when, in those days, there was a lot of flooding on the roads. We used to love walking through them getting our shoes and feet very wet. Our infants teacher had a lot of shoes in her cupboard which we wore while ours were dried by the open fire. In May there was a cattle fair at Loxwood and while going to school it was quite scary to have to face the Sussex cattle belonging to Mr A J Carter which, of course, in those days were driven to the show.

I was twelve when the war started in 1939 and we had evacuees from Peckham Rye. We used to have to practise air raid drill, which meant going up to the church and lying down under the pews, but this never happened for real. We had to share our schooling with the evacuees because there was not enough room in the school. We spent alternate weeks in the old workhouse, part of which is now the village hall. There were four families living in what is now the Vine Room, the hall, the committee room, and an extra building that went across at right angles as far as the church wall. There were two large rooms, one above the other, and here we had our classes. The only way we could get in was by climbing up an old iron fire escape on the outside of the building, where there was a landing and an entrance to the first floor room, and then up again, still outside on the iron steps, to the top room. There was one outside lavatory (with a bucket) in the corner by the church gate, and the iron steps had to be climbed each time you wanted to go. In all weathers! One week we would spend mornings in school and afternoons in the workhouse, and the next week the other way round, with the evacuees at opposite times.'

GETTING THERE

'My sister and I walked about a mile to a private school in Bognor. We lived in the vicarage in South Bersted Street, which has now been replaced by a housing estate. It was backed by fields and there were still more fields between South Bersted and Bognor.

I started school at six years, having learnt to read, write and do arithmetic at home. There were four pupils in my lower division, eight in my sister's upper division. We had lessons in the big bedroom of a private house which had been made into a schoolroom, and played stoolball in the garden. No uniform was worn.

On the way to school we passed the milk float, a cart with an open back, a milk churn and pint measure to fill the milk jugs and billy cans waiting on the doorsteps. Tom Herrington drove the milk float pony and his father had the forge on the corner of Bersted Street. We loved to watch red hot rims being put on wooden wheels with long tongs, while water was poured on with a loud sizzling noise making much steam. This was in addition, of course, to watching the horses being shod.

In the hot summer afternoons the water cart would pass us, spraying the grit surfaced roads, and we loved to creep very near and get cooled down in the water.

I enjoyed climbing on the vicarage wall and sit watching the weddings, Scout parades and funerals in front of the church. The latter were most impressive – the hearse being drawn by black horses with purple plumes, the bearers in top hats and the mourners in deep black. We walked to gym, dancing and music lessons in Bognor, our mother accompanying us and supervising home practice.

At eleven I went to Chichester High School – I caught the bus outside The White Horse in Bersted to Chichester bus station in West Street (fare one shilling return in those days). We walked down South Street, past the gas works to school. We wore green tunics, white blouses and girdles and green, blue and yellow striped ties.

On market day cattle were driven down South Street to the station. It was always exciting, the men shouting, the road full of hurrying cattle. We flattened ourselves against the shops to get out of the way whilst the shopkeepers did their utmost to prevent the cattle from defiling their shopfronts.

I was sad to leave the High School where I had been so happy and go to boarding school. Discipline there was strict and our parents were allowed to visit the school only once a term for tea. The holidays were so happy, wandering on the Downs and through woods all day, watching the birds and animals. Sussex was empty and quiet then, it was rare to see anyone else and quite safe to be alone.'

'I started at Partridge Green school when I was just turned four in 1943. Our official school transport was a lorry belonging to Mr Burfield, a local builder. It was covered in but with only a tailgate at the back. I remember what seemed to me to be a great injustice – on summer days the bit at the front above the cab was opened. We little ones were allowed (made) to stand on the seat and look out and it was quite chilly, but in the afternoons when it was hot and the breeze would have been lovely, the older children considered the gap theirs alone!

Later we moved to the other side of Lindfield and when I passed the scholarship I went to Hove County Girls' School. It was a very long journey to get to school. I left home just before 7 am and walked the first half mile or so to the main road where I caught a bus to Haywards Heath station, arriving about 7.30 am. I then waited until 8 am for the train to Brighton, changed there for the coastway line to Aldrington Halt, from where we walked another three quarters of a mile to school, arriving just before 9 am. At the end of the day the buses fitted better and I'd get home about 5.30 pm. In the winter it was dark for the last bit and my father would leave a hurricane lamp at the lodge for me to carry up the long and, to me, terrifyingly dark drive. If I tried to hurry the lamp would swing a lot casting huge scary shadows – but I was afraid to go slowly. Travelling to and from school took about three and a half hours a day!'

THE WORLD OF WORK

ON THE FARM

◘

Farming has traditionally occupied the majority of workers in West Sussex, though so many changes have taken place, particularly since the Second World War, that life on the land has altered almost beyond recognition. Yet, within living memory, teams of oxen ploughed the Downs and sheep-bells were the only sound to be heard.

LIFE ON A SMALL FARM

'The work was extremely hard, with no holidays except a few hours off on Bank Holidays between attending to the animals. There was no mechanism on farms at Birdham in the 1920s except mowing machines, binders and the threshing engine. Horses were used for all work: ploughing, rolling, sowing, harrowing, cutting and binding the corn.

If the weather was very stormy just before harvest and the corn fell down it would be cut by hand with a faghook and tied into sheaves with strands of corn. It was normally cut by a horse-drawn binder after the headland had been cut by hand to make a passage for the machine. The sheaves were then picked up and stood in groups of six forming a "shock" to dry. The sheaves were then loaded on the waggon with a pitchfork and taken to the rickyard and a rick built with the heads of corn facing the centre of the rick to keep dry. The rick was thatched and the corn threshed at a later date in the winter. The threshed corn was strewn on the wooden floor at one end of the barn to dry. After a few days it was sacked up and weighed. Some was sold and the rest taken to the local watermill to be ground into meal for feeding the animals as required.

The hay was usually made in June. The grass or clover was cut with the horse-drawn mower which left it in swathes to dry. These were turned as required with a long-handled wooden hay fork. It was then heaped up into "cocks" and picked up loose onto the waggon and taken to the rickyard and a rick made. This was thatched for winter feed and cut out with a large hay knife as required The same knife was used to cut out the straw for bedding the animals.

Mangels were also grown for winter feed. These were pulled by hand in the autumn and stacked. The stack was covered with a deep layer of straw and then earth to keep the mangels frost free. They were trimmed of leaves and roots and put through the grinder which cut them into fingers which were then covered with bran for feeding the cows whilst they were being hand-milked. Linseed oil cake was delivered in large "sheets" which were stored on the wooden floor of the barn and ground up in the cake grinder for the cows.

Broad leaf or trefoil clover was also grown and cut with a scythe and fed to the cows in the summer. The horses were stabled at one end of the barn and fed twice a day inside and given a nosebag of oats at midday whilst having an hour's rest from work. The horses were groomed in the evening, by lantern light in the winter. The pigs were fed with barley meal mixed with separated milk in long troughs. They also had any garden waste. Their house and large pen was well bedded up with straw with plenty of room for exercise.

The cows had hovels all round the yard so they could get out of the wind. These and the yard were well bedded with straw and they could go out in the meadows as they wished. Cattle and sheep were walked to market.

The chickens had free range of the rickyard and meadows and gave well flavoured eggs. During March clutches of eggs were placed under broody hens to hatch. The hen and her brood were put under coops and let out to roam during the day. A few hid away to lay their eggs and brought out a brood of chickens. A farm dog and cats were a necessity to keep rats and mice down.

The farms were mainly arable with a four year system – wheat, roots, eg mangels, swedes and turnips, followed by oats and Dutch clover. The clover seed was sown after the oats were up. It was organic farming with farm manure. Farms changed from arable to dairy during the depression of 1920–1930 when many farms went bankrupt due to low corn prices. Some milk was sold locally and the rest made into butter.

There were two large commonfields bordering the harbour. These were divided up into narrow strips and shared out between the farms. Later they were taken over by fewer farmers and eventually turned into building estates.

There was a wheelwright and also a blacksmith in the village who were kept busy and usually had an audience of children. The ring of the hammer on the anvil is a lovely sound.

The engine driver put his hut on the village green to live in during his stay in the district when threshing.

The village pump was over a spring well about seven ft deep and was pumped continuously from dawn to dark. The water was collected in horse-drawn tanks for the farms. Fortunately we had our own well which pumped water into the yard with a second spout for use on the rickyard.'

'We lived on a farm on the outskirts of Horsham (long since built over) where Father kept about 30 dairy cows. Each cow had her own stall in the cowshed and always went to it for milking. They lived inside from October until the grass started growing vigorously in spring, and stayed in overnight for a few weeks at either end of winter. In the late 1920s Father installed what he claimed were the first milking machines in West Sussex. The old die-hards shook their heads and muttered about all the evils, such as mastitis, that would ensue. Fortunately the cows didn't listen and stayed healthy. They were still hand-stripped so the machines can't have been very sophisticated.

The milk was cooled and bottled on the premises and distributed by three roundsmen with vans. Father delivered churns of milk to big customers by lorry. One woman often rang up for an extra pint and my older sister had to cycle off with it – a distance of about two miles – without delay.

On Saturdays my sister had to pot up the cream for the Sunday deliveries. Sometimes a friend helped and was rewarded with a threepenny pot of cream.

The cows were named at random with no clue to their breeding: Daisy, Buttercup, Pulborough (I wonder why?), etc.

When a cow went dry prior to calving she was moved to a loose box where she stayed until the calf was taken from her at a few days old. This caused a lot of distressed bellowing. The bereft calf joined its fellows in a separate pen and had to be taught to drink milk (often the skimmed left over from cream making) from a bucket. This involved putting one's hand into the milk, fingers curled upwards and pushing the calf's head down until it found the fingers to suck. They soon learnt and then managed without help.

Father had learnt some veterinary skill from his father and was keen on homeopathy both for the cattle and the family. Both vet and doctor were rare callers. The doctor came once to remove my sister's tonsils – in a house with no indoor sanitation, a tap in the kitchen and very little heating! She survives.

There was no artificial insemination so each farm had its bull, kept in a small pen. No wonder they got savage. We once had a young bull who still ran with the cows and local boys threw stones at him and made him wild. One day a friend and I, thinking he was shut in elsewhere, were crossing one of the fields when he came galloping after us. We fled for the nearest fence and fortunately, someone in the garden on the other side saw us and pulled us to safety. Farm life always has been hazardous.'

'In the 1920s at Wisborough Green, I can remember each September seeing multitudes of sheep occupying every inch of the village green. They had been born and reared in Kent and brought to await collection by local farmers who were paid so much weekly to graze them through the winter – with sometimes an additional bonus for extra well cared for animals.'

'My father moved from East to West Sussex to farm in 1921–22, bringing with him my mother and two elder daughters and me, aged two and a half, to a house which was partly Elizabethan. There was a large baker's oven reaching from floor to ceiling in the scullery and two big coppers, under which our handyman lit a fire each Monday morning and where all the family washing was done, later being mangled between wooden rollers secured in an iron framework. Morning and evening our cowman would bring in buckets of warm, frothy milk which he poured into big round metal pans in the larder, where it was left for the cream to rise. The farmhands would bring milk cans daily for the surplus milk. My treat occasionally was to be allowed to skim off the cream with a round metal skimmer, with holes to drain off the milk. Sometimes a pan of milk was left for 24 hours on the kitchen range to be scalded for clotted cream and sometimes we made butter which, with wooden pats, we made into interesting shapes.

Each morning, six o'clock in the summer and seven o'clock in the winter, the carters would arrive to feed and water our seven carthorses, which they groomed meticulously and harnessed up for work. The sound of the horses' hooves on frozen cobbles and of roosters crowing at first light is never forgotten, likewise the smell of seed corn being tarred ready for sowing. After harvest, when the Dutch barns were full, we would climb ladders to the top of the corn stacks and watch as many as ten owls blinking at us from their perch on the barn girders.'

A FAMILY CONCERN

'In the late 1930s and 1940s the farm at Scaynes Hill was a family business and the daughter did virtually the same work as the men. While at school she helped her father but at 14 this became a full time job.

It was a mixed farm with 15 milking cows, about eight heifers and two carthorses. The cows were milked twice a day by hand. At first the milk was only strained as it was poured into the churns. Later a dairy was built as the milk had to be cooled before straining. The milk was then taken by lorry to Brighton.

Haymaking near Wivelsfield before the First World War. The whole family came out into the fields to help in what was always an enjoyable part of the farming year.

The full churns were heavy and could not be lifted so they were rolled along on one edge! A difficult manoeuvre which on one occasion went amiss and the churn fell over. The value of the lost milk was deducted from her wages.

Besides milking other tasks included muck spreading using horse and cart, and a special fork to scatter the dung. Slag also had to be scattered and the feed for the cattle was dug and collected by hand. Large kale was also cut before immediate feeding to the cows while mangels and turnips were placed in clamps or stored in the barn. Hand-powered machines were used to chop the mangels and chaff. The hay was also cut into sections, with a large hay knife and then carried by pitch fork. A scythe was used to cut the hay and hedges were trimmed with a swaphook. The trimmings were carried to the farmyard along with any suitable hardcore to reduce the amount of mud.

Eventually things began to change, and an old tractor was purchased. A water pump was installed in the house to replace the outside well with its rope and bucket. Water was pumped by hand to a tank over the cowshed each day.

Haymaking and harvest time were extra busy. A machine cut and made the stooks which after drying were loaded by pitchfork, six at a time onto the Sussex waggon. At the farm the stooks were thrown to the top of the rising square stack that when completed was thatched. When the threshing machine arrived the neighbouring farm workers would join together to help each other.

Wages for the daughter were initially two shillings and sixpence and keep, rising eventually to £2. Even with this smaller sum enough was saved to buy a bicycle for £9!

Breakfast followed two to three hours work. This was a large meal with very stiff porridge and a fry up of all yesterday's leftovers – suet pudding, swede etc all topped with fried eggs. The main meal of the day was at lunch time while tea consisted of large chunks of bread with dripping or cheese and onions, a piece of fruit cake and a large mug of tea. In the summer work continued until 11 pm and supper consisted of two dry biscuits and a mug of watery cocoa.

The weekly bath was taken one after the other in the copper until the ultimate in luxury arrived – a bath, but with only a cold water tap. The effort of carrying hot water upstairs was well worth the luxury of being able to stretch out and soak. Modern amenities were completed with one electric light bulb in the living room.

The family moved into the farm in Scaynes Hill on Lady Day 1930. Quarter Days were the usual days for tenancies to change and the outgoing farmer had to leave a hay and straw stack.'

'All my life I have lived on a farm and have many happy memories. I left school at 14 to help my parents on their farm during the slump in the early 1930s. My mother took in paying guests to subsidize the housekeeping and any casual labour we engaged for haying, harvesting and threshing. In those days it was full board for the sum of two guineas per week! I helped on the farm in my spare time hand-milking the cows; no machines for us then.

In those days farming was hard work. All our cultivation was done by hand or with horses and there were four Shires and two smaller horses for lighter work. As well as corn for sale, all the fodder for the animals was grown on the farm, including oats for the horses and mangels, field cabbage and kale for the cows and sheep. These latter crops needed to be hoed, thinned out and kept free from weeds (no sprays in those days) which was back aching work, but good fun when working in a gang.

We kept 300 pure Southdown breeding sheep and I loved helping when the lambs were born. I always reared the orphans by bottle feeding and was allowed to keep the money when they were sold. I did not have wages, only my keep, which was very good, and my clothes. There always seemed masses of poultry-plucking to be done for the Christmas trade and all year we made butter for our own use and also for sale at Barnham market. During the winter months I helped my father mend corn sacks, ready for harvest time, and also helped him make hurdles which we used to fold our sheep, on root crops such as swedes and turnips.

I well remember the day when my father told me he had entered my name to join the Young Farmers Club. I discovered, at my first meeting, that all members had to be stock keepers of either a calf or a pig and I decided on a calf. The animals were allotted in the spring and we had to keep careful records of everything we did for the calf including food etc. Every year we were entered in the County Agricultural Shows and it was at the Royal Counties Show held at Portsmouth in 1939 that my calf won the first Silver Cup that George VI gave to the Young Farmers Club movement. At our club we had great social times with dances, social evenings, quizzes etc.

I was well pleased when, on my 17th birthday in 1936, my father gave me my first driving licence. There were not many girls driving then and I felt very proud when I passed my test.

At times when the going was hard, I always said I would never marry a farmer. I thought the grass was greener over the fence. However, in 1940 I did just that, so continued adding to my farming experiences. One was to say I would do a milk round in our village, but, at the end of my first day, I just burst into tears and said to my husband, "I will never be able to do this". There seemed endless names and it seemed impossible to sort out what they all wanted, but after three or four days I could not think what I had been making such a fuss about.'

CHANGING TIMES

'At the beginning of this century, Manor Farm at Westergate stretched from Aldingbourne to Lidsey. The then owner, Herbert Neale, would rise at five every day and ride his horse round all his property, taking careful note of barn, stock and fields. He was a far-sighted man, setting up a large dairy herd at a time when such an undertaking was unusual.

In the 1930s waggons and horses, reaper and binder, and large numbers of farm workers were the norm. Will Gillbard purchased a tractor for heavy work soon after he came, and as the decade progressed the number of horses dwindled gradually from six to one. There was an understandable reluctance to get rid of the last one, and the farm did not go fully mechanical until the early 1940s. Those old standard Fordson tractors had an iron seat, and no cab. The driver was open to all weathers. In 1951 there was an exceptionally wet summer and the binder could not deal with the sodden crop. After trying in vain to hire a combine harvester quickly, Will Gillbard bought his own, and finished harvesting on October 9th.

The dairy herd was sold in 1961 and the emphasis shifted to beef rearing. Mechanisation during the 1950s had led to the decline in the numbers of farm workers, until only four remained.'

THE LAST TEAM OF OXEN

'My elder sister told me that she remembered as a very small child, being held up to look over the hedge on the Bostal road at Steyning and being told to try to remember what she saw, for she would not see such a thing again – the last team of oxen to plough that part of the Downs. This was probably 1901 or 1902. I also remember that our old washer-woman once told me that oxen were used on the slopes of the Downs as they were more surefooted there than horses would be.'

A SHEPHERD ON THE DOWNS

'Being the son of a Sussex shepherd, it was taken for granted that I would follow in his footsteps so, at 14 years of age, I worked with my Dad on the Downs above Burpham at a wage of three shillings a week – which in 1922 was considered a fair wage.

Teams of oxen ploughing the Downs were once a common sight, more surefooted than horses on the sloping fields.

147

The busiest time was the lambing, when we would spend long hours in the lambing pens, hoping to double the number of lambs to the ewes.

May was the time when the sheep were dipped. They would be pushed under the water. This was done to prevent the fly and maggots which could be bad in the summer.

June was the time for shearing. After we had sheared our own flock I was given time off to join a gang of shearers and we would visit many farms, taking about a month. We returned year after year to the same farms and could earn up to £5 a week. We thought we were rich.

Our life was out in the open, all day. The sheep were penned in folds made of hurdles and were folded on turnips and kale. They were moved to a new pitch every day and it was quite hard work to make a field of hurdles if the ground was hard with frost.

The sheep in my young days were mostly Southdowns, but later many sorts of breeds were seen on the Downs.

We used to put bells on the biggest ewes. It was the sound of the Downs to hear the bells. Now the Downs are ploughed and the sheep have gone, and the tinkle of the bells also.'

THE LABOURER'S LIFE

'Amos was born in 1877 and died in 1966. His family lived at Eartham where his father was an agricultural labourer for Sir William Bird.

Amos was nine when he started work. He was rook scaring on Sir William's land and he had two fields he had to keep them off. Somehow or other – I don't know how he got his fire – he used to bake a swede in the ashes; a swede that he'd pulled up from the field. He'd bake that and have it for his dinner.

There were 16 children in Amos's family. At some point there was an outbreak of diphtheria in Eartham and four of the children in his family died in three weeks.

When Amos was 16 his father died. There were still four young children at home, so Amos worked to keep his mother and the family until his mother remarried. His mother married the lodger and, indeed, it was common for village families to have a lodger, in spite of the smallness of the cottages and the large size of the families. There were a lot of single men working as agricultural labourers during the 1880s, and right into the 1920s.'

'I started work at Gibbston Bank, Hunston in 1925. I learned to hand-milk there. They used to keep a huge bad-tempered old bull with the cows. One day when the cows and the bull were in the yard and I had to cross it, the old bull went for me. I remembered the old cowman had told me to curl up tight in a ball if this ever happened, so I did. That old bull rolled me round the yard till the other cowman got him off with a pitchfork. I escaped with a cut across my nose but it was scary and I was glad that they had that old bull put down after that.

We worked with horses till after the war when the first tractors came in. We used to work from 7 am till 5 pm having our sandwiches in the field. Two of us would plough the field together but you couldn't talk much, it was hard work. We used to wear rubber boots and when the bottoms wore out we would cut off the tops and wear them as leggings. We used to grow mangels and heap them with long clamps – it was cold, hard work but I don't remember being bothered by it and you used to see lots of wildlife.

Saturdays we used to work till 12 pm and on Sundays we used to go ferreting for rabbits. The funniest thing I ever saw was the day a rabbit shot out of a hole straight into the head of a cow that was grazing there – it knocked itself out stone cold!

After the war I used to take sugar beet to the station at Chichester – even in those days you could get a long queue of cars behind you!

We used to go to the fair at Selsey. One night I didn't get home till 2 am and my Mum had locked me out and said it was disgraceful! I used to win china and stuff and we used it for years. Later I gave it away, but now it is very collectable.'

'In the 1920s my father did contract work to local farms at Parbrook, Billingshurst. He would set off at 6.30 am with his tools and hay knife strapped on the bicycle. According to the seasons he did hay cutting and tying, harvesting and threshing thatching and land work, draining, ditching, ploughing with a horse, hedge cutting and layering of hedges. He was also sometimes hired as a water diviner using a hazel twig. Sometimes he would be away only returning home at weekends and at other times he was able to work locally. He also sharpened blades and shears using a home-made vice he erected in our garden.'

'I married a farm labourer in 1935 and lived in Didling. We had three bedrooms, a sitting room and a kitchen large enough to eat in. There was a wood shed with no floor so wherever workmen were busy in Didling I would go at the end of the day for left over cement and little by little I had a rough floor. The woodshed became a scullery and made the kitchen more comfortable. We bought wallpaper at fourpence halfpenny per roll but it all fell off owing to the make up of the walls, so my friend and I biked to Petworth (over eleven miles each way) and picked up distemper powder from the Leconfield Estate who owned the farm and buildings.

Didling still consists of the farm and six cottages. Four families made their homes there and the other two cottages changed hands fairly frequently. These were usually taken by field workers but it was these families who created any dramas that occurred. I once got hit with a beer bottle when trying to help a family being attacked by a drunken husband. In 1935 there were seven elderly people. My friend and I laid them out one by one over four and a half years just as we helped with the births. Quite an education as I was 21 years old.

The fields were worked with four horses, and cows were hand-milked though we were among the first around to introduce machine milking. Each autumn the cottagers were allocated a hedge, sometimes quite a way off. From this we had pea sticks, bean poles, starting wood and lovely logs – enough to last twelve months. My friend's mother in law was born and bred in the area. She started work at eleven years, walking two miles twice a day to Elsted. The first thing she was asked to do was to pluck a duck. The manservant had killed it and she had nearly finished when the poor thing came round, fluttered out of her hands and made for the pond! Dorcas ran home scared of the consequences.

It was a very happy life and we all got on well together. The men looked forward to moving the young herd from Didling to Harting for the winter and fetching them back in the spring. The wives were busy making up packed lunches (a lot of rivalry there). Money was a bit tight that week because the men walked both ways and there were two pubs on the way but the men loved it.

Harvest time was lovely. I had three small sisters and also Country Holiday Fund boys from London's East End. Every evening the grown ups went stooking and the children had such fun. We got to the middle of the field and bunny beating began. We didn't think it cruel. Nothing got away hurt – it was quick and clean. I would go off before the rest and get the primus going and when they came in and had a wash I had fried rabbit and potatoes – all piping hot for a very hungry family. My sisters talk of it to this day.

War came and all the men were in the Home Guard, going off to Bognor three times a week returning just in time to change for 5 am milking. We had dog fights over us daily and the flying bombs stopped whining near us. There were bomb holes at Bepton but no casualties. A Heinkel dropped its machine gun turret and its ammo in our back yard. The plane ditched on the Downs.

By then we had gone modern. Tractors had replaced horses, the

Downs were ploughed up and in 1949 our farmer died and it seemed that our whole life changed.'

IN SERVICE

For many young girls, going into service at the local 'big house' was the only option available when they left school. In the days when most middle class families and farmers kept at least one servant, such jobs were usually readily available. It could be a good life given a good 'family', but it was hard work for little pay and long hours.

HAPPY DAYS AT UPPARK

This account of life at Uppark was written in the 1950s.

'I had the pleasure of visiting Uppark, Harting, a few weeks ago – the lovely ancient home of Admiral Sir William and Lady Meade Fetherstonhaugh. So much do I admire the house and its surroundings of lovely parkland. I first went there in the year 1880 as dairymaid, to live with her Ladyship, Miss Frances Fetherstonhaugh. I took over the management of the dairy, baked the family bread for the household, also fancy bread. In those days there had to be a great variety of bread and rolls – nine or more sorts, although this was usually only on the occasion of a big shooting party. Her Ladyship kept a large staff of servants then – I should say about 40 in number.

My duties also included making fresh butter and Devonshire cream, cream cheese, butter pats and other butter all sorts of fancy shapes to decorate the breakfast table. Breakfast was served at nine o'clock, therefore I got up at three o'clock in the morning to get these lovely things ready. It is some distance from the dairy to the anteroom outside the dining room where I used to dish up all my butter and fancy breads and butters, creams, Devonshire cream, etc, on lovely silver and china plates, butter dishes, cheese stands and folded serviettes. After I hoped everything was perfect, I would go round the dining room breakfast table, by permission of the butler, to see if everything was alright; that was my every morning job when large parties of guests were stopping at the mansion. I would then return to the dairy and bake a half a sack of family bread, in brick ovens heated with wood, then wash and scrub all the dairy utensils, then go to the bakehouse and clear everything away. Her Ladyship would come to the dairy to show her visitors her lovely marble dairy fixtures and priceless china, which was kept there. A stained glass door led out to a tea room where I used to serve tea if it was asked for; junket, Devonshire cream and fruit. I often got a bit of praise from the ladies and gentlemen – and sometimes more than thank-you!

Lady Frances Fetherstonhaugh was a great lady, fond of company. The hounds met there sometimes; powdered footmen were there to hand refreshments to the ladies and gentlemen on horseback. At the front of the house were the gold gates and the lovely peacocks sitting on the big balls of the gate spreading out their lovely tails; some tame deer would be trotting round, and a few pretty Jersey cows all added to the beauty of the scene. Her Ladyship had three donkeys that lived round on the lawns and front of the lovely house and there were lots of pretty guinea fowl on the lawns as well. Amongst the ladies and gentlemen on the horses Lady Fetherstonhaugh would walk round. She carried her sunshade with a long fringe on it and priceless gold handle and wore white kid gloves and a lovely velvety lace dress, lace toque and a little tint of red in her coat or dress. With her would be Robin, her dog. Lady Fetherstonhaugh was a charming lady and these hunt meets on the front of the house made a wonderful memorable picture.

Afterwards I returned to the dairy to get the butter and milk, junket and all sorts of cheese ready for lunch. Sometimes if I had time I helped Teddy Hall to pluck chickens, partridges or pheasants for the dinner at night The cream then had to be scalded for the next day's Devonshire cream for breakfast and the dairy left spotlessly clean; then milking with Teddy Hall, and sometimes calves to feed and small chickens to see to and shut up for the night.

In 1881 or 1882, Lord Winterton-Turner and his bride, the former Lady Georgina Hamilton, spent their honeymoon at Uppark, at the invitation of Lady Fetherstonhaugh, who went out of residence but left her entire staff to wait on them, with the exception of her own maid and footman. During dinner on their first evening there was a distressing episode. A burglar hoisted a ladder and entered her Ladyship's bedroom. The head housemaid, who was then over 70 years of age, went as usual to tidy her Ladyship's room and found the door locked from the inside. She raised the alarm and soon the watchmen and policemen who were there around the house arrived on the scene. Of the two men involved one got away (eventually to be caught at a London station) and the other fell from the ladder and was captured. Her Ladyship's dressing case was recovered. The burglar was detained in Petersfield police station for the night and then sent to Lewes for trial. Both of these two men were to receive due punishment for their crime. Originally they were at Uppark, with her Ladyship's permission, to sketch, as artists. In this way it is thought they watched and waited their opportunity. But as they had been around for some time they were known quite well to the staff and several of us, including myself, had to go to Lewes to identify them.

In those day Uppark was a very charming home for everyone, also the staff. Her Ladyship frequently gave fetes and dances for the servants and on these occasions the ladies and gentlemen watched from the terrace. We used to have running matches and tug-of-war over the Dog Kennel Pond and plenty of other amusements. Uppark was never a lonely place – plenty of pleasures and, bless your life – plenty of work.'

THE BUTLER

'In the 1920s my father secured a post as butler to a family of seven who owned a country estate three miles from Horsham. He remained in their service for over 20 years. Apart from his normal duties which included being responsible for all the indoor staff of ten, he was expected to arrange all the flowers in the house. He was also valet to his employer and later to the four sons of the house. As they grew up, they would confide in him things they didn't want their parents to know.

The estate was large, giving scope for many leisure pursuits; pheasant shoots in autumn, cricket matches and tennis parties in summer, and badminton matches and an art show in the winter. There were frequent dinner parties and weekend guests staying, which made a lot of extra work for all the staff. The hours were very long by today's standards. My father's usual working day was eleven hours with anything up to 14 hours when the family entertained. But there was no such thing as overtime.

With this job went a large four bedroomed lodge, beautifully cool in the summer, like an ice-house in winter. Four tons of coal were supplied to feed the kitchen range, the only means of cooking, as there was no gas or electricity for us, only for the gentry in the big house who had their own generator, and oil-fired central heating.

For many years my father's salary was £96 a year to feed and clothe his family of four – we were very hard up but happy and made our own entertainment.'

THE MAIDS

'My sister and I both went into service when we left school in the
1920s – we never considered doing anything else, as most village
girls at Halnaker did the same. I started work as a between maid at
Lavant House. I was paid ten shillings a month and my keep, and
had to buy my own uniform. I started my daily chores at 6.30 am
and was on duty until nine or ten at night. During the morning, once
the family were up, I helped the upstairs maid clean the bedrooms,
and in the afternoon I helped in the kitchen. Once a fortnight the
cooking range had to be cleaned down and the flues scraped – a
horrible job!'

'In 1930 I left school aged 14. I helped my mother for a time, then I
went as a housemaid three days a week. I was taught how to wait at
table. The people I worked for moved to a larger house, so I went
full time, 7 am to 10 pm. My wages were five shillings a week. It
was very hard work scrubbing floors, washing and ironing. Silver
and brass had to be cleaned once a week, and that took one afternoon. When I was about 18 I left there and went to work in a farmhouse – not so hard, fewer hours, seven shillings and sixpence a
week and much more friendly!'

ALL FOR ONE

'My mother was a cook and came to Sussex when her "family"
bought a house in Wivelsfield. The house, Coldharbour, had its own
farm and it was part of the cook's job to make the butter. Up until
then buttermaking was not one of mother's skills so it was arranged
for the neighbouring farmer's wife to teach her. Two lessons a week
for four weeks was sufficient. As the farmer's wife had been champion fancy buttermaker of Great Britain at the National Dairy Show
for five years running she was well qualified to teach the craft. It so
happened that the family was usually at home for tea when my
mother arrived and so she met all five brothers sitting round the
table and eyeing her with their wickedly sparkling, intensely blue
eyes. Needless to say it was not long before she was being courted
by one of them, Jim. She always knew when he was on his way to
see her because his dog, Dash, was invariably ahead of him and
scratching on her kitchen door.

On one rare occasion all the servants had been given a day off – a
bank holiday, I think – and my mother and a number of the "girls"
went off from Wivelsfield station to Brighton for the day, although
my mother went on to Lancing to visit her sister. The last train was

Going into service was once almost the only choice for young girls when they left school. Eileen Avard was maid at Stonewick House in the 1940s.

due to leave for Wivelsfield at 10 pm and my mother appealed to all the girls to be sure to be at the station in time. My father was to meet them with the dog cart and transport them the two miles from the station to Coldharbour. The kitchenmaid failed to arrive in time and my mother, being in charge of the party, remained behind to wait for her. The train was just pulling out of the station when the girl arrived. Father met the rest of the party, took them home, switched from the dog cart to the pony and trap and hastened off to Brighton (about 13 miles) for Mother and the kitchenmaid. This took time as you can imagine.

Arriving at Coldharbour in the early hours of the morning Mother found the daughter of the house waiting up for her. Without listening to any explanation, she gave Mother the sack on the spot and ordered her to leave at daybreak. There was no arguing, the sack at a minute's notice it was. So Mother packed her bags. Imagine the surprise of the employers when, in accordance with instructions my mother was ready packed by 8 am – not unexpected – but all the rest of the female staff were also packed and ready to leave! They did not like living in the country and were not staying if Mother went. No amount of persuading at this point could stem the exodus and Coldharbour was left with a butler, coachman and gardeners only!'

THE NURSERY GROWERS

Until the Second World War, the area between Chichester and Worthing was renowned for its nursery produce -- the best tomatoes, so they said, were Worthing grown. Many of these nurseries were family owned and run.

FAMOUS FOR ITS VARIETY

'Prior to the Second World War the coastal district between Worthing and Chichester was famous for the variety of its horticultural produce. The reason for this was its loamy soil between the Downs and the sea which was known as "brick earth". Added to this was the high annual sunshine which helped to warm the glasshouses and produce early crops from the land.

Servicemen returning from the war in 1918 were able to obtain a smallholding and a house under the Government's Land Settlement Scheme. Notable examples of this scheme still exist at Sidlesham where the wooden houses on the nurseries have a Dutch appearance, and at Barnham, in Yapton Road and in Hill Lane where the houses on the holdings are brick built.

The Barnham smallholdings produced everything from tomatoes

and vegetables to cut flowers and hardy nursery stock. A special railway wagon left Barnham station nightly at 6 pm bearing boxes of produce to London's Covent Garden market. A co-operative of many growers was formed called Farmers and Growers Industries (circa 1935) which is still in existence, and now called Fargro.

Because of the greatly increased population and house building in West Sussex three large and prominent nurseries evolved, namely Goatchers Nurseries at Storrington which grew up over three generations, The Barnham Nurseries, over 100 acres in size, and Croftway Nurseries (Toynbee's Nurseries) which was developed from the original land settlement holdings in Barnham in 1918. These large nurseries grew everything for the private garden, including fruit and ornamental trees, flowering shrubs, conifers, hardy perennials and alpines.

Creators of new gardens on the coastal belt had experienced great difficulty in establishing plants in their gardens because of the damage caused by the strong salt-laden south-westerly winds. It was found, however, that by planting a hedge or screen of *Cupressus macrocarpa*, a quick growing shelter belt was formed and a new garden would be protected. The three above nurseries probably grew or supplied over a million of these conifers over the years.

"Macrocarpa", as it was popularly known throughout the district, had a life of about 50 years. Not many are seen today as they have nearly all died or been blown over, but this particular conifer was probably the biggest factor in helping to create the beautiful coastal gardens we enjoy in West Sussex today.'

A FAMILY BUSINESS

'Grandpa and Granny Linfield got married on 1st January 1883. The south road between Lancing and Worthing had been washed away by heavy tides, so the road via Sompting had to be taken. This was gravelly and worried the horse, so the trip took so long that they only just got to the Bedford Row chapel in time (there was a limit to the hour within which marriages could be solemnised).

Grandpa took a small nursery opposite the present entrance to Worthing Hospital Outpatients Department. After a while, he sold this to his brother in law and moved to Bridge Nursery where he built a house for his family. Further west, he took over Ladydell and Chesswood Nurseries on the north side of the railway line. Ladydell had a big flint barn with slits for windows, and here mushroom spawn was "run" into compost for the mushroom beds. There was another nursery added on the east side of Ham Road, running out towards the Wildbrooks, which had a big lean-to greenhouse against the brick wall bordering the railway line. There was also our own particular base, Ophir Nursery, on the front at East Worthing.

A farm had also been bought at Thakeham, just before the First World War, intended for the three youngest boys. Worthing itself was full of nurseries, mostly growing grapes, nectarines peaches and figs in glasshouses, and some of the latter outside, between the greenhouses, as well. Mushroom growing had also started by 1914 – as my mother testified. They had a glut of them the day I was born and Dad was too busy packing them to come home to see how Mother was getting on!

Then came the war. The younger boys, Harold and Wilfred, joined up in 1914 and after training were sent to France, where Harold was killed in 1915, before he had even had his 20th birthday.

A War Agricultural Committee was appointed and made growers take out grapes, peaches and figs from the glasshouses and plant tomatoes. By the end of the war only a few indoor grapevines were left, mostly white muscats. Tomatoes took over in most greenhouses, often with mushroom beds also – traversed by planks raised on bricks (which I and my cousins all learned to walk – and even run – on, and at school they wondered why we all walked and ran rather alike!).

In 1924 a house was built for our family on the Ophir Nursery on the front, and I grew up there. I recall all the men who worked there: Mr Cooper, the foreman; Mr Ayres, older with a long white beard; Mr Pemberton, a bit of a joker, who told me that if I planted the primrose roots in my plot upside down, they would come up pink next year – muggins did, with dire results; Mr Mattens, younger, with a small moustache; Bert Cooper, the garden boy; and Mr Rhodes, painter and decorator, who was colour blind.

By the 1930s the soil, from long use, was getting less productive and land was acquiring building value, so many local nurseries sold their land and moved out. In our case, Ophir was sold to my father's brother, Wilfred, who with a friend, had set up a building firm. The growing side moved to the farm at Thakeham, and nurseries were acquired at Ashington, Sompting, Clymping etc.

By this time mushroom growing had become very scientific. At first it had been rather hit or miss. The spawn was collected from fields, from cowpats and horse-droppings, where the white threads could be spotted by the knowledgeable. We children were paid sixpence each for any promising-looking offering which showed traces of spawn.

When the Second World War started a War Agricultural Committee was once more appointed. It hadn't learned much in the 20 years between. We had two young apple and pear orchards at Thakeham,

158

just due to come into full bearing. The "War Ag" decreed: "Any orchard which has not produced X amount of fruit the previous year must be rooted out." Pleas of future yields went unheeded – they had to be rooted out, and the area planted with Jerusalem artichokes.

We often wondered why the nurseries at Thakeham were not bombed – they were producing food so presumably were a legitimate target. Apart from the food side, an attack would have been lethal to workers. You can't stick paper strips over greenhouses, and anyone working in the middle of one couldn't possibly have got to the door in time. When, in the latter part of the war, we had German prisoners of war working there, they told us why. It was down on their maps as a large lake – light reflecting from the glass must have looked like water!

Finally, the nurseries were taken over by Rank-Hovis-MacDougall, and only a few of the family still work there.'

HAND DUG AND PLENTY OF MANURE

'My father was a nurseryman. He left school at ten years old and went to work on the land at a wage of two shillings and sixpence weekly.

Around 1900 he rented some land in Mash Barn Lane with his brother and they hand dug the whole of this area. As they were undertaking this they were told that it wouldn't produce good crops for some 25 years as this land was under sea water (or tributaries from the river) until the 16th century and then used for salt panning, before grazing cattle. However, with plenty of horse manure it did make useful market garden land. In 1908 they'd saved £200 (George raised some of the money from emptying sewers and Frank delivered milk) and they took over the lease of a large house, The Finches, with land and building attached.

Once a week my father would go to Brighton to meet the carter who'd left home around midnight to walk the horse the eight and a half miles with a loaded van. The night before Mother would boil water to make a special bran mix for the working horse. As a special treat in holiday time I would sometimes be allowed to sit up with the carter for this journey.

As the brothers progressed they built greenhouses for the growing of tomatoes, cucumbers, mushrooms and chrysanthemums. Two were built first with an adjoining stokehole with a coal-burning fire that had to be kept continually stoked even at the weekend, when often my father took on this duty. Before water was laid there were rainwater storage tanks and one of my first memories is of a well for pumping water.

Some of the produce would be sold to local shops and some sent to Covent Garden, London, mainly the tomatoes and 'chrysanths'. They would be packed in boxes, loaded on to a hand cart (two wheels at the back and supporting stakes at the front) and pushed by a worker to the nearby railway yard, for loading on the train.

Both my father and his brother were rejected by the army on health grounds in 1914 and told to go back to work on the land. It was then that they bought up fields adjoining their land and employed prisoners of war.

My father would always commence work at the same time as his workers and complete the same hours; he said "one must set an example". Despite this fact he would spend evenings doing the book-keeping.

As they'd prospered they had purchased the land, built more greenhouses, a new stable and packing shed and later mechanised with a plough etc. Some lower land was sold for building at £1,000 an acre before the Second World War. All the land was eventually sold for building after the war.'

OTHER WAYS WE MADE A LIVING

∽

There were, of course, dozens of other ways in which we made our living in the past, from shopwork to charcoal burning, and these are just a few examples. Sometimes, when times were hard, it was necessary to take on any work that was available, no matter how menial, to keep the family together.

VILLAGE TRADES AND CRAFTS

'Most of the menfolk at West Hoathly in the 1920s were employed by the owners of the "big house". They had their own carpenters, bricklayers, grooms and stable lads, gardeners, farm hands, butlers, houseboys and all the female staff. But also in the village there were the postman, grocers, butchers, bakers, shoemaker, policeman, blacksmith, wheelwright and the school staff. The village policeman was the man who kept law and order, and many a youth felt the swish of the heavy cape he carried, or the toe of his boot. He was a man to be reckoned with and kept the peace in his own way. Our policeman in my childhood had a very large family and nearly always one of his own boys would be mixed up in any mischief, so he dealt with the whole bunch and they remembered it. It was said that nobody would ever be locked up for the night as the cells attached to the police house were used by the family as extra bedrooms.

The wheelwright made the lovely Sussex wagons, wheelbarrows and big farm gates for which the blacksmith made strong iron bolts and latches, and iron tyres for the wheels. All the horses came to be shod, great heavy carthorses and the dainty feet of carriage horses and ponies. The wrought iron gates, made by hand, are still to be seen around the village, with lacy patterns and wonderful designs.

The brickyard opened years ago, started by the brickmakers of Hamsey near Lewes who made a road into the clay soil at the back of West Hoathly station. It is still called Hamsey Road. At that time men were glad of the work, for the wages were much better than for work on the farms, but the work was so heavy that very few were able to do it for many years. Now machinery has taken on the heavy work and many local men are working there today, for the supply of clay still lasts out. Huge lorries now cart the bricks away, whereas years ago they were loaded into railway trucks.'

'Fishing was until recently the main industry in Selsey and by the late 1950s there were three mixed farms in the parish (Grange, Greenleas and Home) but the fourth, Mill farm, was entirely given over to caravan sites. Mr Low-Beer at Norton Priory (the old rectory) specialised in champion Channel Island dairy cattle and had a great many successes at shows all over the country.

Lobsters, crabs and prawns are, and always have been, more plentiful than fish off this coast. The crab and lobster pots or "creels" to be seen on the fishing beach were made of golden willow. Each fisherman made his own pots using the osiers grown in the country around Selsey. In 1910 about 100 men were employed in this industry, but by 1958 there were only a few. The lifeboat was manned by fishermen and though this is not an industry it took up a good deal of the men's time.

Only one factory has existed in Selsey, that belonging to Mr C Pullinger of Ivy Cottage, High Street. Mr Pullinger was a gentleman of a highly inventive nature and on his business card are listed his abilities and the things which were made at his factory. The most celebrated article was "a mousetrap of curious design". This factory employed fishermen during the winter as well as workmen from the village. The mousetrap found a ready market overseas, Germany

161

being one of Mr Pullinger's best customers. As well as mouse and rat traps, farm machinery, boats and pumps were made. Mr Pullinger also hung paper, painted signs, was the village accountant and letter writer and was also grocer, baker and farmer, tax collector and undertaker. The fashion was to line coffins with fine stuff and every two years of so Mrs Pullinger used proudly to display her new skirt made from the "coffin cuttings".

The main business of the village nowadays, namely catering for holidaymakers, has been steadily growing since the beginning of the century. The holiday camp opened in 1932 and since then more and more caravan sites have appeared.'

'Up to the beginning of the 1920s East Preston was a small seaside village, its inhabitants existing by fishing and farming with associated activities, such as the blacksmith, beachcombing and renting rooms to holidaymakers. However, there were two other options which made East Preston with Kingston unique.

In the previous centuries the enormous amount of smuggling indulged in along this part of the coast caused a row of coastguard cottages to be built looking out to sea, with a clear run up to their flagstaff at Kingston. Several coastguards and their families lived here, the cottages having a common corridor through which the men ran whenever an emergency occurred. Flags were used to signal to the coastguard cutter at sea and to receive information concerning the landing of goods.

The other option for employment was in the workhouse. This was the usual grim Dickensian three-storey building surmounted by a large square clocktower and surrounded by barns, gatehouses, nurses' homes, boilerhouses and boardrooms. In my childhood, during the Second World War, the master was Mr Broom, who wore a top hat as he walked about the village and was humbly deferred to by any of the elderly men and women whom he had in his care. At the beginning of the 20th century the village began to be developed and brickfields using local clay sprang up. At the same time flower bulb growing was started commercially, both providing new employment.

People from the theatre and the arts started to buy property here so that gardeners, cooks and domestic servants were required. Jack Hylton and members of the Crazy Gang, Binnie Hale and many more arrived and in turn brought the reigning Wimbledon tennis stars to play at the newly formed club, and the English cricket team to play charity matches on the cricket pitch.'

'The fine culvert and slag heaps at Furnace Pond remind one of the days when Fernhurst was the centre of the iron smelting industry.

The charcoal for it was provided by the forests which surrounded the village on all sides. Cylinders Yard is a reminder of the days when there were large cylinders there for the making of charcoal.

It was a grand experience watching the charcoal burners. The travelling huts in which the workers lived arrived in the wood, plus the tools required. Then the large cylinders of metal were put in position in a chosen place in the wood. During the next few weeks the cylinders were systematically filled with layers of saplings and branches and trunks of trees, with a specially built chimney down the centre. Then one day as you went by, a steady flow of smoke came from the chimney in the centre of the mass of smouldering wood. When this process was completed, the cylinders were removed to show the wood made into charcoal. This was seen in a Fernhurst wood in 1951, and seven years later you could still find perfect charcoal in small pieces and the large empty cylinders rusting away.

In Fernhurst the art of hand spinning was revived in 1912 and many cottages had spinning wheels and spun some very good yarn. At one period the yarn was sent away to various hand-weaving industries in the country or was sent to be knitted into garments by the cottage folk.

A team of Fernhurst men used to perform a very necessary task – they were well diggers. They divined and tracked water and then sank a well. These men were also the bellringers at the church.

There were several industries connected with wood – fencing, barrel hoops, walking sticks, hurdles and oak panels. Oak felled on the Fernhurst side of Blackdown was used in the library of the Inner Temple in London and in its own village hall. Nothing was wasted; at one time the cottages were roofed with pieces of chestnut left when the wood-cutters had trimmed the wood for chestnut paling. Bordering the road from Fernhurst to Midhurst there is still an area of chestnut trees which are systematically coppiced.

There was once a brickyard on Henley Common and until 1920 there was a flour mill at Cooksbridge.'

LAUNDRY WORK

'Some of my earliest memories are of happy times spent in the laundry, a small room built on to our house at Handcross where my grandmother and two aunts were very busy ironing. It was warm in there, the heat coming from a small coke-burning stove. Here flat irons were arranged to get hot, so that when the irons being used became cool, they were changed for hot ones. These were carefully rubbed clean before use so that no smudges were made on the snow-white sheets. These sheets and pillow cases and all white things had been washed and boiled in the two coppers in the wash-house. Soap extract and soda were added to the water – no biological powder in those days. A fire was lit under the coppers which had to be constantly stoked with wood until the water boiled. When rinsed in blue water and squeezed through the mangle, the washing was put out in the yard to dry on rope lines, that were taken down each week after use.

Some of the big houses round about had their own laundry, but some sent to a private one like my grandmother's, and here they also washed the maids' print dresses and aprons, and occasionally a delicate nightie or blouse of the lady's. These were washed separately with great care and the lace goffered, either with tongs, or a little machine rather like a small mangle with fluted rollers open at one end which were heated with small iron bars, often made red hot in the coke fire. A piece of paper was used first to test the heat so that the garment was not damaged.

On Thursdays the washing was taken down from the airers and packed in the laundry baskets, making sure the right articles went in the right basket, with its book of items and prices charged. One very heavy basket was collected by one of the farm workers with a horse and cart, and the smaller baskets were delivered on a trolley by an elderly man, who also delivered newspapers.

Although this was very hard work little money was made, and my grandmother told me that before she received her widow's pension she had to apply for "parish relief" one winter to buy coal. One of my aunts was married, but for the other one this was her only income, but they enjoyed a day trip to Brighton about once a year and bought a new hat and coat each.

Laundry Cottage is now Laurel Cottage, and there is a car in a garage where I used to learn the right way to iron a shirt and drink tea from a saucer.'

THE DRAPER'S SHOP

'When I was 14 years old in 1945 I left school and worked in a draper's shop in a nearby town. I got twelve shillings and sixpence the first week, then it was 17 shillings and sixpence, and we got a rise every year. The war ended soon after and the boss gave us all double wages that week.

I was put in a department which sold household goods and materials. Coupons were needed for most of the goods and they were in very short supply. Coupons had to be added up each night in the same way as money.

In December people started buying things for Christmas and some used to ask for goods to be put by for when they got the Co-op dividend. The second week in December they used to queue up and get their "divi" in a church hall nearby.

Christian names were not allowed and we had to call each other by surnames – Miss whoever-you-were, junior or senior. I was there eight years before I left to get married and just before I left christian names were coming in when customers were not in the shop.'

BENTWOOD

'Before the Second World War a factory was started in Lavant, a bentwood factory, and all they made were the bent wood hoops that used to go round the cabin trunks that people used for their holidays. It was the only factory in England to make these hoops.

Then the war came and they started to build a munitions factory there too, with a huge, tall chimney, but the war was over before the factory was finished. The wood used was brought all the way over from Slindon, more than ten miles across the Downs by overhead cable railway.'

ON THE RAILWAY

'My father joined the railway in 1915 at Eastbourne, and after a period in the army during the First World War, he returned to the railway and continued there until his retirement in 1964. In 1915 it was known as the London and Brighton South Coast Railway.

He started work as a cleaner at the engine sheds at Eastbourne and was responsible for one particular engine. I can remember him telling me that one week he was short in his pay packet, and he asked the reason why and was told, "You did not clean the engine properly one night".

When he first worked on the footplate as a fireman he had to wear his own clothes, and then they were issued with navy blue overalls, and I can remember Mother soaking them in a bucket of hot water to loosen the dirt before she washed them.

Because of electrification of the lines at Eastbourne just before the Second World War, Father could not get promotion to a driver. However, this he obtained in November 1940 by moving to Horsham, where he worked on the steam trains, the Hornbys as they were known, and then on electric passenger trains. I know that at one time he had as many as 13 different weekly turns of duty on his roster, and so Mother had to cope with meals at many different times to fit in with his duties.

The centenary year of the Bluebell Railway was in 1982 and my brother took Father on a visit there to see the "Gladstone" engine on which he used to be a fireman. This engine was brought down from the National Railway Museum at York where it had been on display for about 50 years.'

THE POST

'My uncle was a postman in Lancing. The post office then (in the 1930s and 1940s) was in a wooden hut behind a shop. The hut is a printer's now, but the road to it is still as rough and full of puddles after rain as ever it was. My uncle did three postal deliveries a day, travelling all over Lancing on his bike. He used to park his bike outside The Farmers Arms and it was never stolen. He finished work about 8 pm and his wages were a princely £3 a week.'

'In 1929 I was 25 years old and had been married for a couple of years when my husband obtained the job of village sub-postmaster at Findon. To obtain the job his character had to be exemplary, and he had to supply a reliable timepiece and suitable premises. With the help of my parents, the village bakers, a 20 year mortgage was taken out to build the office and shop, and a telephone exchange to give continuous service. I had been working in a town sub-office for five years, but did not know anything about telephone operating. While the building was being erected I cycled some four miles each afternoon to learn how to manage a telephone exchange by kind permission of the Worthing postmaster.

When we opened our shop, I set up in stationery, haberdashery and wools – a traditional village post office shop – as this would give us some good will to sell when we left, as post office trade was not considered 'good will'.

The mail would arrive in bags from Head Office at 6 am and would then have to be sorted on the post office counter by the two postmen. My husband would deal with and sort the registered bag, starting the delivery about 7.30 am. There was usually a heavy parcel delivery which the postmen would strap on to their bicycles. Christmas was a bumper time for parcels as the post office was the number one service in those days, so we always hoped for fine weather then to be able to tip the parcels out on to the concrete outside, at the back, so as not to hamper movement in the shop. I might add that there were no stated hours for postmen at that time. We reckoned to clear each day and it was not unusual for a man to work until 7 or 8 pm. There was delivery on Christmas Day too – until the office was clear!

At this time the telegram was relied upon for sending urgent or tragic news. The telephone had not come into general use and, if a willing boy could not be found, then the sub-postmaster would have to deliver. There was a time when the sub-postmaster of the adjoining village had a bad accident, and we were requisitioned to cover his area as well as our own. Gratefully the pay was extended also. The Post Office was always very fair, even if somewhat strict.

The only industry in the village was horse racing which provided employment during the winter months. When the horses were engaged at the races, they would be walked the four miles to Worthing station. This would be impossible now owing to the heavy traffic. It was always noticeable when there was a winner. Then during the summer months, there was another source of income. Most of the cottagers would let a couple of rooms, and that meant new faces around the village. The postcard trade would flourish. I kept a record of accommodation available, and earned a few shillings.'

AMBERLEY CHALK PITS

'My father worked at the Amberley chalk pits for a time. I can remember going with him underneath the kilns; the steps down were man-made out of chalk and very narrow and steep. My father had to rake the lime dust out, which he did with a long iron rod. When we reached the surface again more chalk was put on, right to the top, as the kilns had to burn all night and it was not very often they went out. When it was dark they used to glow red. We could not get too near as the heat and sulphur was terrific. On the banks of the pits lovely flowers grew, wallflowers, wild violets and pretty betsey.'

MAKING ENDS MEET

'I was born in Chichester in 1902 and went into service when I was 14. At 18 I went to work at Manor Farm in Lavant but I didn't like it there and I only stayed four months. But it was fate that sent me there for that's where I met my husband who was cowman at the farm. We went to live in one of a pair of old flint cottages where we got our water from a well for many years. Then mains water was laid on and we had an outside tap to share with the other cottage. I remember one year, when we still had the well, that we had a very hot and dry summer and a cart came round with water for us in a milk churn.

During the First World War, before we were married, my husband was in the army and he was awarded the Military Medal. He got ill through having to lie in the wet trenches so much and he had one illness after another and was never really strong again. When he

167

developed dermatitis he wasn't allowed to have anything more to do with the cows and he was off work a lot, once for ten weeks. During this time the only money we had was what I managed to earn for he didn't get any insurance.

For four years I cleaned the village hall. It was Colonel Mortimer who had raised enough money to have the hall built as a memorial to the men who had given their lives in the war. It was built in 1922 but it was very different then from how it is today. There were open fires then and I had to break up all the wood for them. Then there were Aladdin lamps for lighting – they had them all round the room with two hanging in the middle. I had to get the water for cleaning from the river Lavant about 200 yards away across the village green and it took the whole day working hard to clean it up. I had six shillings a week for all that work in the winter, but in the summer they gave me up because they said it didn't get dirty.

There was a lot going on in the hall in those days. There was a whist drive every week and a sixpenny hop. I was never allowed to go till after I was married. Once you went into service you had to be in by nine o'clock so I had never been to a dance until I went there with the girls from next door.

I took in loads and loads of washing. Nearly everyone in the village sent me their washing and I walked into Chichester to fetch more. I used to do the soldiers' washing, too.

Along the Lavant Straight, where the Goodwood airfield is today, there was a military airfield and a Polish squadron was stationed there. Two of the Polish men lodged with me. I didn't have to feed them of course, but I just had to provide them with a bedroom. They were both very nice men, one of them in particular. He used to come downstairs and sit while I was doing my ironing and my son who was a schoolboy then, tried to teach him English. And when he went back home he sent me several cards and also a book of music – it was a Polish opera. I've still got it.

As part of my war work I used to go on Saturdays with Mrs Chapman of the WVS to the NAAFI sites with tea, chocolates, cigarettes and all that sort of thing. And I took in several young soldiers' wives. Some of them still keep up with me and always send to me at Christmas.

In the 1920s and 1930s everything was so different – take the Goodwood races. In those days I used to take in the stable lads and would sleep five or six or even seven of them and get ten shillings a night for it. That was good pay for those days. We looked to that money to buy the children's clothes for the winter.'

WAR & PEACE

THE GREAT WAR 1914–18

With the men away fighting, families in West Sussex found the war years a time of hardship and deprivation. Schoolchildren did their bit, knitting balaclavas for the men at the Front and collecting wild berries for medicines and jams. Women took on the jobs men had vacated, often to find themselves summarily ousted when the soldiers returned once more. And what celebrations there were when the dreadful war was over at last, in towns and villages across the county.

CHEERING AND WAVING

'I can remember so well when war was declared. The people who lived in the workers' cottages all walked up to Handcross village to see and hear what we could of the soldiers. We saw several lorry loads of very young men, all making for France, and they were all cheering and waving as they passed through the village. This was the first time I had seen a lorry. At school at Handcross we were taught to knit socks for the soldiers.'

WHEN THE MEN WERE AWAY

'I came to Southwick in 1914, when my father was sent to France. We lived with my grandparents right on the edge of the Downs. There was practically no building on the Downs then, and our walks were accompanied by the sound of sheep bells and a chat with the shepherds. I went everywhere with my grandfather, "helping" on the allotment and going to collect pennies from the schoolchildren for their savings. There was an army camp on the green and I visited them (I was only nine) and enjoyed their company. They came to our house to play billiards (it was only an ordinary semi-detached house, but it had a very large kitchen which held the billiard table).

Next door lived my great aunt and uncle. He was a retired jeweller and very gifted. He did special work for a man in Hatton Garden, who sent things to him by post, with no stamp and unregistered. That way, he thought, the Post Office would take more care, to make sure of collecting the fee! As far as I know, it worked. I never heard of anything going astray. A letter posted by the late evening post was always delivered next morning and often the reply got to London the following morning.'

'In 1914 my father was sent to France with the Royal Flying Corps. Mother took up work at Goring-by-Sea, delivering meat once a week to the outlying villages of Clapham and Patching – an all day job with a horse and cart. One day it was snowing heavily on the return journey and the horse, blind, began to slip and refused to move on a steep hill in Goring Woods. Mother comforted him and with her shoulders under his neck managed to lead him to the bottom of the hill. She loved the horse and was quite fearless.

Food was very short at that time and there was no rationing as such, so we were lucky if we got something to eat. Fuel was short too, which meant we were often very cold. Influenza was rife. People in the towns and villages died in their hundreds as resistance was low without proper food.'

'During the war I worked at Chichester railway station and at Drayton, which was also a station. I was in the office and "talked" using Morse Code to the other stations. At the end of the war when the men returned, all the women lost their jobs.

Sometimes I was sent to relieve in the Midhurst office and travelled there on the single track line; each train had to have a baton before it could go on the single track, to prevent accidents. The Selsey Tram came into Chichester station every morning bringing loads of fish to be put on the eight o'clock train to Victoria – when the Selsey Tram had a breakdown, the main line train waited.

The ambulance train from Norwood Junction brought the wounded soldiers to Chichester en route to what is now Graylingwell Hospital. "Cicero" tapped out in Morse Code gave advanced warning that Chichester must be ready to receive an ambulance train, sometimes not arriving till 10 pm. The stretchers were taken to the Parcels Office to await transport.

I lived in a small village east of Chichester. In 1914 part of the farm was taken for Tangmere aerodrome.'

'Outside our house at Broadwater there was quite a big open road space. Here, before the war, the horse-drawn buses owned by Mr Town of Worthing, turned round to go back to Worthing Pier (the fare for children for the one and a half miles was a penny). The first motor bus had appeared in 1910 and during the war the top was covered by a huge yellow gas envelope.

There always seemed something to see. Once a week an Italian man and his wife came to play their decorated barrel organ. There was a small live monkey on top and a baby in a drawer. Once there came a really big bear attached to its owner by a chain, and on its hind legs it danced and bowed to us. And, of course, there were the

171

soldiers – on their route march from Shoreham Camp they would come by singing *Sussex by the sea* or *Pack up your troubles.*'

BALACLAVAS AND BLACKBERRIES

'At Goring school our songs became patriotic during the war, and we knitted socks, scarves and balaclavas for the soldiers. Older children were taken out to gather rosehips, elderberries and blackberries and to pick up acorns for the pigs. They were paid a penny a pound for them. The fruits were used for jams and jellies and some were canned and sold at a shop in Montague Street, Worthing, called "Home Industries".'

FOOD WAS SCARCE

'I was born on the outskirts of Dover in July 1907 and am therefore a "Maid of Kent". However, when very young I was more or less adopted by my aunt, and came to live in Fontwell Avenue, Eastergate in Sussex in August 1915.

The First World War was being fought and I was then eight years old. I attended the church school in the village. We had very bad winters in those days and the roads were very bad; if they were covered in snow and ice, we had to walk one and a half miles to and from school. We learned patriotic songs, some of which I can still remember.

There were no ration books, and food was hard to come by. I remember my aunt and a friend being gone all day to Bognor trying to get some kind of food. There were no buses or cars on the roads and they had to walk either to Barnham station or to Bognor, and come back tired and sometimes disappointed.

I have seen my aunt take the cream off the milk and put it into a two lb jamjar and stand shaking it up and down for a long time in order to get a small pot of butter for our bread. Milk was delivered by a horse-drawn float, in large churns, and to our door in a can, where the milk was measured into a milk jug.

Money was very tight and I had one penny a week pocket money. The war was not felt a lot except for the shortage of food, and when we watched Italian prisoners of war being driven up and down to Barnham station from the huge lumber camp at Eartham on long lorries carrying whole tree trunks. These were taken across to France and used as pit props, shoring up the trenches. Now and then, one saw an airship patrolling the coastline. The only news was brought by the daily papers as there were no radios or televisions.

When I was ten years old, I went to stay with my mother at Dover for a few months. The war was really felt there and was frightening. When an air raid warning sounded a huge anti-aircraft gun opposite made the house shake, and shrapnel fell among the surrounding trees. China was always off the dresser and pictures off the walls. The bombardments across the Channel were dreadful to listen to. If out shopping in Dover and there was a warning, everywhere was plunged into sudden darkness and all trams stopped wherever they stood until the all clear sounded. It was all very eerie for a child but I came back to the peace of Eastergate.

On 11th November the following year, the Armistice was signed and we children stood out in the road waving Union Jacks as the Italian prisoners passed by. Their faces were very gloomy. Sometime later I was among the large crowd of people watching the then Duke of Richmond unveil the war memorial in Eastergate where it still stands.'

'I was born one of nine, of whom seven survived, in a new house on a small farm at Birdham, near the harbour. My first memory is of the searchlight apparatus in our field in front of the house, manned by members of a Scottish regiment. I also saw the early and rare sight of aeroplanes and an airship travelling over the Solent.

The shortage of sugar affected us most as there was no sugar for jam making at home. We were allowed to eat plums galore. We were occasionally lucky to get a jar of honey sugar, which was solid honey packed in a cardboard container with tin top and bottom. Bought jam, which contained a mixture of turnip and fruit, was packed likewise. Children went out picking blackberries in schooltime and these went to a depot for jam manufacturers. We were lucky on a farm during the war as we had a house cow, chickens and eggs, and frequently wild rabbits. A pig was killed each autumn. We also had plenty of vegetables and fruit.'

'I remember well how Mother strove to keep us fed and clothed. Grandma was a dressmaker so my sister and I always had nice clothes. Margarine made its first appearance in the shops and each week Mother and I queued for it and anything else on offer. Rationing was a hit and miss affair so we became almost vegetarians, Mother manfully digging and planting a 20 rod allotment two miles from home. Near our house there was a man who kept goats and during the summer months he took them to the seafront where they drew along pretty carriages for children. He also smoked herrings for kippers and bloaters. What a lovely smell when we were so hungry. We used to stand by the barrel sniffing and were told off for getting our clothes smelly.'

THE GUNS OF FRANCE

'During the war the YMCA built a large wooden hut in the cricket field at East Preston to provide billiards, a canteen and a small library for the wounded soldiers housed in the workhouse, whose drunken behaviour disturbed the village every night. At one time the guns in France rattled the doors and windows of the village.'

WHAT FATHER TOLD ME

'As I was not born until 1924 I knew nothing of the war except what I remember my father talking about. He never spoke of the horror of the war, or the awful scenes he must have witnessed during his time as a stretcher bearer, but he told me about the dreadful conditions of the trenches, with water and mud everywhere and so much of the time wearing wet and dirty clothing, and of the cold. Mostly he told stories of the comradeship and cheerfulness of the friends he made in his platoon, of the concert parties he was in and the concerts the band gave whenever possible. He played several instruments – the clarinet, flute, trumpet and piano.

Although he was not 18 until 1917, he saw many bitter battles and so many lives lost. He was in the army of occupation in Germany afterwards and billeted with a family in a small town. They were very short of food and many of their menfolk had been killed or wounded, but he met with nothing but kindness from the family and corresponded with them for many years afterwards.

He met up with my mother's younger brother in September 1918 when Wilfred passed through a trench where my father was standing, and I have a copy of a letter written then letting my mother know about the meeting: "Wilfred said, don't worry about your boyfriend George, he is out of the line at present." A few days after that Wilfred was killed – he was 18.'

PEACE AT LAST

'One of my first memories is of Armistice Day, 11th November 1918. It was a rather gloomy, misty day but we walked up to Halnaker with the pushchair, waving flags and shouting, "The war's gone over" and it seemed as if a great weight had been lifted from all the grown ups. Flags were poking out of cottage windows and everyone seemed happy. The next summer there was a celebration party in Goodwood Park for all the children. We drove up from Boxgrove in a farm waggon, ran races, had a lovely tea and were each presented with a medal on a red, white and blue ribbon.'

'At the end of the war the Armistice was celebrated with great enthusiasm in Findon. It was known as Peace Day in 1919 and the whole village was decorated with flags. A marquee was erected at Findon Place for a great party. Everybody was invited. The West Chiltington Silver Band came over to play. There were sports and games for the children and for the adults – a great and long remembered event.'

This item has been taken from a newspaper cutting dated 1918.

'The little village of Scaynes Hill was gaily decorated for Peace Day, and everyone was out for enjoyment. The proceedings commenced with a "Victory" cricket match between two home elevens.

At 1 pm the men (some 50 to 60) adjourned to the Anchor Inn, where they found an excellent and generous repast prepared by mine host. The large dining hall was prettily decorated with flags, and the tables with flowers, the whole having a charming effect. Under mine host's supervision ample justice was done to the good things with which the tables were laden.

After luncheon play was resumed until 4.30 pm when an excellent tea was served under the trees on the ground and was greatly appreciated by all who were present. The match was voted to be second to none ever played in the village. Also in the afternoon there were sports on the village common, which were kept going until dark.

At 4 pm the children sat down to a capital tea which was followed by another for the "grown ups" and old folk.

A large bonfire, which had been prepared on the common, was set alight at 10 pm and was accompanied with a good display of fireworks. About midnight the National Anthem was sung, amid loud cheering. This brought to a close a most enjoyable day which will long be remembered in Scaynes Hill.'

THE SECOND WORLD WAR 1939–45: DODGING THE BOMBS

Twenty years after those Peace celebrations in 1919, we were again at war and this time faced the terror of bombing raids and aerial machine gunning. West Sussex, thankfully, did not suffer the blanket bombing which tormented some other counties, but we learned to live with the threat of sudden death nonetheless.

WAR BRINGS CHANGES

'Many changes were brought to the village of Sidlesham by the Second World War. Men called up or volunteering left farms and smallholdings which were then turned over to growing corn. In the empty houses soldiers from English and Welsh regiments and French Canadians were billeted until D-Day. Early in the war, evacuee children were billeted with local families and the parish church and Methodist halls were used as classrooms.

Women went into the Women's Forces, became land girls on farms, ran officers' shops and also those in the towns, Housewives joined the WVS and ran a canteen for HM Forces billeted in the village. The WI knitted woollen garments, made pickles and jams. Older men became special constables, Home Guard and Auxiliary Fire Service and ARP Wardens. Both sexes became Red Cross, St John's Ambulance workers and fire watchers.

At first all was quiet, and many evacuees went home. Then the Battle of Britain started. Around Sidlesham were the aerodromes of Tangmere, Ford, Thorney and later as D-Day approached, the emergency one at Church Norton. German bombers came over the peninsula of Selsey in huge numbers. Sighting by Chichester Cathedral spire, they went off north to London and east to Portsmouth and Southampton, pursued by a very small number of fighter planes from these local airfields. German planes were shot at and bombs jettisoned but despite this no one of the village was killed and only slight damage was done to housing.

As D-Day approached every wayside tree sheltered a gun or truck; a Mulberry Harbour appeared near the entrance to Pagham harbour and landing craft in Chichester harbour. Sighted by a solitary German plane, an air raid followed and all the guns ready for D-Day blazed forth – the noisiest night locally! Shortly, at night with pin-

176

point lights and nose to tail, the soldiers who had been gathered locally, together with all their equipment, quietly departed. Local people lined the road; all the canteen chocolate and cigarettes were pressed into the men's hands and we wished them God Speed.

As dawn broke on D-Day we heard the drone of planes with gliders attached, rank on rank, stretching from Emsworth to Littlehampton. On the ground everyone went to their action post and the sound of gunfire towards the French coast was heard. We did not need the news by radio at 8 pm to tell us that the invasion of the French coast had begun.'

'On the Sunday morning when the news of the declaration of war was handed to our rector at Balcombe as he was finishing his sermon, I was weighing up sweets for a customer in our shop and there were several people waiting to be served. Mother rushed in to tell us. I can remember the deathly silence as everyone looked at each other, then very soon afterwards the first siren was heard and nobody knew what to do.

During the Battle of Britain, Balcombe saw many air battles overhead and witnessed planes being shot down. There were bombs jettisoned just below Balcombe church and many bomb craters in fields around the village. Army units were stationed in and around the village and large houses had to give up rooms for officers' messes and offices. Balcombe Forest was packed with troops for the impending visit of a high ranking officer – my brother in law's unit, so he said, had to "sweep the forest of leaves and branches"!

Members of the Ardingly ARP, most of whom were related to each other. The air raid wardens performed sterling service through the war, as did other local men who joined the Home Guard or the Fire service.

There were many bomb scares whilst travelling by train and quite frequent detours were made because of damage. The stations had their names removed, so great care had to be exercised in counting your stops – no blackout could be raised to see why the train had stopped or where it was. Many passengers ended up at the wrong station, and one or two fell out as we were not actually in the station when they opened the doors. Sometimes the train stopped if there were a lot of enemy planes at night as the driver thought the sparks from the funnel might be seen.

The last two and a half years of the war I spent in East Grinstead, which had suffered badly when bombs were dropped on the cinema and shops in London Road and over 100 people were killed. We moved there the following year and rebuilding had started, but many premises were still in ruins.

Father became an ARP warden and the air raid alert post was opposite Wesley House, where we lived. It was badly damaged early one morning when a doodlebug came down in the London Road, in almost the same place as the bombs, and we lost every pane of glass except in one window where my mother was standing. All the ceilings came down and the door frames came away from the wall. It was very frightening hearing my father shout a warning from the ARP post opposite when he saw the flying bomb turn back towards the town. The King and Queen came through the town in the morning, on their way to stay with friends at Uckfield, and they stopped and walked about the ruins for a considerable time. It took days and days to rid the house of glass.'

'We were on the beach when they declared war. Already Bognor fire station and Town Hall had sandbags in place. Soon the sands were out of bounds, huge steel barriers erected to stop invaders. Lights disappeared behind blackout curtains and the air raid siren sounded daily as the enemy flew overhead bound for London. Travelwise along the coast we were in a restricted area, no further east than Littlehampton. We'd beat the ban by changing buses there and hoping no one checked identity cards.

Mother was a firewarden, smart with steel hat and bucket. This latter was often used to collect manure, left by the dairy's horse, to improve our allotment in Mead Lane. Stepfather happily joined the Home Guard, part of a team that manned a naval gun at the sea end of Aldwick Avenue. Their children's Christmas party was enlivened when someone put too much gelatine in the jellies, but we beat them vigorously.

We watched the dogfights over the sea as we walked to school. The pier was now HMS Barbara. We saw near there a huge black spiked sea mine floating. Our Villa Maria convent school closed for a year during the Battle of Britain and we were sent to relations on a Surrey farm, where we saw London burn nightly from the stairwell window. Mother wrote that Tangmere and Ford airfields had been flattened.

Back home we found troops in the Rock Gardens Hotel, between us and the sea. The Americans' dustbins overflowed with discarded eatable food. Kept late in school hall for a lecture, we escaped the shattered glass in the corridors when a bomb fell in Albert Road. Troops guarded the shops that day. The Germans had machine gunned the High Street, but fortunately it was half day closing. Bognor's few bombs were dropped as the planes returned home. A doodlebug fell near Shelley Road, where a resident of a seaside hotel died of shock. A German plane crashing into an empty gasometer led to a gallant rescue by a local man.

War years to us children meant sleep interrupted by sirens; queueing on Saturday for over two hours to buy the famous Mance sausages; cycle rides as far as Midhurst, as the beach was out of bounds; and evacuees, including the bored 16 year old who soon returned to brave the Blitz.

One uncle died in a civilian road accident in Brussels, his jeep hit by a lorry load of drunken soldiers celebrating peace declared that day. VJ night the other uncle returned, we opened a bottle of champagne and joined the crowds in the Marine Gardens, where the fountain played and they switched on the fairy lights.'

THE FLYING CIRCUS

'As Chidham was very close to Thorney RAF aerodrome and was vulnerable throughout the war, anti-aircraft guns were set up in Chidham and nissen huts built to house the troops; old cars were distributed over the farms as an anti-invasion precaution.

The south-east room of the west wing of the vicarage was used by the Home Guard as an observation post with a clear view over to the RAF station at Thorney Island. There was a considerable amount of activity with crashing planes and falling bombs but no casualties other than Germans in the village, although the vicarage had the dubious distinction of receiving the only direct hit – an incendiary bomb through the roof which was quickly dealt with by the local voluntary fire service and the Home Guard.

An entry in the Parish Register recorded that "Heinrich Liekerman died in November 1940 aged 21 and was buried in the churchyard under Defence Regulations."

Another event was reported in the local paper: "On October 8th,

1940, a bomber crashed at Chidmere on its way to Thorney Aerodrome. Three of the crew escaped with slight injuries and the plane burst into flames with a badly injured man inside. Mr George Parker of Knapp House and Mr Len Hackett of Roselynn dragged him out although his parachute was entangled. Mr Parker is an ex-serviceman of 46, a poultry farmer and Mr Len Hackett a smallholder. Mr Parker suffered burns to his face and neck and Mr Hackett was affected by flames." '

'In the early 1940s there was much air activity in the Thorney Island area. As children, we would watch the dog fights, as they were called, between the Spitfires and the German planes coming to drop bombs on Portsmouth and Southampton. At that time Thorney was a front line RAF airfield, and as soon as the air raid warning sounded about six planes would take off and circle fairly slowly over the airfield until the all clear. They were known as the "flying circus" and, presumably, were intended to prevent the German planes from getting close enough to bomb the airfield accurately.

One day we counted seven planes circling round but thought nothing of it, until bombs started to fall from the last of the seven, which then broke away and flew off! We learnt afterwards that this RAF plane had crashed in Germany without too much damage, been repaired, and, with a German crew, returned to carry out this very cheeky raid by tagging onto the end of the circus.'

A BEAUTIFUL SUMMER'S DAY

'It was a beautiful summer's day, my mother had packed a picnic and planned to take my three year old sister Julie, the three evacuees, Reggie, Dennis and Kathleen who lived with us and myself to see Boxgrove Priory. The "vaccuees" as I called them, had come from Southend and so had never seen the countryside or farm animals.

We set off from West Bognor with the picnic and lemonade safely packed in the Tansad pram. The day was very hot and soon the boys all removed their shirts. On the road we met a former neighbour, on her way to meet a young airman from Tangmere. Our ways parted at Colworth. We carried on towards Oving and the Royal Oak public house.

Suddenly from the distance came a droning noise which grew louder and louder, planes came screaming out of the sky and from the surrounding area all the anti-aircraft guns opened up with a tremendous roar.

My mother told us to get into the ditch, the boys complaining bitterly, as having removed their shirts they found themselves in a bed of stinging nettles!

Then over our heads appeared Hurricanes from Tangmere and we witnessed a dog-fight at first hand. How long it lasted I do not know. The pram was still on the road and the driver of a passing car spotted it and stopped to investigate. It turned out to be our family doctor, Dr Durgeon on his way back from Chichester. He packed us all into the car and with the pram safely stowed in the boot took us home. Aged only six it was the first car in which I had ever ridden!

It was years later that I discovered that the day of our proposed picnic was the day Tangmere was almost wiped out by the Junkers dive bombers, 16th August 1940 in the second month of the Battle of Britain.'

FISHING IN CHICHESTER HARBOUR

'During the war, all traffic in the harbour was subject to permission from the Admiralty and fishermen were included in these permit holders. Often the fishermen were older men or perhaps those who were exempt from call up to the armed forces.

No fishing was allowed during the hours of darkness for a variety of reasons. The more obvious one being the very real risk of enemy agents landing or leaving the country using fishing boats as cover. Lights shown on board, indicating the whereabouts of the harbour would have been a threat to Thorney Island Air Base. Fast patrol boats did occasionally come upon a local fishing boat who had risked putting to sea at night to supplement their catch or pick up nets or pots that bad weather had prevented them retrieving earlier. It was then after receiving a harsh warning about permits being withdrawn or worse – being blown out of the water – that a fat plaice or sole found its way on board the patrol boat.

During daylight hours fishing was carried out normally as fuel would allow and with severe food rationing, the fish was essential. Strangely, its importance was not reflected in an inflated price as it would be now in similar circumstances. Possibly this was because transport was difficult as petrol rationing was in force and most catches could only be sold locally.

There are many sad tales told by fishermen of the war years. One tells of the night Portsmouth burnt and you could read your newspaper on deck by the light. There was no fear for themselves, only a deep compassion for the people of Portsmouth. In their own way these men who fished the harbour made their own contribution to the war. No doubt when the young men returned to fishing after hostilities ceased, there were many 'fishy' stories told over a pint in the local. Nothing changes!'

BOMBS ON THE ROOF

'My mother and I were sitting by the fire in 1940 discussing my wedding arrangements for the following month, and my father was attending a parish council meeting, when Ratatatat! Ratatatat! Someone knocking on the door? Of course, my father had forgotten his keys. So I opened the door and to my horror the whole road was ablaze with the most eerie light. I rushed to the back door and this weird light was even penetrating the black-out curtain.

My first thought was to ring 999, but having done that, I remembered that the Auxiliary Fire Service team was stationed at the end of the road. As I raced toward them shouting "Fire! Fire!" they jumped onto their machine and rushed to the rescue; I found them a little over-eager to man their first job.

My father returned to find his house on fire and choppers and hammers being rained onto his roof and all he said was "Hey, don't smash my house up!"

One of the firemen decided to take a broader look at their handiwork and stepped backwards down the garden with his eyes on the roof, when splash! He hadn't seen the goldfish pond. I have never heard such expletives before or since.

Suddenly, a cry of alarm. The roof of the nursing home, two doors away, was ablaze, so they left us to rescue the patients and to find willing neighbours to give them beds. I slept in my own bed with a tarpaulin sheet over the hole in the roof and a most unpleasant smell, a mixture of incendiary bombs and smoke.

A few months later my father decided to remove branches from a tree near the kitchen window. We were watching him fearfully on the ladder when we saw him put his hand into the middle of the tree and remove a cylindrical object: an unexploded incendiary bomb!'

TIP AND RUN RAIDS

'My father was a special constable and had served as such since the First World War, and at the commencement of the last war was on duty at one of the siren posts in Worthing when he received the Red Alert. Not knowing that war had already been declared on Germany, he and his colleague let off the alarm imagining that the Germans were going to raid us before war had been declared – my father was in such a state of shock that he quite forgot he had cycled to his post, and walked home, leaving his bike behind!

There was a certain amount of rivalry between the local specials and the ARP wardens, and on one occasion during the black-out a local air raid warden rapped on our door demanding to see Father. He was in a great state and very angry and demanded that we put our lights out at once as they would surely attract enemy aircraft; in vain my father tried to persuade him that there were no lights on and our black-out was adequate. The warden demanded that my father should go down to the gate with him and see for himself. This he did, only to discover that the "lights" were in fact a large bed of white daisies near the front gate upon which the moon was shining causing them to resemble a well-lit area!

The most terrifying experiences, to me, were the tip and run raids. We lived in Grand Avenue in Worthing, and the German bombers would come in off the sea and drop their sticks of bombs and/or fire their machine guns as they flew up the road at a very low level. One afternoon we were having tea in our kitchen at the back of the house when we heard one of these bombers approaching. My mother yelled at us to take cover and we raced out of the room and hid behind the doors to the scullery and the hall. There was a loud explosion, and when we went back to our tea we found a cannon bullet had come through the window and our tea table was covered in glass – no doubt we would have been quite badly hurt had my mother not acted so promptly.'

'During the Second World War I was working in Woolworths, in North Street nearly opposite The Slippery S. This is a twitten which is the Sussex name for a narrow alley with walls on both sides. We had some excitement about four o'clock one afternoon when a bomb dropped on Geerings' shoe shop just opposite Woolies, and then bounced into St Martin's, just behind the shop. I was on the top floor at tea break with my mate when we heard it and we fled down the stairs, all three flights of them. It blew the windows out, there was glass everywhere and when I got to the bottom I realised my friend wasn't with me so I went back and found her sitting stunned in the sand bucket, which was where the blast had blown her. After we cleaned up I retrieved my bike from round the back of the building and found it was buckled so I had to walk home.

I didn't get home till nearly 7 pm, over an hour late, and my Mum didn't half go for me and gave me a right telling off for being late for tea. When she finally let me speak she made me sit at the kitchen table and put some newspapers over it. Then she combed all the glass out of my hair.'

'On 10th February 1943, eight bombs fell in or close to Midhurst – one just behind the present police station, which took the backs off a row of cottages and broke a lot of windows, one at the corner of Sheep Lane, and the remaining six in Cowdray Park.

Because the plane dropping the bombs, a Dornier 17, was flying at a very low level they were still travelling horizontally when they reached buildings. The second bomb (which must have had a delayed action fuse) took a chimneypot off a house on the west side of Church Hill, crossed over to a house on the east side and entered under the eaves; it travelled through the house in a gradual downward direction leaving a clearly to be seen trail of damage – holes in walls, splintered woodwork etc, and then on into the base of the house next door on the corner of Sheep Lane, where it exploded killing the three occupants. I remember being taken by my father to see the track of the bomb through the house on Church Hill. A lot of damage was done to houses round about, and most if not all the windows in the parish church destroyed. In addition to the three fatal casualties there were about 30 people slightly injured by cuts from flying glass etc.

On another occasion a large bomb was dropped on the A286 at Cocking Causeway between Midhurst and the turning to Heyshott, and I remember seeing buses running a shuttle service up to the crater on each side and the passengers had to get out and clamber round the edge of the crater to continue their journeys. This made a vivid impression, and I still visualise the crater almost every time I drive along that stretch of road.'

'One of the first bombs of the war fell on the corner of Grinstead Lane in Lancing, where The Britannia is now. Many bombs fell on Lancing, but one memorable incident occurred when a German plane was shot down. The pilot's parachute caught on the drainpipe of a house in First Avenue, giving the lady of the house a shock when she opened the door to find a German airman hanging there!'

THE FIRST FLYING BOMBS

'As a child in the Second World War, I lived in Horsham where my father was an Inspector in the then West Sussex Constabulary.

Not long after the D-Day landings, we were woken up one night by an urgent banging on the front door, and my father hastened downstairs. He hurriedly got dressed and left the house. He soon returned and I heard him tell my mother to get me up and take me over to the Horsham police station. It was usual for us to do this and take shelter in one of the cells when there was an air raid in progress, but this night there had been no siren.

As we lived almost opposite the police station, we were there in a moment and then other wives and children of policemen started to arrive. Why are we here when there is no air raid on, was the question being asked by everyone. Was it an unexploded bomb or perhaps a landmine? No policeman would answer the question and we were all kept inside the thick-walled cell for some hours.

Not so many hours later we found out the reason for our incarceration. The first flying bombs, or doodlebugs as they were called, were coming over, and the police throughout the southern counties were being alerted by our Observer Corps.

Like everyone else, we were then on the alert for the unforgettable sound of that machine of death, or perhaps to cheer on a Spitfire chasing one and trying to tip its wings, when it would go off course and crash.'

HE'S A SPY!

'I went to work for Bishop Bell, then Bishop of Chichester, as his private secretary in 1937. While I was at the palace, Bishop Bell sponsored 40 German Jewish pastors and their families to come to this country. My parents were very good Christians and offered to have one pastor to live in our house. He was a young man and probably very bored with nothing to do, so he often walked to Tangmere, about a mile away, where there was a big RAF fighter station. Just before war broke out he returned to Germany, having been told his family would suffer if he did not go back. Despite this, my mother thought he was a spy!

I joined up as a VAD in 1940, but was on leave when there was a very bad raid on Tangmere. My father and I lay against a barn in a bed of stinging nettles, holding two terrified dogs as shrapnel was raining down. One or two bombs fell in fields near the village, but mercifully the 11th century priory was not hit. Sadly, Tangmere itself had quite a lot of damage and a number of personnel were killed.

My father was in command of the Boxgrove Home Guard in 1940, and was told that they must defend Tangmere if the Germans landed parachutists on the Downs. Luckily this did not happen – the Home Guard was very like *Dad's Army*.'

'It was reported at some point that signals were being sent from a house on Marley Common, Camelsdale, to German bombers. When the occupant was away in London on diplomatic service, his house was entered and signalling equipment was found, as well as full German uniform.'

'The war came to us all in one form or another, but the residents of Fernhurst will not forget the shock of the shattering noise made by the bomb which fell at the crossroads in 1941. Property was extensively damaged and people shocked and hurt. One lady remembers that as she looked across the road from her house, the walls of the house opposite just crumpled and fell. Windows of houses were blown in and roofs torn open. Trees were uprooted and hurled from their places.

Neither do they forget the treachery of "Lord Haw-Haw", William Joyce, who spent his honeymoon in Fernhurst and frequented The Spread Eagle. Presumably while in the district he was spying, for from Germany later came the "news" over the air that military installations in Fernhurst had been destroyed. By this he meant the precision parts section of Burrows & Payne and the camp at Henley – but the story was false.

Ribbentrop and his friends visited the home of Lord Riversdale before the war and enjoyed the beautiful district of Fernhurst. Lord Riversdale had large steel interests in Sheffield and frequently entertained steel magnates from Germany, who also enjoyed the countryside and came to know the area well. After the war, proof was found that Fernhurst was the place chosen by Ribbentrop for his adoption when Germany won the war.'

'From the mid 1920s onwards, Sir Oswald Mosley with a troop of Blackshirts regularly camped at West Sands on Selsey during the summer season. They frequently marched through Selsey – what an unexpected sight in a little Sussex village. The infamous William Joyce was a frequent guest of the Blackshirts as he had relatives in the village.'

LIFE GOES ON

Despite barbed wire on the beaches and increasing shortages of food and other necessities, life had to go on and we all did our bit for the war effort. Soldiers and other 'strangers' became a part of everyday life, some more welcome than others!

IT'S NOT DECENT!

'With the outbreak of war and the call-up of nearly all able bodied men, Barnham became a village of women, children and older men. An invasion of pregnant young women from the East End of London totally upset life at The Murrell Arms, our village pub, where the nursery workers used to take their lunch bags and have a drink in their lunch hour. It was unheard of for a woman, especially a pregnant woman, to go into a bar without her husband and even with him she would only come now and again on Sunday evenings – but during the week and pregnant "wasn't decent" the older men said.

After the fall of Dunkirk the Coldstream Guards were camped in the meadow at the bottom of our garden. By this time I had a brand new four bedroomed house with a bathroom and I must have bathed every Coldstreamer there (not personally, I hasten to add). Poor men, they only had what they stood up in and looked shattered. For a time they "stood to" with the Home Guard. Because of the threatened invasion and the closeness of the coast, the Home Guard had guns, but the Coldstream Guards at that time hadn't been rearmed.'

'One of the main changes to affect Partridge Green was the arrival of evacuees. At 14, and naive, I and my friends were astonished when children of our age actually went on the bus without an adult and even went into Horsham. This brought about a change and I was allowed to go by bus too – what a special day, I remember I really dressed up and even took my handbag.

Another thing that shocked us villagers was the way the evacuees went out of the house with their rollers in their hair. They even went to the pub – and fancy going to the pub! Women never went to the pub, let alone with rollers in their hair.

Excitement came when the air raid warden cycled down the high street blowing his whistle. This was our air raid warning and instead of all going inside, this was so unusual that we all ran outside to see what was happening. A plane was brought down on the outskirts of the village, and debris was all around. I found a wallet in which there were photos and I handed this in, but it made you think of the great loss the war had caused.'

PART OF EVERYDAY LIFE

'The armed forces were part of everyday life. With an air-sea rescue unit based at Shoreham Airport, air force ground staff were billeted in the town, so there was a continual flow of young men living in our house. Having an old-fashioned geyser, Mother offered baths for one shilling to armed personnel billeted in empty houses, so the army also came visiting; not the navy – the sailors were catered for at Lancing College and King Alfred Baths at Hove. I remember cooking shepherd's pie and jam tarts for them for my Guides cook's badge.

Dad was a special constable, combining a full day's work with night duty, guarding Ricardo Engineering Works when there were rumours of a German invasion on the South Coast – two policeman armed with truncheons against German paratroopers! They did once stalk a suspected lone German along the river Adur towpath, only to discover when jumping up the bank and shining their torches that it was a swan! Dad also captured a German pilot who crashed on Erringham Hill.

I suppose that being an evacuee was my most traumatic experience. We were all to meet on Worthing station for a special train; no one knew where we were going, and I remember passing my house and waving to my mother in the garden. We travelled many hours, boredom being relieved by word games, puzzles and books. At midday, the teachers came along with mugs of tomato soup, then a hot pie and lastly rice pudding. This was revolting, even to those of us used to plain fare because of the pre-war depression. One and all, we threw that pudding out of the window. I have often wondered what an air observer would have made of the long white trail along the line.

We eventually reached Newark-on-Trent and were taken to the High School, where we were given a meal, two blankets and left to sleep on the hall floor. As well as being disturbed by the strangeness and the tears of the homesick girls, we had two air raid warnings and each time had to go down to the shelter. Some lucky girls got seats, and the rest of us lay on the concrete floor – result, we spent our first week as evacuees with streaming colds.

The following morning we were taken in coaches to outlying villages and waited in the church hall for the WVS ladies to take us to our foster homes. My group went to Old Balderton, a linear village with one long street. Gradually my friends disappeared, while those left felt very alone. Eventually I was the only one left. I have never forgotten the awful sensation of being forsaken and wondering if anybody wanted plain, bespectacled me. I was quite convinced I had been forgotten, but of course I was not and spent a happy summer with part-time schooling, plenty of homework and time to wander the countryside.

One incident I remember was at the time of the fall of France. We considered that France had let us down, so refused to go to our French lessons and speak French for a couple of days. How we got away with it, I do not know, unless perhaps our teachers sympathised.'

'We came to live in Bosham during the war. My husband was a wireless "ham" and an expert at receiving Morse Code messages. Because of this MI5 asked him to move to the coast so that he could pick up radio signals from the Continent more easily.

The only approach then to our house was through a lane called Brook Avenue, which was, and still is, very narrow. Our furniture had to get through the lane. Bosham was a quiet village with hardly anybody about, which was to be expected as most of the menfolk were away at the war. There were no cars, only horse traffic.

Soon after our arrival there was a bad fire in the village involving a thatched house. Our nearest fire station was in Chichester, over four miles away. My husband was horrified at the lack of fire protection and at once got in touch with the Fire Service Headquarters. They were most helpful and said that if he could find six to eight young men who might help, they would send a representative to talk to them. This was done and they agreed to supply a fire appliance for the village. Mr Hine, who kept a grocer's shop in the village, said they could use his garage for the appliance until they could build something permanent for it – and that came about in the early 1950s.'

'Compared to others we were exposed to little danger. However, we did have one or two scary moments when returning German bombers offloaded their unused bombs before recrossing the Channel.

Living by the coast, we witnessed the tremendous build up of men and equipment that culminated in the D-Day landings. The night before the crossing, tanks and lorries full of servicemen rumbled non-stop along the lanes and roads to the ports. At first light, the weather was discouraging. The sky was leaden grey with great wild clouds. Nevertheless, it soon filled with aeroplanes taking gliders packed with ammunition and troops. It was an awe-inspiring sight that I'll never forget.

When they finally disappeared from view, everything seemed so empty. It was a feeling of anti-climax. All we could do was wait, listen to the radio for news – and hope for the best.

My family are forever teasing me about my wartime brush with the law. I managed to get my name on police records when I went for a walk on the beach with Brian, a young family friend, and a sailor I'd met. The beach was defended with barbed wire and pill boxes. We walked around one of the pill boxes. I thought we were on the right side of the defences, obviously we weren't because a policeman accosted us! Brian and I were fined 15 shillings each. I don't know what happened to the sailor but I suspect he was in worse trouble.'

FINDING A HOME

'I did not arrive in West Sussex until the summer of 1949 when my husband was posted to the Royal Air Force Station at Tangmere on his return from Germany.

We had only been married for about 18 months, so imagine our joy at being allocated a married quarter; No 48 to be exact, one of the "not so old", built in the 1930s. Then it was heaven to have our own first home, but looking back at the conditions and contents of the house, how did we manage? An old back-to-back range was our cooking facility, so it was fires every day (yes, even in the heat of summer) to cook on, or boil a kettle. A huge hot-water tank – heated from the same fire – took up a large chunk of the kitchen, with no cupboard to hide it; the furniture supplied by the RAF was of the meanest economy style – one armchair only ("for the master" we used to say), white wood table and windsor chairs, iron bedsteads, and no such luxuries as carpets, washing machine or fridge. It was a happy life, all the same. Other than the NAAFI or local store it was a walk into Chichester to shop, with the luxury of a bus-ride home!

My main reason for writing of Tangmere, however, was to capture the memory of Ma Maxwell and her family, a grand lady who, throughout the war and afterwards, kept the little cafe and shop just outside the main gates of the camp. She was open all hours for the benefit of the lads and lassies on the station. Air raids and bombs did not prevent the door being open for that welcome cup of coffee and a chunk of home-made apple pie; not to mention a sympathetic ear to all the moans, whilst having a warm by her big range fire in the kitchen.'

'After losing our home owing to enemy action, returning to Sussex in 1943 was peace, perfect peace comparatively speaking. It was impossible to find a house in London, but I knew there were empty houses in Sussex, for it was my home county before I married. For military reasons the West Sussex coast was a "restricted" area, and only those with a pass could gain entry. My husband had been conscripted into the Army and had a pass, so I begged him to go to Sussex and find us a house even if we could not live in it till the war was over. One leave he returned triumphant with the lease of a dear little cottage in Goring, then he had to return to his unit. Kind though our parents were in giving us shelter, I longed for my own home again and

190

racked my brains to think of a way of overcoming the regulations. Suffice it to say that I did, and in September 1943 I moved back to West Sussex with our three year old daughter and 15 month old son. We still had the sirens and bombers passing overhead, but I felt safer than in London especially as we had a Morrison shelter in the dining room in which we all slept.

The cottage had a cheery coal fire which kept us warm and dried and aired the clothes; no disposable nappies then nor washing machines. We loved the walks to the village where there were a few shops, and over the railway bridge in Shaftesbury Avenue to pick daisies in the fields beyond. A real treat was to wander in Titnore Lane looking for wild flowers, and sticklebacks and dragonflies in the pond. Pram-pushing into Worthing was quite an adventure, and we always met someone we knew to chat to and compare notes on the night's alarms and the latest news of our husbands.

For a young family basic food rations of milk, butter, cheese, sugar, bacon and meat were adequate, and local fruit and vegetables were plentiful. September was a busy month jamming and bottling, salting beans, pickling onions and making chutney. Clothes and fabric were rationed too, and the ingenuity of mums and grannies in making do had to be seen to be believed. A happy little nursery school nearby saved the children from being bored by these wartime activities. When coal was short each child took along a lump to keep the fire burning.

It seems an anomaly to say these were happy times, but they were despite the anxieties and the heartache.'

'In 1939, feeling war was imminent, my husband was anxious to find property on the south coast, where he felt I and the children would be safe. In June, we decided to have a place built in Ferring. After war was declared and my husband left for France, the builder was having difficulty in getting supplies and it wasn't till October that I was able to take possession. In the meantime I found local accommodation, the landlady being pleased to take us as by this time evacuees were arriving in Ferring (few of them stayed long – they hated the quietness and the lack of fish and chips).

There were only a few people in Ferring during the war but it was and always has been a very friendly place. It became a banned area and a number of Canadian troops were billeted in empty houses. Women were required to register and were allocated jobs such as fire watching (those with young children being exempt).

It was fairly peaceful as planes passed over without incident, but a bomb was dropped on a bungalow in Sea Lane, killing the parents of a small boy.'

POSTED TO SUSSEX

'I first discovered Findon in 1941 when my small "F" Section Royal Signals was billeted in the servants' quarters of Findon Place, then in the ownership of the Hartridge family. We were attached to the Regimental headquarters of the 146 Field Regiment RA whose orderly room was the main south facing sitting room, with Colonel Richards established in the ballroom and his officers and staff in or about the remainder of the accommodation. The MT park was the walled kitchen garden. The three 25 pounder gun batteries were positioned strategically in the area, with one at Angmering.

The Colonel soon found he required the servants' quarters for other purposes, so my section was cleared out and we were accommodated in the whole of Nepcote Lodge and its stabling and outbuildings at the top of Steep Lane. To the east of Nepcote Lodge and reaching down to Nepcote Lane the land was vacant except for a very large indoor riding school building, which had been taken over by REME for servicing all the vehicles of the 38th Welsh Division of which the regiment was a part.

In 1941 it was considered quite a possibility that the German forces might invade Britain along the South Coast, and would use the valleys through the South Downs to proceed towards London. This emphasised the vulnerability of the main south/north roads like the A22 (Eastbourne), A23 (Brighton) and A24 (Worthing).

In this area a huge tank trap was constructed which ran down from the top of Church Hill to about the present car park of the garden centre and along southwards a little way, then up the southern slope of Cissbury. The trap was about 20 ft wide with irregularly placed rows of four ft concrete cubes. Seen from the top of Church Hill or Cissbury Ring it was a depressing sight. Fortunately it was never required, and was removed eventually after the war.'

'I first came to West Sussex in the summer of 1942 when I was on my way to join 94 British General Hospital mobilising at Goodwood House. A group of us left Victoria for Chichester and had to change trains at Three Bridges, which was then in East Sussex.

On arrival at Chichester we went by Army transport to Goodwood House. The interior looked bleak; all the walls were covered with some sort of boarding. The Sisters' Mess was in the basement, as was the little whitewashed chapel. Bedrooms were shared; I shared with three or four others. There were bars at the window – a former nursery? Many years later I went with a WI outing to a flower festival at the house and was able to see it as it should be. I hardly recognised it.

For several weeks, while awaiting further orders, we were not working. I remember the groans the morning after a session of Army drill! We were able to explore our surroundings, including the extensive grounds. We would hitchhike into Chichester four miles away or walk to the crossroads near where the motel is now, from where we could catch a bus. Eventually I brought my cycle from home which increased my mobility. What is now the busy dual carriageway A27 was then a pleasant country road suitable for cyclists and walkers. Quite often I found my way to Bognor along quiet country lanes. On one occasion I had cycled there and met up with some Sisters who had travelled by bus. I left when they did and when I reached the main road near Chichester I had to wait for their bus to go past before I could cross the road. I was back at Goodwood House well before my friends were.

Some of us used to go to services at the Cathedral. One Sunday we decided to go to the Methodist church, which if I remember rightly was in South Street. There we were made very welcome and several times were entertained in people's homes.

In December we were told we were leaving, but were not told our destination. There was a flurry of last minute trips into Chichester for shopping etc and soon we were "confined to barracks" until we were conveyed to the station for the troop train to Currock where we boarded the *Arundel Castle* for Algiers.'

GETTING THE RATIONS

'During the war when food was scarce everyone had to register with one particular shop for any items which were rationed; however, if you had more than one ration book in the family it was possible to register each book with a different retailer. It was therefore my mother's bright idea to register at several shops, this had the advantage that one might be more likely to be able to buy scarce, but unrationed items, eg biscuits, at more than one shop, as most shopkeepers kept scarce goods for their registered customers. This was all very well for my mother, but it was a perpetual grouse for me as, on Saturday mornings, I would be sent off to queue for the shopping. First I would be sent to Sainsbury's, where I would queue for bacon at one counter until Mother arrived, usually just as I was about to be served – she would then take over, and I would have to go, say, to the butter counter again, until she arrived. This would continue until we had finished at Sainsbury's, which was in Goring Road to the west of Worthing, then I was off to Tarring on my bike to queue for groceries at a shop called Teetgen's – again, Mother would come along on her bike and take over. From there, it would be down to

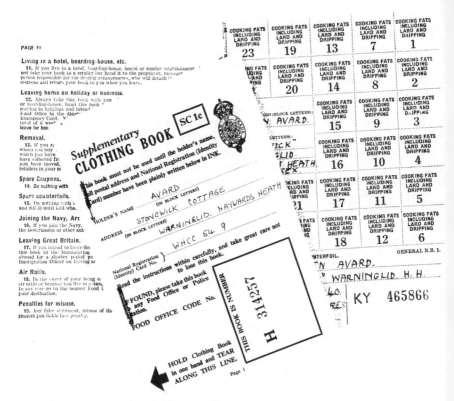

We all had ration books during the war, and had to register with named shops for each category of goods. Even with rationing, goods were still scarce and queueing became a way of life.

the centre of Worthing to another little grocer's for more items, then, believe it or not, back to Tarring Road, a distance of well over a mile, to the butcher's for our meat rations.

All the shopping was done on my bicycle, and following behind me I nearly always had my two dogs, a spaniel and a mongrel, rarely on leads running along quite happily down the main road. There were no hygiene laws then prohibiting dogs in shops and it was considered quite natural for customers to take their dogs into shops – had any shopkeeper queried this practice I feel sure their valued customers would "have taken their custom elsewhere" and probably told their friends to do the same.'

'My parents at Lower Beeding dug up the garden in the early 1940s to produce food and meat for the family, keeping ducks, chickens, bantams, bees and rabbits, and growing fruit and vegetables. Much of the surplus was sold locally to hotels or through the WI market. We had a spare bedroom so there were always guests, mainly evacuees and trainee land girls, but we were all well fed despite the shortages.

Village Produce Associations were formed when the government asked everyone to Dig for Victory. A contemporary leaflet describes how "in 1940 it was thought that country gardens might produce more vegetables than could be used locally, and that this surplus could be collected and marketed for distribution in the towns. In the summer of that year the Ministry of Food therefore set up Garden Produce Committees in most of the counties of England and Wales, with the joint support of the National Allotments Society, the National Federation of Women's Institutes and the National Council of Social Service, and charged them with the work of organising the disposal of surplus vegetables from the villages. Not long after these committees were formed, air raids and the subsequent evacuation from town to country led to considerable increases in population in many rural areas and local surpluses quickly disappeared. In these circumstances it became evident that increased and planned production in the villages must be the aim for the immediate future, and accordingly the Ministry of Agriculture, by agreement with the Ministry of Food, assumed responsibility for the administration of County Garden Produce Committees in 1941."

The first one I know of in this area was formed as West Grinstead and Dial Post VPA in 1942. Later on a Federation of West Sussex VPA was formed and still exists today, although quite a few clubs have changed their name to Horticultural Societies.'

WE ALL DID OUR BIT

'In September 1939 everything changed and we all became involved. We collected a penny a week for the Red Cross, a local fire service was started, air raid wardens, fire watchers and, after Dunkirk, the Home Guard. By that time, we had a telephone and electricity followed. Main drainage did not arrive until about 1950. One of my jobs was to call out the Home Guard. I leapt out of bed and on my bike and it was a real job to wake up men who had been hard at it all day in the fields, many of whom had no doorbell or knocker! Our only casualty was a Home Guard man who lost his moustache!

The village hall was requisitioned by the Army. The Canadians introduced us to square dancing but the French Canadians did the dance differently and we were sometimes almost involved in a free fight!

I was working in Chichester and had to have a pass in case transport broke down and we had to drive through Tangmere Aerodrome. The buses which went near Tangmere had black curtains and when we got near the aerodrome, we all got up and drew the curtains. We could easily have had a peep but nobody ever did!

Towards the end of the war, I and a friend ran an art exhibition in our hall for the Red Cross. We had our own ambulance and we used to collect things from far and wide. The idea seemed to catch on and people were ringing up from all over the place. It ran for three days and apart from raising a lot of money, it also brought together people who had no idea that they had kindred spirits living so near.

In 1945 I was working in Worthing and we were doing long hours and had short lunch breaks. If we were lucky, we got to the "British Restaurant" before the food ran out. If not, we had to find a place without too long a queue. The old ladies (who had presumably lost their domestic help) used to get out early and eat everything up before we could get there and *how* we hated them; I don't suppose they had any idea how we felt!'

WOOL, JAM AND MEAT PIES

'At the outbreak of war a number of members of Crawley Down WI undertook to collect and arrange for the mending of evacuated children's clothes whilst others made the new black-out curtains for the hall. A Wool Comforts sub-committee was formed in 1940 and organised the knitting and despatch of socks to men in the forces, and gifts were sent to soldiers stationed in the village. Knitted items were sent to the Russians and to prisoners of war of the Merchant Navy and proceeds from carol singing were sent to the Russian Red Cross. Dances were organised to entertain the troops.

A Pie Scheme was started in April 1944, the pies to be sold in the hall, and an application was made to the Food Office for a licence to sell meat pies. By August the scheme had reached 750 pies and one member arranged for pies to be left at her house for distribution in the Copthorne area, the van driver being given two shillings and sixpence for doing it. The Pie Scheme was a great success and by the end of 1948 91,000 pies had been sold, but it was finally closed in May 1949.

Another project which proved very successful was the organisation of a fruit preservation centre in July 1940. Three centres were arranged for the cooking of surplus fruit at which 14 members assisted, and 750 lbs of preserves were made in the first year. In 1949 a member offered the use of an outhouse and a permit for ten cwt of sugar was obtained. A total of 1,100 lbs of jam was made by a small nucleus of members and this was sold to the local shops, but any jam falling below 100% mark was sold at a reduced price to institutions, chiefly the nursery school at Great Frenches, although wholesalers did take some of the surplus. In the first three years over 2,500 lbs of jam were made and sold. The Ministry of Agriculture Inspector said Crawley Down was one of the best centres in the area and letters of thanks were received from Lord Woolton, the Minister of Food and Lady Denman. The centre was in operation for a total of five years.

There were, of course, lighter moments, the Dramatic Circle giving many performances of plays at WI meetings, entering festivals at Eastbourne and Lewes and giving public performances. During the war open air performances of Shakespeare were given and on one occasion the Battle of Britain was in progress overhead while *The Tempest* was being performed – very impressive.

A RIVETING STORY

'The older women in Fittleworth wanted to do something to help the war effort in 1939. Mrs Roylance at Little Poynes and my mother at Tripp Hill made our houses available as sorting centres for duralumin rivets. These were delivered to us in large sackfuls from an aircraft factory in Surrey. They were supposed to be clean but often they were very dirty. We tipped them on to the floor or on to tables in our drawing rooms, which were given over for the duration of the war. Our helpers came in at any time of the day to suit their convenience and often visitors from the nearby guest house joined in. We started off by sorting out the heads – they were either flat or round. Then we sorted them into 34 different lengths, putting them into jamjars. Finally there were ten different widths to be separated out. We packed them into twelve inch square cardboard boxes and they were collected by the factory who paid us by weight. It was lovely when we had the big rivets to deal with. In all we made over £300 for various charities.'

IT WENT ON AFTER THE WAR

'In the bleak days of 1949, luxuries such as canned fruit and tomatoes were unobtainable in the shops. Many of the members of Chidham WI grew their own fruit and vegetables as indeed did most people in these post war years and it was suggested that there would be no shortage of customers if the WI started up a canning service. The decision was therefore taken to purchase a canning machine and plans made for the service which was to be run by voluntary helpers.

Our first canning session was duly arranged and I can still recall arriving at the village hall at 8.30 am on a Thursday morning with a pushchair laden with produce and utensils. An early start was essential as there was a lot to do in just a few hours and while the canning machine was being set up and the brine and syrup prepared I was busy booking in the fruit and sugar left by our customers who had now started to arrive.

The first task was to wash and drain the fruit, placing apples and pears into a salt water solution for a short period and then thoroughly rinsing so that they retained their colour during canning. The canning process itself was not at all complicated but it was laborious and time consuming especially the sealing of the cans. This involved turning a handle rather like that on a mincer a total of 20 times for each can while the can and its lid were being compressed between the top plate and base plate of the machine. Once the cans were sealed they were sterilised in the copper then allowed to cool in a large galvanised bath full of cold water which was kept outside the village hall.

Our customers would return soon after 4 pm to collect their cans of fruit which we sold for sevenpence halfpenny each and to reclaim any unused fruit or sugar. There was never time to label the cans and we overcame this problem by scratching the customer number and the produce code on the lid during canning. With each can costing fourpence halfpenny the WI only made a small return upon the canning operation once our gas and electricity costs had been taken into account. Our aim had been to provide a service to the local community and looking back I am sure that we achieved this.

When we discontinued the canning venture in 1952 my mother purchased the canning machine and I still have this packed away in the loft. I have calculated that we used over 3,000 cans from 1949 to 1952 and although canning was undoubtedly hard work we thoroughly enjoyed working together as a team.'

'I came to West Sussex in 1947 with my husband and five year old son, and was lucky to find my first real home was a good sized summer let bungalow at Elmer Beach. House building having been suspended during the war, accommodation was a major problem for most, especially for young couples married during and just after those years.

The Rural District Council had powers to requisition any empty property if the owner did not find occupants within a given time. So many families were housed in this way until sufficient council housing was built, when the owners were handed back their properties.

Then came the furnishing. My Yorkshire mother in law acquired some redundant ARP blankets, grey and brown. She bleached them and then dyed them a lovely mid blue in the bath; we thought and hoped they could just be mistaken for velvet. We begged margarine boxes from the stores and turned them into dressing tables with paint and shelves and a curtain all round. Floor covering was rationed, but most pre war houses had good wooden floorboards, so we polished them until they really shone and I believe the most effective results were with dark brown shoe polish.

We took our shopping lists and coupons to Sainsbury's each week, usually one Mum had the children and the other took the bus to Bognor from the Elmer Hotel, ninepence return, small children free.

On Friday the order was delivered to the door, the milkman came each day, the baker twice a week. The village greengrocer called for an order twice a week also and delivered next day. The laundryman came from Chichester once a week and a pleasant young girl cycled from Bilsham to help with the housework twice a week for four shillings an hour.

There was a lot of excitement when such items as dessicated coconut and bananas returned to the shops, when we quickly turned to Mother's recipe books to make good use of them.

The baby clinic was held regularly in the Methodist church at Felpham. It was a great help and blessing to all the young mothers who met and got to know each other. Free orange juice and cod liver oil was available to all children, and such items as Marmite, dried milk and Farex were sold at slightly below shop prices. There were nurses and a midwife at hand to help with any problems, and each baby or child was weighed.

Clothing coupons were still in operation so "Make Do and Mend" was the order of the day. From one pair of men's corduroy trousers I made three pairs of dungarees for my three sons. They laugh at the picture now, not at the dungarees but the fact that I had mended their carpet slippers with leather toecaps. "Gosh Mum, we must have been poor then". An old Army camel hair cape became dressing gowns, which incidentally guaranteed they were in the front line for shepherds in their infants school nativity plays.'

A CHILD'S WAR

For many children, war brought tremendous changes. Evacuees arrived in the peaceful Sussex countryside and found a new way of life opening up for them, while local children had their schooling and families interrupted by the new arrivals.

EVEN BEFORE THE WAR

'In 1935 we held a children's fancy dress party at Sompting and I remember we invited about six little Basque girls, refugees from the Spanish civil war, who were billeted with their teacher in a large old house nearby. One of our little girls wore a dress covered with "magic" symbols and we noticed the Basque children muttering amongst themselves. Suddenly they made a rush at her, because one of the symbols was a swastika. They would have hurt her but for the intervention of their teacher. We little knew the meaning of the swastika then, but evidently they did, poor little souls.'

A NEW SCHOOL

'I was evacuated from Streatham in September 1939, aged 15 years, to Chichester High School for Girls. With three other girls I was billeted in a large house in Whyke Lane owned by two spinster ladies. There was a large garden, run by one of the ladies, with outhouses where fruit was stored in trays and a still room used for storing jams. The ladies had a niece aged about 18 who was deaf and dumb and she enjoyed spending time with us. We learned how to do deaf and dumb sign language and we had great fun together with lots of laughter. We were not allowed out after dark as Chichester was a garrison town, but we were able to have our own bicycles and cycled for miles in the Chichester area – there were few cars in those days. In 1939 Bishop Bell was Bishop of Chichester and he kindly allocated a large room, probably the dining room, in the Bishop's Palace for use by the girl evacuees in which we could meet our parents when they came to visit us at weekends.

A high spot of the term was when Queen Elizabeth came to the school. I remember she wore black with an off the face hat and a spray of lily of the valley as a corsage.'

'I can remember bowling along in the train, well labelled and with a small suitcase and gas mask, and being told we were going to Chichester; I wonder how many of us knew where it was?

There were five of us in our first billet, looked after by two old ladies. The second "home" was with a lady whose husband was in the Army – while the cat was away the mouse played and on Sunday, left to our own devices, we could find nothing but jam and potatoes to eat. Our third billet was far more like home.

We attended Chichester High School for Girls, but had our own teachers and classrooms. That first winter it was so cold the rain froze on the trees. At the time of Dunkirk I can remember waiting at the level crossing for the hospital trains with their red crosses to go through.

We had our Sunday dinners in the Assembly Rooms to begin with; on the day Queen Elizabeth dined with us, onions were off! Later the older girls had lunch in the pantry of the Bishop's Palace, and the day it was my turn to help with the washing up we always seemed to have fish and chips and suet pudding with syrup to follow – what a greasy mess.

We sat our exams in the Palace that first summer. If the siren went we moved to a small "place of safety" and no talking was allowed.'

'In 1940 the Royal Naval School was evacuated from St Margaret's, Twickenham to Verdley Place, Fernhurst, a large house owned by Miss Schuster. The school had been bombed and with numbers reduced was hastily moved to Fernhurst and remained there until 1942, when it was moved to Stoatley Hall, Farnham Lane, Haslemere, where it still is.

I taught music at Verdley Place for a short time and can remember the difficulty of shepherding the girls down the twisty stairs and along unknown passages to safety in the lower part of the house when the air raid sirens went in the night. The teaching staff had to dine in the billiard room, having been told to be careful not to damage the table. In "free time", even on a hot summer's day, the girls had to wear hats and gloves when walking in the grounds and the headmistress admonished me for cycling to the shops in Fernhurst without a hat or stockings and in toeless sandals.

Discipline was strict and rigid and everyone, staff and girls, had some naval connection; not so now. Teaching there was enjoyable, however. On Sundays I used to cycle home to Teddington to play the organ. Women were welcome to do so because most male organists had joined up and were unavailable. As in other professions it was a breakthrough for us. Guildford Cathedral, which I cycled past, was then in 1941 about two ft high and I have watched it grow up out of the hill.'

A CHANGE IN LIFESTYLE

'It was towards the end of our annual seaside holiday at Ramsgate that my mother and father returned earlier than planned with me, to our home in inner London. War against Germany was declared on the Sunday morning after our return and on the very next day Monday 4th September, I, an eleven year old schoolgirl joined one of the evacuation-special trains taking children away from the danger area of London to safer places in the countryside.

The tears and anguish at leaving parents behind were greatly softened by the extremely kind people we found after leaving the train at Worthing and proceeding by coach to the very beautiful village of Findon.

The sudden change in lifestyle I and my schoolfriends experienced was both great and dramatic. I remember so well our contingent arriving at the village school. I wondered where I would be staying that night. Would I be on my own or with others? In the event I and a schoolfriend were taken to Graywalls, the house of Mr and Mrs Clarke. We were wonderfully received and we both fell in love at first sight with this beautiful house.

The village school with its existing pupils was far too small to accommodate our party from London consisting of perhaps as many as 50, mainly schoolgirls and a few schoolboys in the age group of eleven to 14.

The solution to this problem was that we had classroom lessons in the afternoons. In the mornings we went for walks in the village and the surrounding area learning about the history of the village and being intrigued by Cissbury Ring and highly excited at the sheep fair on Nepcote Green. This schooling arrangement did not last very long and after about a couple of months we were accommodated in the village hall thus leaving the village school for its own pupils. This went on for some time and after that we were bussed to a school in nearby Washington.

It was whilst I was living with the Cundalls that I reported to my teacher that I thought their German maid might be a spy after I saw her ironing a blank piece of paper and seeing writing appear. Teacher informed the police who quickly investigated. My suspicions however were not well founded!'

'My first memory of Sussex is not really a very happy one! On Friday 1st September 1939 I became a very reluctant evacuee, aged nine, sent from London to stay "indefinitely" with a distant relative in the rural depths of Sussex, not far from Hassocks. I was a London child born and bred and quite unprepared for the removal from my modern London home. I began to feel uneasy at Victoria, where I

202

was placed on a crowded train full of other children labelled and carrying gas masks, waving sadly to my rapidly receding mother on the platform.

I was told (falsely as it turned out) that I was just going away for a few days "until we know what's happening". When the train reached Hassocks quite a number of children got out, and I was eventually found by my "aunt" (not really an aunt but a very distant cousin). She had a rather ramshackle car, and we drove into the depths of Sussex, which to me seemed as remote and uninhabited as Tibet! Auntie's home was a thatched cottage, some way from any other habitation, and to which we had to walk along a very muddy lane and then across a field full of thistles and nettles.

Needless to say there was no electricity or mains water, so that for many years the word "Sussex" evoked for me the smell of paraffin lamps and somewhat brackish water coming from a well in the garden. The place would have seemed primitive to most Sussex people, so you can imagine the effect on a rather precocious Londoner. All the time I stayed there I remember feeling cold, as well as very depressed at being separated from parents and friends.

On the next day, Saturday 2nd September, we walked along by the railway and watched an endless procession of trains speeding by, full of children being evacuated from London. I waved to them and wondered what was going to happen next. What would a war be like?

Next day, Sunday 3rd, my aunt got out her battery radio and we drove up to the Downs overlooking Brighton. At 11 am we listened to Mr Chamberlain. An air raid siren went off which was rather frightening, but I gather it was a mistake, as the all clear sounded soon after. We drove down to the coast and watched the soldiers putting up a barbed wire barrier all along the seashore. Then we went back for lunch.

It was several months before I saw my parents again (although they wrote regularly) and there was no telephone at the cottage. I never saw any of my London schoolfriends again until we were all nearly grown up after the war. In the following months I became used to primitive country life, and quite enjoyed fetching milk and eggs from the farm nearby, and riding on the splendid shire horses. Eventually I moved to our new family home just outside London, just in time for the Blitz and the Battle of Britain which filled our skies by day and night.'

LIFE WITH GRANDFATHER

'During the war we were evacuated from London to our grandfather's large house, and as he was old-fashioned we must have lived a life dominated by Victorian ways. West Stoke House was very large (17 bedrooms, I think), and one wing was used by evacuees: three teachers, a blind husband and 24 infants' school children. I joined them for lessons till I was old enough to be sent off to boarding school like my elder brothers and sister. Later this part of the house became a Mess for troops camping in the woods before D-Day.

Our father stayed in London as an ARP warden, and our mother always worried until his morning phone call to say he was safe. She worked three days a week at a Toc H Forces canteen and two nights at the County Hall (Air Raid Warning service).

Life was traditional and not always comfortable. It seemed natural that the wood-fired radiators were usually cold, and that in winter there could be ice on the bedroom water jugs. There was a puny electric fire, and I remember my chilly bare knees.

Lunch had to be nearly silent while Grandfather listened to the one o'clock news, which I thought very boring. I loved supper in bed with a book – especially during the fruit season when we could pick as much as we cared to eat, except for the peaches or any grapes which survived the cold greenhouse. Strange to think that Grandfather still had gardeners and two elderly maids in those days.

We still had early morning prayers until the cook struck and said she was too busy. We hated having to read the day's Bible passage and be criticised for faulty diction. Of course we never realised how difficult Grandfather must have found this invasion of four lively grandchildren.

The nearest shop was four miles away: we were allowed petrol for one journey there per week as the bus route was a mile and a half away. But there was plenty of home-grown food – vegetables and fruit, hens, geese, bees and goats. We children helped to milk the goats Gert and Daisy, though Gert was an alarmingly good kicker. Pigeons and rabbits came from the woods, and in the spring there was squab pie from the breasts of young rooks (I doubt if I could face this now!). My mother used to eye the village "invasion rations" of tinned food which was stacked in a cellar, but it never got used.

The cellars too were where my mother held what I thought were "cellar parties" – all night affairs which involved family and many neighbours. Only later did I realise that we were taking refuge from the air raid! Later we used to count the bombers out, and then the sadly reduced numbers coming back.

How far away this all seems now.'

IT'S AMAZING WE EVER LEARNED ANYTHING

'I was only nine years old when the Second World War started in 1939. My earliest memory is of the first air raid siren. My friends and I were playing in Orchard Way, Lancing and heard a siren which we thought was a fire engine. We all ran towards First Avenue to see where the engine was going when an elderly lady (at least she seemed old to me) came up and said we should all go home and lock our doors as the war had started. We all did as we were told. The only snag was when my mother came home from the WI with two little evacuees in tow she was unable to get in.

We were only expecting one evacuee but the little boy wouldn't be parted from his sister, she was only five and he was only eight or nine, so that is how we started with evacuees. We had about four different evacuees altogether through the war. If it wasn't evacuees it was airmen or people who were working down here. We eventually ended up with a land girl who seemed to be with us forever.

A lot of my schooldays were spent in the air raid shelter, as soon as the siren went we were escorted to the underground shelter. I remember we used to have a lot of spelling bees and play Hangman. The only light was a hurricane lamp. If we were down the shelter at lunchtime we were given Horlicks tablets and Rowntrees pastilles. If we were lucky to have somebody reliable to pick us up we could go home but it had to be by transport and we had to be returned back to school as soon as the all clear went. I was one of the lucky ones, if my brother was available he would come on his trade bike and put me in the big wicker basket. He was an errand boy for the Co-op.

It's amazing people of my age ever learned anything at school but we all seemed to manage to get good jobs when we left.'

'I was at Bosham school during the war. I had to spend two days a week digging for victory – never mind my schooling – on ground given by Mr Brinkman of the nurseries. I was also a WVS messenger, which entailed bicycling, suitably attired with an official armband, with messages from Thatched Railway Cottage (an old railway carriage believed to have been used by Edward VII which stood next door to the Critchfield Garage, now the Bosham Service Station) up to Woodend, waiting for a reply and returning.

In the holidays when the threat of invasion was in everyone's mind, I helped to build a gunpost in Govers Field behind Green Lane. I also helped to fill sandbags to place on Heavers field, alongside Delling Lane, to prevent enemy gliders landing. At this time, my father was in the Home Guard and two nights a week in Smugglers

Lane manned a look-out for possible invaders armed only with a thick club.

I recall two Austrian gentlemen running a cheese factory making "Chissick Cheese" in Broadbridge Farm House. The cheese was not very popular and two or three days before the declaration of war, the gentlemen disappeared. The local theory was that they had been spies.

A searchlight battery was placed behind Brooks Farm at Broadbridge, and was the target of two blast bombs. Many houses were damaged, including the railway gatehouse, but the only injuries were to two carthorses that, to the great distress of the owner had to be destroyed. Another time a German dive bomber crash-landed nearby, which gave all the local children many happy hours of souvenir hunting.'

'When the war started I was seven, living in Lancing and attending South Lancing JMI school. In 1940 there was an influx of evacuees and the school became so overcrowded that we had to use other centres in the village as classrooms. It was very confusing and I used to get so worried and frightened because I couldn't always remember where I ought to be and I remember running to and fro looking for friends in my class who seemed to know where they were going.

The air raid shelters were across the playground and field, dug into the bank of the unfinished new railway bridge. When the sirens sounded we all had to run across the field and into the shelters. Although I was quite plump I ran very fast as I was scared, and on one occasion I arrived first but tripped as I was going down the steps in the dark and as I lay there everyone rushed over me. By the time the teacher heard my cries I was black and blue. Once we were in the shelters we had to recite our tables or learn pieces of poetry, our voices getting louder as we heard the guns going off and felt the vibrations of exploding bombs. The teachers had to light hurricane lamps.

When I was in the top class in the junior school the desks were in tiers, with the back row quite high above the floor. If you were in the scholarship group you sat in the top row and if you weren't very bright you sat at floor level. Our teacher, Miss Royal, was very strict and we were all quite frightened of her. One day I bought my sweet ration on my way back to school after lunch (no school dinners then), and during story time surreptitiously opened my desk to eat one. It was a two ounce bag of pink and white spearmint balls and I unfortunately tipped them out and they clattered down the steps from top to bottom. In the hush Miss Royal said, "How kind of you to share your sweets, Mildred. Those of you who can reach them may pick them up and eat them after school." '

WE MOVED TO RUSTINGTON

'In 1939 my father was due to return to his station in the Far East and he would not agree to my being evacuated from London and away from my family. So it was arranged, the month before the outbreak of the Second World War, that I moved to Rustington with my uncle and his family to the house he had just purchased. Cousin Eleanor and I then attended, as day scholars, the French Convent of the Holy Family in Norfolk Road, Littlehampton.

One lovely sunny day I returned to the convent for the afternoon lessons to a very subdued class, and Denise, a French girl, was sobbing uncontrollably – "Paris had fallen". The Sisters were equally desolate and in the next two days it was very sad to see the odd quiet tear trickle down the Sister's face.

One morning shortly after this, Eleanor and I left the bus at the bottom of South Terrace and Norfolk Road and found it necessary to walk in the road as the pavements in South Terrace and a short way up Norfolk Road held the bodies of exhausted soldiers. The lads were still there at lunch time and at the end of the schoolday. Next morning some soldiers were still there, but we were able to pick our way through and walk on the pavement. By lunch they had all been billeted.

Also about this time an Italian family living in our road had received their internment instructions. It was sad to part with our new friends but I became the owner of the daughter's bicycle. Thereafter, Eleanor and I cycled to and from school through the Whapple, and on to Berry Lane. I always had a thrill when riding along the bridlepath of the Whapple, feeling that I was part of the history of travellers from Roman days. There used to be a weed growing there, it was fairly common, segmented like a sugar-cane, easy to break into pieces, and which I understood was a type of primitive grass. The elevation when riding the bicycle enabled me to look over the low hedges of the bridlepath. Eleanor and I used to look out for the Local Defence Volunteer, with a band on his arm, holding a rifle, and with his back to us as he looked out to sea. Later in the war I worked in the City of London with two robust young men, over six feet tall, broad, strong and healthy looking, who had been invalided out of the army with rheumatism, and week by week their bodies curled into a bishop's crook. Their job had been as coastal watchkeepers in all weathers.

My family had a direct hit in the first London night raid and

Mother moved to Rustington. We had a house in Broadmark Way. This introduced me to my badly constipated dragon, as there were very loud groans which seemed to come from the ground near the entrance to Bushby Avenue. I believed the noise related to the pumping of the water supply to the private Sea Estate. Every self-respecting village should have a dragon.

Finally, there is my fond memory of "Old Harry" who dug up our back lawn – "Dig for Victory". He also kindly advised us on the does and don'ts of vegetable growing, which included going into the garden in the gloaming to collect and dispose of slugs.

Old Harry had a round rosy face, and the most amazing beard. His face was clear of all bristles, but from ear to ear, travelling under his jawbone and chin in a half circle was a well trimmed but luxurious beard. Old Harry's throat-warmer, so his daughter told me, was the true "Sussex Underdowns" style.

'Our London home was bombed in August 1940. Our next London home was blitzed a month later and we moved to Rustington. I was still very lame having broken my ankle a year earlier and was about five and a half years old.

We rented a house in Broadmark Way, on the southern side of that road. The fence and hedge at the bottom of our garden formed part of the barrier cutting all civilians off from getting to the beach. All the houses further south of that line had been evacuated. I can remember seeing the Home Guard parade and march. They all seemed such very, very old men – almost as old as my uncle (in his seventies!). It seemed funny to see them parading with broomsticks instead of rifles – one man had lost his left hand and two of them were as lame as me, but Rustington couldn't compete with the Worthing Home Guard, they had three Generals in their ranks, two of whom had fought in the Boer War at that rank.

Buses were restricted to Worthing Road, Mill Lane and Station Road, Rustington – Broadmark Lane, Sea Lane, North Lane, The Street and Ash Lane were out of bounds to anyone who did not live or work in the immediate area. My mother was indignant at the number of times she had to prove that she lived on the very edge of the Forbidden Zone. This seemed even worse as she had been asked by the local shopkeepers and ARP to translate for some Frenchmen – I think that they were part of the Free French Army, as we left Rustington before the French Canadians arrived.

I can remember seeing dog fights between our fighters and the German bombers and fighters, and praying that the poor pilot coming down by parachute would land on the beach and not in the sea a hundred yards out. We also saw our fighter planes encircling the parachuting pilot – German pilots justified their shooting of the helpless pilot as within the Geneva Convention.

In the summer/autumn of 1941 there was little fruit at the green-grocer but a near neighbour told my mother that most of the houses on the Sea Estate were empty and locked up. She took us on a foray – they seemed big houses with enormous gardens but we knocked on a front door and were told to help ourselves and that one neighbour had pears and another might still have plums. (Remember there was no means of collecting or delivering this fruit except on foot.) In 1942, when coal shortages began to hurt, fir cones and broken branches were also collected. My aunt kept chickens and if we visited I was supposed to collect a bag of snails for those greedy birds.

When after the war we returned to Rustington, and in September 1946 I went to Chichester Girls' High School, we were told of the many boats that had gone from the Adur and Arun rivers, from the Chichester Basin and from Selsey, and of the amateur and professional fishermen who steered to the smoke of Dunkirk.'

LANCING IN WARTIME

'On the morning of 3rd September 1939 my sister and I were on the beach at Lancing, playing on the sand, when our father came down to take us home. That was the last time we went on the beach for six years, as within a few days the army was laying mines and building anti-tank traps. Few people realised that the beach green at Lancing was once very much lower. After the outbreak of war the whole area was filled with huge concrete blocks topped with rolls of barbed wire. After the war the spaces in between were filled in and the whole grassed over to make the present green.

My brothers were in the army, and one day my sister and I arrived home to find four strange boys in the house. They were evacuees from Brixton and were like creatures from another planet. They were, in our eyes, very rough and rude, spoke unintelligibly, and as well as having an aversion to washing, were always hungry and ate everything in sight. My parents were very kind and patient, however, and soon "tamed" them and we had some good times with them. The boys were not with us for long and went back to London as their mothers missed them and thought the "phoney war" would soon be over.

My father worked in the railway works in Lancing. He went to work every day on his bicycle, and we always knew when he would be home for dinner as the works hooter sounded at twelve o'clock, and as the great gates opened in Bessborough Terrace hundreds of men poured out on their bikes, taking up all the road. They had an hour then went back again until 5.30 pm when the hooter went again. Wherever you were in Lancing you could hear the hooter. The railway works were a target for enemy bombers and there were many raids. My father had to do a lot of firewatching at night, going off at eight o'clock with his flask and tin helmet, coming home at 7 am for a wash and some breakfast, then going off again to do a day's work.

One day my mother and I were walking down South Street towards the sea when an aircraft flew low straight up the road. My mother shouted, "Blimey, it's a Jerry", and we flung ourselves down behind the fence outside the fire station and heard the machine gun bullets ricocheting up the street. When we picked ourselves up my mother remarked drily that it was all right as we were just by the mortuary. At the age of eight this was small comfort to me. I remember walking home from school when a bomb dropped nearby, and as I huddled against a wall the big plate glass windows of the bank blew in and out like chiffon until they finally burst out into the road with the blast. The bungalow at the back of our garden in Chester Avenue, was hit by a bomb and my mother climbed up the debris to help an old lady who had been blown on to the roof.'

UNDERNEATH THE BALLOON

'I remember vividly "the day war broke out". My Mum and Auntie were listening to the radio and crying! We youngsters were sent off to the shop for ice cream, a rare treat. When the first air raid sounded my Dad filled the bath with water in case the house caught fire; poor Dad, how we pulled his leg later.

We had a shelter in the garden that regularly filled with water during the winter months. We also had an Anderson shelter in the dining room, horrid thing it was too, so big it stuck out halfway across the doorway. Many a bruise we got from its sharp edges.

And then there were the gas masks. How I cried because I couldn't have a Mickey Mouse one, I was just too old. We had to take them everywhere, I used to pack my sandwiches in my case.

One day our school, Nyewood Junior, was machine gunned! The siren never went so we were not in the shelter. Fortunately our teacher saw the plane coming and shouted for us to get under our desks. It was a miracle no one was hurt, but we lost all our windows. Normally when the siren went we all used to file out to the shelters and sing "loud" until the all clear went.

I shall never forget when the planes and gliders went over to France for D-Day. The sky was dark with aircraft for hours.

Of course the worst hardship for us children (my Mum had six evacuees) was the sweet ration; only two ounces per week. There was a little shop (Grants I think it was called) near our school where we used to buy washed carrots and munch them on the way home.

My mother had shingles very badly during the war, about 1943–44. Anyway the evacuees were sent to another home. I was sad to see them go because I am an only child, but when the doodlebugs started in London my cousin Margaret came to stay. She was great fun.

One night Margaret, Mum and I went to the pictures in Bognor. My Dad had been sent to Bermuda in 1941 as an overseer in the dockyard there. We got in rather late and just fell into bed. At about 2 am, there was a loud banging at the door, so Mum went down to see what was happening. An airman stood there. "You are to be evacuated," he said in a loud voice, "Get the kids up and get down to the village hall". Mum stood there in a daze, thinking she was having a bad dream (Margaret and I were still fast asleep), so she went back to bed! Ten minutes later another loud knocking, same airman. "Come on," he said, "Are you ready?" At this Mother really panicked, pulled us out of bed we couldn't find anything, what a to-do. At last we got ready, and the airman led us down the garden path. As we got to the front gate, we looked up and nearly died. A huge barrage balloon was sitting on our chimney pot! The fire was still "in" and though banked down with damp tea leaves as usual, it was still jolly hot. Did we run. I have never run so hard in my life. Mind you my Mum nearly killed me because I ran back for my doll. We spent the night in the village hall. The Army managed to get the balloon over in the nearby field to deflate it, and of course next day all the village youngsters tore bits off for souvenirs. I kept my piece for years.

Well, at long last the war ended, and my Dad came home after being four years away. I didn't know him. He brought home with him a great hand of bananas; I didn't remember them either.'

THE LAND ARMY

As women were conscripted, one of the ways they could serve was to go onto the land to replace the agricultural workers who had been called up and to help with the increased production demanded of farms which now had to feed an increasingly hungry population. They were the Land Army, and they coped with a demanding job (many of them with no experience of farming or of country life) with resilience and humour.

A POOR INEXPERIENCED LAND GIRL

'In 1939 I found myself working as a member of the Women's Land Army at North Stoke near my beloved Arundel. I was billeted in the home of the cowman and his wife and small son together with a paying farm pupil who greatly resented the fact that I was being paid 28 shillings per week and he was paying to work! In addition we had two evacuees to share the three small bedrooms. The privy was halfway down the garden but had a plentiful supply of neatly cut up newspaper which provided an interesting source of up-to-date war news.

I was privileged, as was also the farm pupil, to have a can of hot water brought up to our bedroom but everyone else washed in the washing-up bowl in the kitchen cum living room. When one of the evacuees had a rather nasty ear infection I remember feeling a little disturbed!

My work was hard. Hours of monotonous "dung carting" to the top of the Downs. The old-time carters were not kind to me – they always left me with the youngest and most excitable horse. The army were enjoying an "exercise" and would come down from their camp at breakneck speed in their tanks and other transport with no thought for a poor, inexperienced land girl coping with a highly strung chestnut who had never seen or heard anything like it! However, we survived.

On a happier note – at the end of the day's work the carthorses would return to their stables and after being unharnessed they would all leave their stalls and amble down to the water trough whilst their carters bedded their stables down. They would return in their own time snatching the odd piece of grass en route. The end of another working day. A tired land girl would also return to her high tea – working out how she could eke out her butter ration and looking forward to reading *Gone With the Wind* in bed by candlelight before beginning another day all over again.'

FULL OF PATRIOTIC FERVOUR

'I came to Bosham first in August 1939. I was No 1817 in the Women's Land Army; full of patriotic fervour, I had joined in February 1939. One week's "training" on Mr Torrance's farm – then back to my London job as a dental nurse until war broke out and I returned to Sussex. I loved Bosham with its boats, sea smells, distant hills and green fields.

For my first six weeks I was "tatty picking" for nine hours a day; 30 shillings a week, £1 of which was for my landlady. No uniform in the early days but this came gradually. Milking machines were installed in the cowshed and I changed to dairywork. This meant rising at 4 am every day (no half-day). I carried the milk from the shed to the dairy, put it through the cooler and into the churns which had to be labelled and put on the platform outside by 7 am ready for collection. After lighting the boiler I could then go home for breakfast – starving hungry!

After breakfast all equipment had to be scrubbed and sterilised. Break then until afternoon milking.

After six months service I received my armband and half-diamond. Then came an invitation to London to take tea with HM The Queen (three of us from each county went). On arriving at Goldsmiths Hall our Honorary Director, Lady Denman, instructed us on curtseying! Her Majesty was beautiful – in mauve velvet – and spoke to each of us. How we cheered her as she left!

After 18 months' service at Bosham I moved to Parham and worked for Lady Denman's brother. Modern cowshed, Red Poll herd and a cottage for the four land girls employed (two in the dairy, two tractor driving). One other girl lived in the village and was relief milker.

In 1942 I was asked to train new recruits in dairywork. Women were now conscripted. I moved to Todhurst Hostel where I had four trainees every month. Land Army girls from this hostel worked in gangs on nearby farms, threshing mainly but also seasonal jobs on the land.

In 1943 I became a Milk Recorder, working for the Milk Marketing Board. Based in Petworth, I visited farms within a very wide area, on a bicycle, quite often carrying a heavy wooden box of butterfat samples on the back! I checked yields, lactation records etc, and earmarked calves, cows and even goats! Much less monotonous than the daily routine of milking, it also gave me long weekends off.

We worked long and hard in those far-off days but gained so much in return and I still retain a deep love of Sussex.'

LEAKING WELLIES AND HUNGER

'I was four years a land girl at 45 shillings a week on a thousand acre farm near Chichester. Five ft two inches and city bred, I turned my hand to ploughing, cultivating, sowing and reaping, as well as the odd bizarre job like bagging up flue dust, hot from a rail track, this being a new scheme for fertilisation at the time. Ours set fire to the bags and was a burnt out case.

We were always up against weather conditions and discomfort of

A rare quiet moment for the land girls Janet, Audrey and Marjorie, who worked at the Manor Farm, Chidham during the war. Most remembered their service as a time of 'leaking wellies, damp socks, hunger and fatigue'.

214

some kind or another, and not being supplied with underwear, I wore my father's combinations in winter for extra protection. I later transferred to the cowpens and worked with another girl. Here I escaped the weather but suffered the tongue of two embittered cowmen, who got the most out of us. When milking machines were introduced we had to break the old cows in and they didn't take kindly to it. We were severely bruised in the initial period.

Three of us shared a cowman's cottage which was pretty basic. There was no indoor plumbing of any kind and only a tap in the yard for water. In the kitchen we had three buckets for drinking water, washing and slops. Our washing water had to be thrown out in the field and we frequently lost our pan scourer, usually to be found hanging on a bush. A kitchen range was our only means of cooking and this was always going out as we were not there to attend it. Paraffin lamps and candles provided lighting and I have only to smell a paraffin stove today to get a flashback of our 5 am start, drinking tea from a a flask before the morning milking.

Furniture was in short supply. In the kitchen we had an outsize basket chair which would take two and a dog, a deal table and three upright chairs. The parlour was empty, but upstairs were the all important beds, the odd chest of drawers and a wash basin.

We were given a spaniel who chased the cows in the wrong direction. His menu was worse than ours. If he was lucky he got a bone from the butcher which he nervously buried, but mostly ate bread and marg with gravy and would moodily chew coke for something to get his teeth into. Our own meat ration was unreliable, as it was sent up on the bus and invariably went to the wrong village. We lived mainly on bread, cheese, dried egg, jam and tinned meat or fish when available, apart from the meagre allowance of bacon, sugar, marg and butter which came in ounces rather than pounds. Occasional fresh eggs or sausages (a rare event) were a supplement, and we also grew a few vegetables.

Our privy was a bucket which had to be emptied more often than we could have wished, but it was marvellous for the tomatoes. Later a flying bomb demolished it, and the roof and windows of the cottage were stove in. We were in bed at the time and amazingly none of us were injured, but we had to be billeted in the village, and it was milking as usual the next morning though we were in shock and hadn't slept.

Our life was haunted by leaking wellies, damp socks, hunger and fatigue, and our idea of luxury was a hot bath once a week and going to bed early. As Vita Sackville West said "It is a plodding story of endurance rather than heroics." Nevertheless we talk about it yet with nostalgia.'

I MARRIED THE FARMER

'In 1942 conscription came in for women aged 18. I was persuaded by my father to join the Land Army. I was given the job of milking at a farm at Birdham four miles away from my home. I used to set off at 5.30 am and work through till about ten o'clock, leaving everything shipshape for the afternoon milking. I returned at two o'clock and went home at five, so completing 16 miles a day on my bike.

One morning I was convinced that I could hear church bells, which were the signal that the German invasion had begun. "Don't worry," said the cowman, "that only be the water dripping on that there bucket!"

Just before my 20th birthday I married the farmer – correction, I married the farm. The production of food had great priority and as my husband was managing three farms he was not allowed to join up, a bitter pill at times. As a member of the Home Guard he did many duties manning the beaches at night. I remember gathering up my baby when the air raid warnings went and creeping down to a rat infested shelter. At about this time there was much activity in the village, with many barges and two Mulberry Harbours being prepared for the invasion. Troops, tanks, jeeps and guns were everywhere.'

THE TIMBER CORPS

'From March 1943 to February 1948 I served as a member of the Timber Corps of the Women's Land Army. My work was to measure the trees felled, the cordwood cut, and count the pit props. The timber fellers were paid on piecework and from these figures their wages could be calculated. The equipment we had to carry to do this work was a long tape measure, a quarter girth tape measure, a timber sword (a tool by which one could pull the quarter girth tape under the tree), a pot of paint (the butt of the tree had to be numbered), a scribe knife for marking and a book to record the work done.

We worked outside in all weathers, the only thing to defeat us was snow, when it was impossible to uncover the work done.

The office was usually a wooden hut in the forest, and lodgings were in the nearest town or village. Transport was by bicycle. Uniform included breeches, shirt, green jersey, greatcoat, green beret, brown socks and shoes. For work we wore dungarees and jackets, boots and gaiters or wellington boots.

Timber Corps girls could be found driving tractors and lorries, working as sawyers, felling trees, and any other jobs needed in a forest. During these years I worked in the forests at Arundel, Poynings, Lewes, and finished my service at Southwater.'

HIGHDAYS & HOLIDAYS

HOLIDAYS AND OUTINGS

Holidays spent on West Sussex's beaches have remained cherished memories for many children between the wars. What need did we have for foreign shores when there were sandcastles to be built and donkeys to ride?

OUT FOR THE DAY

'August Bank Holiday was our favourite as the whole family packed into the waggon and went to the beach at Bracklesham. A big basket was packed with sandwiches and cake and we stopped at the Old Bell Inn to collect bottles of ale, ginger ale and fizzy lemonade. On reaching the beach the waggon was unloaded and the horse tied up to the hedge on a plot of grass. There was a large rock at the top of the shingle to sit under. We knew all the people on the beach as they were all locals. After many paddles and enjoying our lunch and tea, the horse was allowed to paddle, and we returned home early evening, tired and happy.'

'In 1914 I was a boy of seven and was one of a Sunday school class at Tangmere. Our outing was almost due – we were going to the seaside at Bognor, which was about six and a half miles away, and I was excited as I had never been to the sea.

On the day we gathered at the vicarage, our transport a large farm waggon, one huge horse and its driver. Boards were put across the waggon as our seating. We wended our way through miles of lanes – it was great.

The beach at Bognor was lovely, with donkey rides, Punch and Judy and children's tricycles. Before leaving we were taken to the nearby Toy Bazaar to buy anything we wanted up to one shilling and sixpence. I've never forgotten it.'

'Before the First World War we would travel from our home in Hampshire to visit our relations who had a holiday cottage in Bognor.

Dressed in our best frocks of embroidered voile, wearing straw hats with elastic cutting our chins, and brown strapped shoes polished to a high gloss, we came "over the water" to South Parade Pier to catch the open deck Southdown bus to Bognor. We jogged along at a stately 12 mph and by the time we reached Chichester the

218

radiator was boiling. We sat on the top deck, admiring the graceful lines of the Cathedral and the picturesque North, South, East and West Streets, until the driver returned with his watering can. We then headed for the sea, crossing the West Sussex Plain, rather like the waggoners of early America must have felt. Would our journey ever end?

At last Bognor Pier came into view, and our relations were waiting with a picnic hamper. The summer visitors were strolling along the prom, everybody wearing a hat. Some of the gentlemen sported boaters, whilst others had on hard felts with curling brims which they would raise to passing acquaintances.

Because of the danger of our spoiling our shoes we were not allowed on the beach, but walked to the Marine Gardens for our picnic. We spoke in low voices and ate delicately. It was all rather like being in church. Bognor was so very select.

There were families holding picnics on the firm white sand, dressed in navy blue bathing suits, the children with sleeves to the elbow and legs below the knee, ladies with skirts sown to their suits, wearing rubber caps with rubber carnations clipped to the side.

At low tide, the wet sand looking as polished as our shoes, the beautiful horses of Sussex were brought for exercise and we watched them gallop along the water's edge, kicking up the spray, their manes flying in the breeze, whinnying with delight.

Our visit to Bognor ended by our having tea in a subdued restaurant near the pier, poached eggs on toast followed by cream horns. Then away we were driven, sitting on the front seat of the lower deck, watching the driver manipulating the gears in his lonely cabin.

Darkness had encroached on the fields when we reached home, and we were tired, but we had enjoyed the quiet serenity of Bognor.'

'On our birthdays in July in the early 1920s we went in George Bowles' village taxi to Bognor, having prayed fervently for a fine day. If wet you had to make your sandcastles under the pier. Another exciting treat was the annual WI outing. We boarded the green Southdown charabancs outside the almshouses at Halnaker. Each row of seats had a door at either end and they rose in tiers towards the back. The huge hood was folded back and we had a wonderful view as we whirled through the summer air with hay and bean fields smelling sweetly on either side. We would pick up outlying people as we headed for Brighton or Worthing or Littlehampton. Mrs Dykes always wore a wide brimmed black lace hat with a wreath of different garden flowers round it, sweet peas one year and roses another.'

DEAR OLD BOGNOR

'Bognor Regis in 1934 and my first seaside holiday after a long illness. The thrill of the long train ride and smell of the sea on arrival. We were hiring an apartment, own bedrooms and dining room with landlady doing the cooking, meals at your convenience.

The clothes trunk had been collected by Carter Patterson the previous week, you put a cardboard CP notice in your window and the horse-drawn van called, took the luggage to the nearest railway station and arranged for it to be delivered the other end.

We explored the local shops, all pleased to deliver orders. Mother chose the food and then we went down to the shore. There was a Punch and Judy show, and a man drawing sand pictures, different each day of our fortnight. I think this one was of Arundel Castle, but always there was a collecting cap for contributions. Next morning on an early walk we watched Ralph Lynn's racehorses being exercised along the sands and had our own pony rides on much quieter steeds after breakfast.

I had always wanted a pair of beach pyjamas like the film stars but instead was bought a "playsuit", an all in one shorts and blouse, white pique with blue pattern which did up down the front with buttons, but I did get my "gipsy sandals" which had bands of embroidered canvas, plaited woollen tie ups, sling backs and wooden heels which made a satisfying clacking sound as you walked along.

The following year we hired a beach hut on stilts with its own steps down to the beach; the sea came right up at high tide and my younger brother tried fishing from the balcony. Those huts have long gone, together with the Esplanade Theatre where we first saw Tony Hancock, and the burnt down Pavilion Theatre with London-like revues. There was also a show on the pier, Eric Ross and his wife Ida with their company at the Rex and Uncle Duggie and his pierrots in the Bandstand. "If the day is hot and muggy, come and see your Uncle Duggie" etc.

We had walks along to the Craigwell Estate past Craigwell House where King George V convalesced and other large mansions where the Aga Khan and guests stayed during Goodwood Week.

The Marine Gardens were lit up with coloured lights amongst the plants at night and there was a Butlin's Amusement Park on the front. My mother won a set of saucepans on an early version of bingo (several wins cashed at once) and my brother and I were sometimes lucky enough to win a bar of chocolate on the penny in the slot machines.

My parents went dancing at the end of the pier and my father fished for our supper from the jetty. Men walked around the beaches and waded into the sea taking photographs; one of us was used in a publicity book, much to my mother's pride and our embarrassment. After the war nothing was quite the same. Our landlady had retired, most of the specialist shops had gone, and most of the big hotels were demolished and high rise flats built, but I will always remember those golden days.'

'When a child I spent many holidays in Bognor, and later, settled there. My childhood memories are still very vivid.

West of the pier, a sand-artist carved outlines of famous castles and, nearby, the Bognor Clown gave two daily shows with performing dogs and an unforgettable line of "patter". His daughter, "Miss Vi and her Living Marionettes", had a cheeky style we all enjoyed.

We sat on the sloping rocky sea wall on which living winkles and limpets awaited the next tide. Scuffling over those sharp shells was very unkind to tender bottoms!

Bognor shops used to be small and welcoming. Kings the bakers sold delicious buns for a penny, and locally caught prawns cost the same at stalls on the pebble beach near the pier.

Saits' Dairy (long disappeared) served ices at table in little glass dishes shaped like scallop shells; ices rich and creamy, unlike any sold today.

The pier had slot machines showing what the butler saw; a tin woman being rescued from a burning building by a tin fireman; and a palmist and phrenologist waited in their booths.

At a dance on the pier I first saw the "Cakewalk", and in the pavilion at the seaward end was a skating rink.

From the pier, onlookers watched summer regattas, and on one occasion clapped vigorously at a mock battle between two local boatmen; but the applause ended suddenly when it became obvious that the battle was in earnest, a real grudge fight.

Poor old pier – its seaward end, damaged beyond repair in the gale of February 1965, was recently demolished.

In the Olympian Gardens on the seafront a pierrot party, which once included Seymour Hicks, gave nightly shows, changing into full evening dress during the interval. How we children loved the ladies' dresses!

Disused railway carriages were for years the only buildings on Pagham Beach, and used exclusively for holidays. They had no gas, electricity or sanitation, water came from a pump that froze in winter, and cooking was by oil. One cold Easter, too much wood piled on a make-shift fireplace set the tin chimney afire and nearly burned our carriage down.

In a cornfield west of Bognor a railway carriage converted to a public toilet was beloved for its novelty, and a tea garden nearby (cream teas, one shilling and sixpence) had a robin that ate cake from one's hand.

In North Bersted, two miles distant, was the Jubilee Stamp Room in the Rising Sun Inn, where walls, ceilings, furniture, ornaments, were all plastered with used postage stamps, while more stamps strung on thread festooned the ceilings as well. We children enjoyed the visitors' book for its often ribald comments.

Dear old Bognor – I have so many happy memories.'

GOLDEN LITTLEHAMPTON

My first memories of Sussex are from the late 1920s and early 1930s when my mother, father, sister and me came to Littlehampton on holiday. We would be joined by aunts, uncles and their friends. We travelled down from London by Timpson's charabanc but the uncles came on their motorbike and sidecar. We stayed in East Ham Road and Gloucester Road and on one occasion had to change addresses after one night as the place was bug infested! We bought our own food which the landlady cooked for us.

I seem to remember walking through cornfields to the green and beach, though these days it seems improbable. When the corn was cut it was stooked and we had our photo taken sitting against a stook behind the sand dunes. There was no Butlin's Amusement Park then, but a lovely green where it was safe for children to play. Every morning the holidaymakers assembled on the green for a keep fit display. It catered for everyone from the youngest child to the oldest adult. Then a bathe and afterwards a run along the front to buy a whipped cream walnut. The modern ones do not taste a bit like those of the late 1920s.'

'Many years ago I was helping with a company of Girl Guides which was attached to what was known as a Residential School, where the children of broken homes or orphans were sent to be in the care of the London County Council. They had never seen the sea, their holidays spent with relatives in the dismal streets of the inner city.

We thought it would be a good idea to take them for a day at the seaside, so, by dint of many raffles and whist drives, we got enough money to hire a coach and drive to Littlehampton. Our driver was a gloomy man, and the children, not used to travelling, soon became queasy and we had sudden stops when we were told to put them on the verge and tell them to take big gulps of fresh air. It seemed a long journey.

Bury Hill was a delight to them. They had only seen hills crowded

A stroll along Pier Road, Littlehampton in the 1930s. The old ferry boat ticket office is on the right. Many people remember holidays at West Sussex resorts with great affection and nostalgia.

with houses and flats, the view of a patchwork quilt of corn fields and meadow lands was their idea of what heaven must be like.

In those days there were no bypasses and we rattled down Arundel's hill. The castle, rising up high at our side, could only have been built for Sleeping Beauty.

Soon we were turning in to Banjo Road. The sun was shining, the sky was blue and before them stretched the endless azure of the sea, the white frilled waves dropping softly to the golden sand. We had taken the precaution of telling them to wear their swimming costumes under their uniforms. They ran for the beach, shedding their clothes as they went. Mothers grabbed their toddlers and hurried to safety, dogs barked and old men took their newspapers off their faces. The hordes rushed into the sea, and as invaders to our shores did of old, wrecked castles and created havoc.

It was with difficulty that we managed to persuade them to stop trying to drown each other and come to lunch. We had won for ourselves a nice length of beach, and they stretched to catch the sun's caressing rays. Grass was familiar to them, and concrete and soil, but they squealed with pleasure as they trickled the sand through their toes.

After another dip they begged to be allowed to visit the Amusement Park, so we shared some of the raffle money among them, and we could hear their shouts, as could the citizens of Littlehampton, as they drove the Dodgem cars and rode the Big Wheel.

Too soon for them, the coach came back to Banjo Road and we

counted them aboard and left as they sang, "There's a hole in my bucket dear Georgie". On we went, singing the camp fire songs, through the quiet lanes of Sussex, startling the cows and fluttering the birds from the trees.

We arrived home to the school, pale faces aglow with the sun. We gave our driver the remainder of the raffle money and saw the flicker of a smile. They went to their dormitories. For them it had indeed been Golden Littlehampton.'

CAMPING IN THE 1930s

'Tomato nurseries lined the lane, at the end of which was the entrance to our campsite at Goring-by-Sea. A wooden shop, gaunt, black tarred and raised on stilts stood guard. Everything from Camp Coffee to paraffin and sweets was available. The sensations engendered by liquorish laces and four a penny gobstoppers linger still.

Seaweed, a constant problem, was collected, tossed into high-sided horse-drawn carts and taken to be used as manure.

Standing in isolation was the hand operated water pump where we filled our containers.

Two straggling rows of vans faced the sea. The rent for the southern line was more expensive than the back row. Every van had its own chemical toilet usually housed in a shed at the rear, and they were emptied by the campers into a pit a couple of fields away. Strangely there is no recollection of obnoxious smells! Accommodation varied from purpose-built trailers to old railway carriages and buses. A motley sight even then.

The sun shone, but one wet day we children were ushered into a double decker bus to play with board games or Lexicon, or Happy Families, or to rush up and down the stairs in a rowdy chase while our elders gathered in a neighbouring van to play bridge or whist.

Breakfast smells wafted across the field. The aroma of paraffin stoves mixed with frying bacon, tomatoes and newly gathered mushrooms was irresistible. Midday meals were usually cold, but we tucked into hot dinners at night, after spending long days on the beach where the sea receded for miles, leaving rock pools, and the sound of gulls scavenging along the tide line.

We swam on the incoming tide, and when it was full we used the stone bank which held back the sea, sliding down the steepest slopes on a sack or tin tray. Late in the season when the sorrel, which grew profusely below the stones, was red and ripe we collected the seeds into paper bags, twisting the tops to make "bombs". Teams were chosen and war declared, the bombs flying, thrown so hard they burst on impact.

Scouts and Guides encamped nearby, and before leaving they always had a sing-song which we managed to gate-crash.

In the 1950s I made a pilgrimage to Sea Lane. Change had begun. Today only the sea is the same, the nurseries and fields are under tarmac, bricks and cement. The lane is a dual carriageway. Progress? So we say!'

A TREAT AT SHOREHAM

'We lived on a farm near Horsham so Father was tied to twice daily milking, seven days a week but sometimes we went for a picnic dinner. I don't think he was keen as there was always a crisis which demanded his attention until almost midday. Consequently we tended to picnic only a mile or so from home. We did get to Leith Hill once!

A rarer treat was to go for an evening swim at Shoreham beach. My older sisters and their friends rode on the flat back of the milk lorry while I rode inside with my parents.

Once, in about 1933, we rented a bungalow there for a fortnight's holiday. All our luggage was packed in a trailer behind the lorry and it broke loose on the way. My eldest sister was left to guard it while Father took us on to Shoreham. I remember sitting on Mother's lap in floods of tears, but whether for the loss of my sister or our goods I don't recall. The bungalow was made from two railway carriages parked parallel with the space between made into a living room. The compartments of the carriages were the bedrooms. Fascinating to a six year old. Father stayed at home but joined us when he could and used to take the others midnight bathing – I was put to bed at the usual time, protesting loudly. At low tide there was enough sand exposed for digging and playing hopscotch. All swept away by development now.'

STAYING AT THE LIDO

'It was in the 1950s that Rustington was discovered by us and where we went each August for a two week holiday for nine consecutive years, staying at the holiday camp at Mallon Dene, which was called The Lido.

Travel for us in those days was by public transport, so it was the train from Weybridge in Surrey to Guildford, changing on to Horsham where we were escorted across the rails by a porter to join the one to Littlehampton, then usually the luxury of a taxi to The Lido. One year there was a bus strike in the area and it was impossible to get a taxi, so there was nothing for it but to walk, not easy with the two week's luggage for three, but we fortunately had the pushchair so child and cases took turns.

The camp was smallish by normal standards, not a Butlin's or Warner's. The buildings were like blocks of flats of two storeys, these housed the bedrooms with the toilets at the centre of each block, no en suite in those days! Luxury was the washbasin and constant hot water n the room. The reception, dining and ballroom were in the first building facing the sea, and these were all set in very well kept grounds, with playing fields, tennis courts, putting green etc. There were two outdoor swimming pools, one a children's. An activities programme was arranged for both adults and the children which was most acceptable, as the Augusts of those years were often wet. I remember my husband and son often wearing raincoats to go down to the sea for a swim!

After dinner each evening we walked along the greenswath through East Preston village, and through the village of Rustington. On return the dancing would be underway, but should you need an alcoholic drink then it would have to be a visit to the Mallon Dene hotel, as the Lido was called a dry camp.

We were very disappointed when quite suddenly, the site was sold for house building, and our happy holidays here at an end.'

BREAKING THE SOUND BARRIER

'I was in Lancing on holiday, and on 7th September 1953 I sat on the beach waiting for Neville Duke to break the sound barrier. He flew low along the shore and passed in a flash. The noise was amazing, even to someone who was on duty during the blitz in London.

I have since discovered that the plane he flew in is in the museum at Tangmere, and Mr Neville Duke is president of the Tangmere Military Aviation Museum. The curator at the museum told me he was in Marks and Spencers in Worthing at the time, and customers who didn't know what was happening all got down on the floor, thinking it was a bomb.'

MAKING OUR OWN ENTERTAINMENT

⟨⊙⟩

Once even the smallest village could boast a little dance band or a group of enthusiastic amateur actors whose latest show would play to packed houses. We were used to making our own entertainment before the days of television, and would travel miles to the nearest 'hop' or whist drive. Sports too had a keen following, particularly that Sussex speciality, stoolball.

THE MUMMERS OF BOXGROVE

'The Tipteers were active at Boxgrove before the First World War, and then faded out until the early 1930s when they were revived by Mr Sharp from Fishbourne. They performed a mummers play loosely based on the story of the Crusades. One lady remembered that they "did like a play and sang songs. We used to go up the village hall and we used to have a good evening's entertainment." During the winter the Tipteers performed at Goodwood House and most large houses and hotels in the area. They even performed at the Albert Hall on one occasion.'

'In the 1930s improvements to the parish room at Horsted Keynes – the installation of electric lighting and coke-fired central heating – were financed mainly from the proceeds of the fortnightly dances: live music by The Jubilee Boys, playing accordion, drums, piano, violin and clarinet. It cost a shilling and the girls always wore long dresses and the men evening suits.

Girls joined the Village Club where they wore home-made gym tunics, white blouses and red ties. They did road drill, skipping and Indian club work. There was a boys' night once a month.'

'In my youth all our entertainment was home-made. Our little village hall's dances were to a real dance band, and the local Womens Institute's drama group put on regular plays and concerts. We had a lovely band of people called the Bobs and Shingles, named after the hairstyles of the day, who gave excellent performances to packed houses, admission threepence, sixpence and front row a shilling.

There was no piped heating in the hall, only two huge coal fires. When an interval came a volunteer would rush and get a bucket of

MONDAY, AUGUST 4th, For Three Days **WILL HAY, CLAUDE HULBERT** in **THE GHOST OF ST. MICHAEL'S** (ʊ) Also **BASIL SYDNEY** in **THE FARMER'S WIFE** (ʊ)	THURSDAY, AUGUST 7th, for Three Days **NORMA SHEARER, ROBERT TAYLOR** in **ESCAPE** (ʊ) And **JOE E. BROWN** in **SO YOU WON'T TALK** (ʊ)
MONDAY, AUGUST 11th, for Three Days **Margaret LOCKWOOD, Derek FARR** in **QUIET WEDDING** (ʌ) Also **WILL MAHONEY** in **COME UP SMILING** (ʊ)	THURSDAY, AUGUST 14th, for Three Days **ALICE FAYE, BETTY GRABLE** in **TIN PAN ALLEY** (ʊ) Also **GUY KIBBEE** in **STREET OF MEMORIES**
MONDAY, AUGUST 18th, for Three Days **CHARLES BOYER, IRENE DUNNE** in **BACK STREET** (A) And **NOVA PILBEAM** in **SPRING MEETING** (ʊ)	THURSDAY, AUGUST 21st, for Three Days **WALTER PIDGEON, ROBERT TAYLOR** in **FLIGHT COMMAND** (ʌ) Also **HARRY LANGDON** in **MISBEHAVING HUSBANDS** (ʊ)
MONDAY, AUGUST 25th, for Three Days **Martha SCOTT, William GARGAN** in **CHEERS for MISS BISHOP** (ʊ) Also **CONQUEST OF THE AIR**	THURSDAY, AUGUST 28th, for Three Days **Gary COOPER, Madeleine CARROLL** in **NORTH WEST MOUNTED POLICE** (ʊ) (Technicolour) Also **W. C. FIELDS** in **THE BANK DETECTIVE**

―――― COMING NEXT MONTH ――――

Judy Garland in LITTLE NELLY KELLY   Paul Muni in HUDSON'S BAY
Gary Grant in PHILADELPHIA STORY   Rex Harrison in MAJOR BARBARA
Ray Milland in ARISE MY LOVE   Deanna Durbin in NICE GIRL

COMPLETE CHANGE OF PROGRAMME EVERY SUNDAY.

The programme for the Luxor Cinema at Lancing in August 1941. Going to the cinema once or even twice a week was common before the days of television.

coal. If you had a seat far from the fire you took a hot water bottle. Lighting was by gas. The hall's caretaker was paid ten shillings a week, plus an extra one and sixpence for clearing out the grates and changing the gas mantles.

Our nearest approach to a theatre was when a repertory company would come for a week and put on a different play every night, which the village appreciated a great deal.

In the mid 1920s a local garage owner opened the Imperial Picture House and my father took me to see Charlie Chaplin and the other comedians of the day. It cost my Dad eightpence and I had a penny sherbet dab.

In the early 1930s a nearby small town opened a very posh modern cinema, the Regent, and in 1935 I went with my fiancé to the presentation of a marvellous Wurlitzer organ which rose up from underground and gave half an hour's beautiful music. This was a spectacle not to be missed and the Regent was packed every night for a few months until the novelty wore off. We went twice a week.'

'Whist drives and social evenings were held in the old school room at Findon. As it wasn't a very big room, it was necessary to get there early. The social evenings for the most part consisted of singing and recitations, long narrative poems, and usually performed by women. Similar evenings were also held in the upstairs room of the Wattle house on Nepcote Fair Green (wattles or hurdles were stored in the lower half of the building for use at the sheep Fair in September). The curate, Mr Percy Leonard, used to sing cockney songs.

Amateur dramatics were staged in the big room of Findon school, the stage being made from wooden boards on trestles. Everything had to stop when the school clock struck the hour, as the works were in a large case at the back of the stage. A pantomime was written and presented by Mrs Clark, a villager, bringing in the local events and the people involved, all of which was a great success. Entertainments were given by the Girl Guides and others in the Old Comrades Hut next to the then Grey Point Hotel in the High Street. Dances were also held there. All these events and many others were held in aid of a fund to build the village hall, which with generous support from villagers and local traders, was finally built and opened in 1938 with a Grand Fancy Dress Ball. The Findon Dramatic Club, led by Barbara Coleman their producer, staged many three-act plays and film shows were given; during the war, weekly dances were held with a local band.

Yearly flower shows were held in a field at the bottom of Church Drive, with the West Chiltington Band in attendance. The Silver Jubilee of King George V and Queen Mary was celebrated by a special day on which, following a morning Thanksgiving Service, sports were held in the afternoon, and in the evening bonfires were lit on Cissbury Ring and other places. I remember coming home to the village from Cissbury and hearing the nightingales singing.

Commercial entertainment was available in Worthing where there was, at first, a roller skating rink where the Dome Cinema now is, and there was also the Picturedrome Cinema (with its entrance from Chapel Road), which is now the Connaught Theatre. Another cinema was the Plaza in Rowlands Road, which latterly became a bingo hall. Of course there was always the Pier Pavilion where many shows and dances were held.

There were some private tennis courts in Findon and public courts in Worthing, all of which were popular. Ice skating, relatively new and rare in the 1930s, was available at Brighton, and very popular. Cricket has always been popular in Findon with its beautifully located ground a short walk from the church. County Cricket was played at the Worthing Manor Ground until the mid 1950s.'

'In the late 1940s and early 1950s, the main source of entertainment for young people in Horsham was the three cinemas, where you would know nearly everyone, at least by sight, in the full theatres. Then there was dancing every Saturday night to a live band at the local Drill Hall. These dances were attended come what may, unless you were actually dying, and it was there that most of us met our future spouses. On Sunday afternoons us girls would walk around Horsham town centre, dressed up to the nines, hoping to meet the boys we'd seen at the dance the previous evening. This was known locally as the "monkey parade".

LISTENING TO THE RADIO

'At the weekend usually a fire would be lit in the dining room or perhaps the front room, where the family would listen to the radio – Luxembourg and The Ovaltinies was a favourite and Children's Hour with Uncle Mac reading out all the names of children with birthdays. It was a great thrill to hear your name over the air. As far as I can remember 1924 was the first time I heard a radio, when it had to be listened to through earphones, but it was very soon after this that the radio had a separate loudspeaker in the shape of a trumpet. The early radio was run on a battery – this had to be sent to a garage to be recharged every week, so there were always two batteries on the go – one being recharged and one in the set. As the batteries were quite heavy they had to be taken to the garage in a pushchair or small truck, this was usually Father's task, as there was no car.'

LEATHER ON WILLOW

'Chidham Cricket Club was started in 1921 with matches played at home on the Manor Farm. The vicar wrote:

"June 1st. Cricket match in Manor Meadow between Chidham and Ashling. Chidham won. Dance in the evening on Manor Lawn arranged by Mr and Mrs C Goodger and the cricket committee. One hundred villagers and friends present – perfect weather.

July 9th. A cricket match between a team from Portsmouth banks and Chidham. Chidham won by 20 runs, Mr Charles Goodger, our churchwarden, scoring 17 runs."

Chidham Cricket Club in 1927. Cricket and other sports were part of the social activities of town and village, and keenly contested.

The cricket club flourished and later persuaded the Women's Institute to provide them with teas at a cost of one shilling for tea, bread and butter, jam, watercress, lettuce or radishes (when available), cakes and buns. The WI managed to make a profit and kindly gave the club a donation at the end of the season.'

THE VILLAGE GYMNASIUM

'In 1912 a scheme was afoot to convert the vicarage barn at Fernhurst into a village gymnasium. The idea was well received by the villagers and was carried through. The cost of altering the building and fitting it up with the necessary apparatus was to be about £50. A committee was formed to make the club self supporting and Mr Dudley Paul promised to provide an instructor for three months. This gentleman was the chief supporter and other local people promised generous help. The village gymnasium was a great success and the people who remember say the social contacts and healthy exercise made wonderful recreation periods. Miss Russell also gave much pleasure by teaching country dancing in the barn such good old favourites as *We won't go home 'til morning* and *Sellenger's Round.'*

STOOLBALL

'Stoolball is something like cricket in that it has eleven players, field-

231

ing in much the same positions, but there are more balls to the over and the wickets are only 16 yards apart instead of 22.

The bowling crease is ten yards from each wicket and the hard, kid-covered ball must be delivered underhand. The batsman is out very much as he is in cricket, except that bbw (body before wicket) takes the place of lbw. The bat is held in either hand, defending a wicket consisting of a one ft square board mounted on a stake four ft eight inches from the ground to the wicket's top. The bat is something like that used for table tennis but larger, more oval, and a good deal heavier. Well-sprung, it can drive the ball a most satisfying distance!

In Sussex the game was played a great deal during, and just after, the First World War, and it was somewhere about 1917 that I joined the village club – and played with it until I married and left the district.

It was about May that the fixture list with other clubs came into action, and, in those far-off days, the members of the team who did not bicycle would sally forth to play the away matches in a horse-drawn waggonette, the farmer who drove it acting as umpire on arrival. Later, when the local coal merchant invested in a motor coach as a sideline to his business, we were able to get further afield and the away fixtures took on the form of an outing – with at least one stop on the way home to "treat the driver" and to buy fish and chips for the family's supper.

Among our keenest and most expert players were the blacksmith's wife and her three buxom daughters – all of them possessing remarkable hitting power and ,the daughters at any rate, very nimble in the field. When "Mum's" rheumatics grew too bad for her to take an active part in the game, she returned to the pavilion and took over the job of scoring. By this time she had two daughters-in-law in the team, and little difficulties arose with so many of her family in the field.

On one occasion when the umpire from the opposing team gave one of her daughters "out" she disagreed with his decision.

"You wasn't out, Gert!" she bellowed from the score-box. "You stay in!"

"She is out and out she goes!" asserted the umpire, swivelling round on his heel to address the pavilion.

"Don't you dare come out, my gal!" threatened the irate parent, and finally our captain had to intervene and pour oil on the troubled waters.

There was another occasion, I remember, when "Mum's" feelings overcame her. We were playing a team very evenly matched with our own and everyone was rather keyed up in consequence The opposing team was in and, realising they were unlikely to reach and pass the score we had put up by the agreed time for drawing stumps, they were stone-walling and obviously playing for a draw. This always annoyed our spectators, and rude remarks were heard very plainly from all parts of the field. When the draw became actual fact it was too much for "Mum".

"Milky lot!" she yelled to the departing guests as their coach bumped its way out of the gate of the recreation ground; and it was a long time before the red flush of the fury faded from her creased and, normally, kindly face and she felt able to pack the crocks away in the clothes basket in which the tea utensils were stored nearby in the local policeman's cottage – by kind permission of his wife. She always boiled our urn for us and cut the bread and butter, which was supplemented by some delectable penny buns made in the village and known by most of the team – very unfairly – as "Plum 'Eavies".

The first match of the season was always against the local cricket club, giving rise to a great deal of fun and badinage and providing an entirely free entertainment for most of the village, young and old.

Everyone knows it is a butter-fingers who drops a catch, but, gradually, this became changed in our village to subtle remarks as to how much butter or marge the unlucky fielder had been buying at the local shop. Eventually "you bin shoppin' then?" became the accepted query from onlookers whenever a catch was dropped.

Sometimes, when the cricket and stoolball clubs met together on the field of battle, they did so in fancy dress – the men in top hats and smock frocks and the women in anything they happened to have laid by from a village dance – maybe a fortune teller's gay attire or some sort of pierrette costume. It all lent colour to the field and afforded even more scope for comment from the spectators!

The Second World War, alas, brought a number of village clubs to an end, but many have since re-formed and the game is still being played in many villages in Sussex and in quite a number of schools.

Those of us who have defended our wickets – who have experienced the diversity of bowling from the slow and easy to the swift and deadly, not to mention the peculiar slow motion, high-pitched balls which used to be unexpectedly and surprisingly delivered by our captain, and described by the blacksmith's family as "them donkey drops" – and have known the thrill of a good drive to the boundary with a well seasoned bat – we should be sorry indeed to see the game die out, and the happiness of this feature of village life in early spring and throughout summer months relegated to those forgotten customs of the past.'

233

CELEBRATIONS AND OCCASIONS

Royalty and West Sussex have long had a close relationship and when it was time to celebrate Royal Jubilees and Coronations, towns and villages did so with enthusiasm. There were other great occasions too, such as when Edward VII opened the new sanatorium named after him, and less formal sightings of the Royals at Bognor.

1905: OPENING THE SANATORIUM

'In 1905 there was a general holiday at Fernhurst when Edward VII passed through the village to open the King Edward VII Sanatorium. The children were given special places along the route and a very charming arch was built at the crossroads. The king came by brougham from Haslemere station and travelled up King's Road, to which he gave the name. He would have appreciated the beautiful countryside through which he travelled but was apparently very much perturbed when he thought the horses went too quickly down Fridays Hill. Lord Roberts accompanied the king and stood at his side during the ceremony. Stands were erected in the pine woods, in which the sanatorium stands, for invited guests. The children from Fernhurst school walked from the crossroads up the sanatorium drive,which was then a very rough road, and had a wonderful viewing place close to the actual stonelaying. One scholar remembers that the stone looked very large and the amount of mortar very small in quantity at that time. The king was in a specially built box and the children saw and heard all he said. They were fascinated with the plumes in Lord Roberts' helmet which waved in the breeze.'

THE ROYALS AT BOGNOR

'I have lived in Bognor Regis since 1917 when my family moved from Crawford Street in London where I was born. In the early 1920s my parents bought a large house in Clarence Road which my mother ran as a guest house. This she called Crawford House after our London address.

In 1928 I well remember King George V and Queen Mary arriving in Bognor to stay at Craigweil House where the King convalesced after a serious illness. On their arrival he looked extremely ill, but when he later returned to London after his convalescence he looked very much better and was sitting up in his car waving to everyone. He was a very good advertisement for the Sussex sea air! During their stay I also recall seeing the present Queen as a very young girl hand in hand with her grandmother in local shops. Queen Mary was also a weekly visitor to the Princess Mary Convalescent Home at the corner of Clarence Road and the Esplanade which she had opened before becoming Queen and was named after her. Her red Daimler became a familiar sight each week when she arrived with a large basket of flowers to be met by the matron. Unfortunately this building along with many other lovely old buildings in Bognor has been demolished and the site is yet another block of flats.'

1935 AND 1937: JUBILEE AND CORONATION

'At Pulborough in 1935 the costs for the celebration of George V's Silver Jubilee were itemised as follows:

Teas for 360 children at sixpence	£8 15 00 (!)
Presentation mugs	£7 10 00
Meat tea for 200 over 65 at a shilling	£10 00 00
Band or music	£20 00 00
Fireworks and bonfire	£10 00 00
Sports	£10 00 00

All the events and the teas took place in the field in front of the rectory.'

'The day of the Jubilee the schoolchildren of Balcombe assembled at the school and were presented with a Jubilee Mug each. We then all marched with the Scouts and Guides to church for a Service of Thanksgiving. In the evening we listened to the description on the wireless of the celebrations in London, and the next day saw the pictures in the newspaper, and better still saw the newsreels at the cinema.

The wedding of the daughter of the Earl and Countess of Athlone (Princess Alice) caused great excitement. The Earl and Countess were regular worshippers at St Mary's church when in residence at Brantridge Park. The organist and choir came from, I think, Westminster Abbey, but my father had to sit on the organ stool as well, just in case the organ "played up", as it could at times – according to the weather, Dad said. Queen Mary was in one car with the Duchess of York (now our Queen Mother) and Princess Elizabeth (now our Queen) was sitting beside her in a pale blue velvet bridesmaid's dress. King George V was unwell and could not attend. It was a fine and very warm day and there was a long, long time to wait to wave our flags and cheer – we all got rather tired and a bit bad tempered and we really hadn't seen a great deal!

The death of George V on 20th January 1936 plunged us into gloom and sadness. The wireless was continually switched on for every bulletin and when we heard the words, "The King's life is

---

STORRINGTON, SULLINGTON AND DISTRICT

Programme of

★ JUBILEE ★
CELEBRATIONS

On Monday, May 6th, 1935

7 a.m.	**PEAL OF BELLS**
10 a.m.	**CHURCH SERVICE** (costumes may be worn)
11.45 a.m.	**DECORATED PROCESSION** (with the Band). Assembly 11.15 a.m. at Chantry Cross Roads. Judging, 12.30 p.m. in Recreation Ground. Three Good Prizes for each of the following:—Private Cars, Trade Vans, Farm Wagons, Cycles, Perambulators, Pedestrians (Adults and Children), Mounted Section
2.30 p.m.	**SPORTS** (Children and Adults) Flat Races, Sack Races, Egg and Spoon, Three-legged Race, Obstacle Races, Skipping Race, Tug-of-War (Teams of 8), etc. The Band will play during Sports
5.15 p.m.	**CHILDREN'S TEA** (For all Children attending school)
6.15 p.m.	**COMIC FOOTBALL MATCH**. Recreation Ground
9 p.m.	**TORCHLIGHT PROCESSION** from field at Nightingale Lane, led by the Band
9.30 p.m.	**BONFIRE ON THE DOWNS**
10.30 p.m.	**JUBILEE BALL** (in Guide Hall). All Entrances and Admissions Free

GOD SAVE OUR KING AND QUEEN

The 1935 Royal Jubilee was was celebrated with day-long activities at Storrington, from the early morning peal of bells to the Jubilee Ball in the Guide hall.

slowly ebbing to its close" it was clearly only a matter of time. There was only solemn music on the wireless all the day he died and on the day of the funeral. Prince Edward was proclaimed King – then the American papers disclosed that he was in love with Mrs Wallis Simpson and we were back to doom and gloom and the wireless on for every bulletin! There was a general feeling of relief when the Abdication was announced.

The Coronation of George VI took place at Westminster Abbey in May 1937. It was a very exciting and jolly day in the village and we children were given a commemorative beaker and a very fine tea in the Victory Hall. The cinemas were packed for the Pathe news film of the day – there were special showings at the Broadway Cinema at Haywards Heath and my mother took me more than once!'

1953: CORONATION OF ELIZABETH II

'Do you remember the rain on Coronation Day? At Henfield we had a parade of floats through the village. Some members of the WI had, as part of their amateur dramatics, created a "circus". We made ponies with hobbyhorse heads and ostrich feather plumes; an elephant which housed two or our largest members, with a big head and small hole where the mouth should be, through which the front half put her grey-stockinged arm, waving it like a trunk; clowns; a tightrope walker with tutu and parasol; a bandmaster, complete with evening dress and dapper black moustache, followed by various musicians with accordions, pipes, saxophones, anything that would play a tune, even a comb; and a ringmaster, a superb figure in top hat, breeches and carrying a whip.

We were asked to join the parade and gaily we agreed, then, thinking of the back halves of the three animals struggling along for at least two miles, we hired two trucks and two tractors – horses on one, elephant on the other.

I was a weightlifter, with red tights and leopard skin, running beside the elephant, and the clown slipped on the high pavement and fell into the road under the truck wheel. A phone was handy so I rang for a doctor. When I got back I found her surrounded by help, and my eyes turned to the elephant (who could not see or hear). Its trunk was waving, but its back half had fainted and was sitting down!

We quickly unzipped the army blanket and took her in to the chemist, who gave her sal volatile, and she carried on her journey.

When we reached our destination the doctor drew up with our battered clown to say she was only bruised; her whalebone corsets and fur coat under her costume had saved her.'

'In 1953 girls from the Lancastrian Girls School in Chichester took part in the celebrations in Priory Park and acted in a pageant depicting the first Elizabeth. We were joined by the boys from the school next door to ours – normally we were not allowed to speak to them and woe betide any girl caught hanging around the dividing fence trying to communicate with the opposite sex! A memorable day in more ways than one.'

'The Coronation was celebrated at Washington by different firms and organisations decorating a float for the parade, and the children in fancy dress were paraded round the recreation ground and judged. A supper was held in the village hall and we went to a bonfire and firework display on Chanctonbury Ring.'

THROUGH THE YEAR

Certain events came round every year, and were eagerly awaited breaks in the working routine. Some are now memories only, such as Stopham Regatta or the great harvest suppers of the turn of the century -- or indeed, Empire Day, once celebrated by every child on 24th May and now gone the way of the Empire it commemorated.

EMPIRE DAY

'This was a special event at school celebrated each year on 24th May. Parents attended our school at Billingshurst and Britannia and her attendants were always represented on a stage while the rest of the children represented the countries of the British Empire. All schoolchildren took white marguerites to school on this day. It was always celebrated in the morning and then we had a half day off.'

'If you wanted to visit Priory Park in Chichester in 1920, keys were issued to various prominent citizens and croquet was played on the lawns. Later on it was opened to the public at certain times of the day. Mr Matthews was the park-keeper and lived in the little lodge inside the gates. He wore a dark suit and a pillbox hat with a peak. He was very strict as there were certain times the Park was opened and closed. When it was time for closing he rang a huge hand bell and everyone cleared out very quickly, otherwise they got the sharp edge of his tongue.

However, on Empire Day we visited the Park. It was quite a big day for all the schools in Chichester and the outlying districts who attended. The mayor and his chaplain were there. We sang hymns and *Jerusalem* and, of course, *God Save the King* and had prayers. Then we had to march past the Mayor, eyes right when we got to him (this we had been practising for weeks at school, when an old oak tree was chosen to be the "mayor"). The Mayor gave a speech and then gave the schools a half day. You can imagine the three cheers which were given for him!'

'On Empire Day at Goring, the whole school assembled in the playground around the flagpole. The Union Jack was hoisted and everyone sang a song called *Empire Day*, followed by *God Bless the Prince of Wales*, prayers, *God Save the King* and the lowering of the flag.

A few days later, on 29th May, Oak Apple Day was celebrated. Oak apples were worn by the children to commemorate King Charles hiding in an oak tree while fleeing to France from his enemies.'

ROGATIONTIDE

'In the 1920s Rogationtide was very special. For three days at Charlton there would be a short service at a farm as soon as the men had finished their work. They would come to a barn and have a mug of tea and buns, especially for the children. Then we would have the service and perhaps there would be 20 or 30 there who would start to beat the bounds of the parish. That was a long way, which is why it had to be spread over three days. The barn where they came in Charlton was where they made bundles of wood for the fires in the Duke of Richmond's house. On the day they got over to Singleton they had to go right up the hill on Cucumber Farm (that name doesn't mean anything to do with cucumbers, it is from old words meaning "cows' shelter") and it was really beautiful up there; you could see right over to the Isle of Wight on a clear day.'

GOODWOOD RACES

'When I was very small, from about 1910, we lived in a cottage at West Lavant where my father worked on a farm.

Goodwood Races were held in the third week in July and all the schools round about were closed for Goodwood week. The people who were going to Goodwood used to arrive at Singleton station on the train and go to Goodwood in carriages drawn by horses. The rich people used to stay at the big houses like West Dean – that was where King Edward VII always stayed with his friend Mr Edward James, whose wife was the mistress of the King. Other upper class people stayed at Arundel Castle or Goodwood House or at Adsdean which was the house where Lord Mountbatten lived later on before he moved to Broadlands. Adsdean was the house that interested us most as the people staying there had to pass our cottage in their carriages to go to the races. My sister being in a bathchair, they sympathised with these two little girls sitting outside and as they went along they would always wave and throw coins out to us, and if they had done well at the races they would throw us more on their way back.

I remember well one day a man stopped his carriage by us and said he would back a horse for my sister and if it won he would give her his winnings. And he did! I don't know exactly who he was, whether he was royalty or not, but he was certainly a man of Society.

Thursday was the Goodwood Cup Day and my father had a holiday from his farm work from twelve o'clock on that day. He and my mother pushed my sister and me all the way up the Trundle – that is the steep hill which overlooks the race course and it was about two or three miles from our house. If you went up there you could see all the racing without having to pay as you would if you went into the enclosure.

I can remember my parents pushing us down near the enclosure so that we could see Queen Mary and King George V. I can't remember seeing King Edward VII. Royalty *always* came to Goodwood in those days.

There were fortune tellers up on the Trundle and I can remember a strangely dressed man who called himself Prince Monalulu – he used to take bets and you would hear him call out "I've got a horse!" And there was someone with an enamel bucket full of yellow lemonade that you could buy, but my mother wouldn't let us have any of that – so we just sat there and watched.

Lavant was completely full during Goodwood Week, and so were Singleton and Boxgrove. People used to book up from one year to the next. And all the inhabitants the likes of us used to help with the house cleaning where the people were staying, and with the bed-making and the food and the washing up. All the grand people were entertained at dances and balls in the evenings.'

THE VILLAGE FETE

'The Balcombe village fete before the Second World War was usually held in a field which belonged to Balcombe House, near St Mary's church. There were several large tents housing home-made cakes, jams and marmalades and other delicacies. A painting competition was held every year and another competition for buttonholing and drawn thread work. The flower, fruit and vegetable tent was lovely and there was much rivalry, and mutterings and grumbling at the judges' decisions.

There were coconuts to be won, roll the penny – and a "Win the Pig" competition. This fascinated me and I would pester my mother for extra pennies so that I would stand a chance of winning the little pig, which in my innocence I thought I would be able to have as a pet if I won it. My mother did her best to keep me away from the wattle pen. Little did I know the winner received the "dear little pig" at a later date as bacon!

A circus came to Balcombe and the elephants were paraded through the village each day during its week in a field at the bottom of Mill Lane. The whole circus came by train with the animals in goods wagons and there was much excitement at the railway sidings at the unloading. Pocket money that week was spent sitting on hard slatted benches for each early evening performance. Many gardens were treated with very unusual manure in the hope of bigger and better crops for the summer fete.'

STOPHAM REGATTA

'Stopham held a regatta every year from 1908 to the First World War. The trees and bridge were festooned with lights. Races were held, rowing upstream. The boats were decorated and people from other villages could take part, so some of the younger staff at Stopham House were allowed time off for practice for the honour of the village. One gardener told how he rowed in a two-man boat with a housemaid as cox. The staff at this time amounted to about 15 indoor staff and six outdoor staff. Even the rectory had three sleeping-in maids, cook, parlourmaid and housemaid with a village woman for the rough work and all washing sent out – and an outside staff of two. There was plenty of competition on the river!'

THE FAIR

'The fair came two or three times a year to West Chiltington before the First World War, and on the day games and races were held. The older gents played Churchwarden's Pipe – long clay pipes to be lit and smoked during the race. The pipes started at a foot long but were fragile, so when they became really short they were smoked upside down to protect the nose!'

'On the last Monday in May, Horsted Club Day was held. This meant the arrival of Alfred Bond's Fair. Children would walk up the Birch Grove Road and put their ears to the road listening for the vibrations made by the steam engine Bing Boy with its polished brasses and other engines, which could be felt long before it could be heard. Roundabouts, swingboats, shooting galleries, coconut shies, whelk stalls and a gingerbread stall would all be set up on the green. After school the children would race up the hill to the green to take advantage of the free rides allowed on one afternoon.'

'Lindfield Fair was the event of the summer. We saw our very first Smith's potato crisps there, including the blue bag of salt. It was all magic, especially the Fat Lady who, just for sixpence invited you to prod her leg to prove it was real – the dent stayed in. Ugh! Well worth the money.'

'Adjoining Manor Farm at Wivelsfield was Moon's Field, now the local recreation ground. It was on this field after the First World War, in the height of summer, that the annual World's Fair was held – the location then was known as North End Burgess Hill but over the years it became known as World's End and the name sticks to this day.

The fairground gipsies had exquisite caravans, drawn by horses. During the period of the fair these horses were turned out to graze at Manor Farm and as a result we children were privileged visitors to the caravans. To a five year old the interiors were like Aladdin's cave. Mirrors and fancy china abounded, every piece of flat wood had flowers, birds etc painted in brilliant colours on it. Pretty little cupboards opened to show even more treasures. It was a world apart.'

WIVELSFIELD FOOD PRODUCTION SHOW

'I really only remember one Food Production Show at Wivelsfield and I think it must have been the last, or nearly the last, to be held there. It was, if my memory serves me correctly, in 1926 or 1927 and though of tender years the events are vividly etched on my mind.

In those days every housewife made her own jam, bottled her own fruit, baked her own cakes from recipes handed down from genera-

PC Connor, the local bobby, shows a keen interest in the dahlia exhibits at the Storrington Flower Show in about 1938. Flower and Produce Shows involved the whole village and there was a great deal of competition amongst proud local growers.

tion to generation. All the cooking was done on coal-fired kitchen ranges. Sewing and mending too were an important part of a woman's day-to-day duties – cash was hard to come by and "ready-mades" had not yet come into their own. All the men grew their own vegetables and spent many hours tending their gardens with great pride. The most wonderful displays of flowers and vegetables were raised from seeds costing one or two pennies a packet. Even the children tended their own little gardens where marigolds and mignonette rubbed shoulders with parsley and potatoes. Many cottages had their own bees, quite a few using only the old-fashioned skips, though I don't know how the honey was gathered from them. So, when the Annual Food Production Show came round there was intense competition. It was an easy going affair with no particular rules or regulations. The Show, so far as I can remember, took place in September just before Harvest Festival.

Now, my Aunt Janie knew her limitations. Her slapdash nature ruled her out of the needlework and cookery classes. She came into her own with her fruit and vegetables since the farm supplied unlimited nutriment for her crops. However, this year her apples had failed. It so happened whilst calling on one of the local beekeepers for some of his very fine honey and being proudly shown round his garden, she noticed a tree covered in the most luscious looking apples. She exclaimed how lovely they looked and asked if he could spare her a couple of pounds. Dear Mr P, overwhelmed by Janie's appreciation, was only too happy to oblige and that evening he took her a trugful of his choicest specimens.

Came the day of the Show. It was a feast for the eye. Every type of vegetable and fruit mouth-wateringly arranged – I particularly remember kidney potatoes, alas never seen today, and lettuces and cabbages as beautiful in their way as the prize roses, fruit cakes displayed on best china plates, and a kaleidoscope of bottled plums, marmalade, lemon curd, chutney, home-baked bread, meat pies, sweet peas, roses, dahlias and children's collections of flowers. There seemed to be no end to the delights.

The judging took place in the morning so by two o'clock when the Show was officially opened, the victors were known. As expected Janie had been very successful with her garden produce but – oh shame – had beaten Mr P with his own apples! On the credit side, she did admit her deception and Mr P rightfully received the cup – they remained good friends!

I have no memory of any subsequent Food Production Shows. Perhaps rules were drawn up which dampened enthusiasm, perhaps even Janie's nerve deserted her, or perhaps it was simply that times were changing. It is difficult today to imagine the almost total involvement of everyone in the village in these and similar events but it was good while it lasted.'

SHEEP FAIRS

'I have a remembrance of looking down upon the street in which we lived, crowded with sheep. Seen from the bedroom window, the jostling, bobbing multitude appeared as a cream coloured carpet moving steadily up the hill. No doubt there were drovers and dogs, but I have no recollection of them, nor of bleating, barking or of any noise whatever. All I can remember of that moment is that slowly moving mass of sheep.

When I was a boy sheep, cattle and pigs were driven through the streets to and from the market, but the huge flock below me was probably on its way to the Race Hill where each autumn a Sheep Fair was held. In those days the flocks travelled on foot to the fairground, the majority over the hills from Downland farms, but a few from valley farms could not avoid the narrow streets, as they were obliged to cross the river by the old stone bridge in the lower part of the town. Once over the bridge, the High Street could be bypassed by shepherding the sheep through East Street and West Street, where we lived, and Paddock Road to Race Hill where from time immemorial a fair had been held. Here the whole ground was laid out with a chequerboard pattern of hurdle pens, with passageways between.

Arriving at irregular intervals, the flocks caused considerable commotion in the alleyways should two arrive together. Many had been travelling since the grey light of dawn, moving steadily toward the fairground. Some perhaps had started the journey the day before, and had stopped overnight at a farm within easy walking distance. Hundreds of sheep were on the move on such days, urged on by the shepherd, their dogs and a host of small boys.

This was also a social occasion for farmers and shepherds, and the voices of man and beast added to the hubbub of that jam packed fairground. I remember being fascinated by the patter of the auctioneer and could never understand how he knew who was bidding, as no one seemed interested in the pen of sheep he was selling. I also remember the dogs, the shaggy Old English breed which had not yet been ousted by the smoother coated collie.

The most pleasing sound in all the clamour was that of the bells. Whether made from an old can, with an iron bolt for a clapper, or a work of art forged by the local blacksmith, the range of notes and tones produced was magical. The magic of the Downs was in those bells, the springy turf and the tangy breeze, the brilliant skies and the freedom of those vast smooth hills. I have five of these treasures. Their notes bring back many memories of youthful summers, when the only man-made sound to be heard on the hills was that of the tinkling bells as the flock slowly quartered the turf.'

'Since 1790 there has been a Sheep Fair at Findon in September. Mr Norman Groves, born 1912, told me that in his youth there would be 20,000 to 30,000 sheep sold on Nepcote Green where the sheep were auctioned by Messrs Burt & Sons of Steyning. The sheep would have been driven for many miles to the fair and there was a strict rule that none were allowed on the green until the day that the selling would take place. The sheep would be rested up on the Downs above Findon and brought down through the village during the night, to arrive as soon after midnight as possible when they would be permitted to come on to the green where pens had been put up to hold them. Every householder made sure that his garden gate was securely fastened before he went to bed on the night that the sheep passed through the village.

245

On the day of the fair, as well as the auctioning of the sheep, there was great fun to be had: roundabouts, swings, music sideshows and many other forms of entertainment made this a great event. This was particularly true for the children who were given a day's holiday from school. Next day the fairground equipment had to be packed and moved by noon.

There was, it seems, another event, the Spring or Lamb Fair, but I was assured that it was nothing compared to the great sheep fair.

Sometimes a lad might be asked to help with the sheep and would help to herd the flock as far as Amberly Mount, about eight miles away. He would then walk the same distance back to the village. The shepherd would give him threepence for his trouble so he did not mind the 16 miles he trudged with that money in his pocket.'

PETWORTH CHARTER FAIR

'The Petworth Charter Fair still takes place annually on 20th November in the Market Square (closed to traffic for the day) but is now very different from the fair that I knew in my childhood in the 1920s. Although then smaller than it had been previously, it still covered both Market Square and part of Golden Square. It was run largely by the Smith and the Hammond families. The Smiths lived in their caravans parked in New Street, notwithstanding which traffic continued to flow up and down the street. Tom Smith owned the large roundabouts, always sited at the south end of Market Square and his old father, Andrew Smith (a well known character) ran the coconut shies nearby. Chairoplanes were tried one year but were considered too dangerous in the limited space and were not repeated but now they are there every year!

The Hammonds lived in caravans in Lombard Street and ran (among other things) the miniature replica of the large roundabouts (with galloping horses and cockerels) for small children, which was powered by old Mr Hammond cranking a large wheel in the centre, all for one penny per ride of about five minutes. Hard work for sometimes only a few pence but very hard work with a full load aboard!

The fair started mid afternoon when the nannies from the larger houses in Petworth and around would be there with their charges and mothers with young children, the children riding on the small roundabouts and visiting the stalls. By mid evening (after their dinners) it was the recognised thing for the "gentry", professional folk and tradespeople to attend and generally enjoy themselves on the rides and at the stalls. Only after the public houses closed, up to the closing of the fair at midnight, did a somewhat rowdier element

246

enter in but this never got out of hand. Then boys and youths were very much in evidence, with "squirters" bought at the fair (something like a toothpaste tube filled with water) which they used to squirt water over unsuspecting persons.

Many persons lived round Market Square in those days and most of them used to entertain friends on Fair Day and spend the evening at windows overlooking the fair, rendered bright from the strong electric lights on the roundabouts, seeming all the brighter as electricity had not yet come to Petworth.

Only on Fair Days Miss Knight (generally known as "Fan" Knight) at the baker's shop in Lombard Street would bake a special kind of ginger biscuit known as "Fairings", which always formed part of tea that day.

Fair Day was always a highlight of my childhood winters and from then Christmas was exactly five weeks away!'

CHICHESTER SLOE FAIR

'I remember the Sloe Fair, a Charter Fair, during the late 1920s and early 1930s. The gipsy caravans would arrive in Chichester with all the children and dogs. They were all pulled by horses, large and small. The children wore boots, thick jackets, woollies and often had peak caps on their heads. Some sat on the wooden steps, others ran by the side of the caravans as they came down the street. Most had dogs and a chicken in a coop hanging on the caravan, and a canary in a cage.

There were steam traction engines which supplied the electricity for the roundabouts and switchback. There were hurdy gurdies, sideshows, boxing booths, coconut shies, roast chestnuts, toffee apples, home-made rock, water pistols and confetti. If it rained you got covered in mud as well. The ground is now a car park and not half as much fun.'

HARVEST SUPPER

'In the country around Hindhead at the turn of the century, the great event of the autumn was the annual Harvest Supper. The big kitchen became the scene of much activity and preparation and the cook's young man, the postman, and anyone else who happened to be handy at the time, were pressed into being of use and – with the promise of a share in the feast – to help to carry in the huge joints of meat, with all their accompaniments, and the foaming jugs of ale to the long tables at which presided, respectively, the foreman and the head gardener.

Grandpa, framed in the ivy-entwined doorway, would say Grace and wish them all a happy evening and later on – when the feasting was over and the clay pipes lit – Mother and her sister and brother would creep down the back stairs and listen to the time-honoured Harvest Songs. With chairs turned sideways and fingers lovingly encircling their mugs of ale, the guests' tongues would loosen and one after another would be called upon for a "sorng".

> "Come out, it's now September,
> The hunter's moon's begun
> All through the wheat and stubble
> You hear the frequent gun . . ."

would drift into:

> "I married with a scolding wife,
> 'Bout twenty years ago,
> And ever since I've led a life
> Of misery and woe . . ."

with everyone joining in the chorus – and many female titters:

> "She worries me, she flerries me;
> It is 'er 'eart's delight
> For to bang me with the fire shovel
> Round the room at night!"

Someone would start the first verse of *Come all you jolly ploughmen*, and it would not be long before *Pulling hard against the stream* with its excellent advice of helping our less fortunate brothers, would echo through the long, cheerful, firelit room. Others who did not possess great vocal powers would propose a toast, and after the Master and Mistress had been so honoured all sorts of excuses for an extra drink would occur to the younger members of the party, including – "A 'ealth to the ole man as scratched 'is 'ead to make 'is 'at fit!" suggested by a ploughboy, who was instantly sat upon severely for "imperence" by his mother.

"Oh Grandma, you did have some fun!" I would sometimes exclaim rather enviously – to which she would reply that there was no "gadding about" such as young people of today thought necessary, but they made their own fun, in their own families, by their own firesides, and mostly with their own talents. "Yes," said Grandma, with a reminiscent twinkle in her eye, "Yes – it takes one back talking of the old days . . . sometimes I think you young people miss a great deal of the romance of life . . . but no doubt you think me very old-fashioned!" '

'By autumn Grandmother's old tea caddy was half full of pence saved from her weekly washing. This was to pay for a pony and trap to take us to her sister Bertha's farm, a few miles from Arundel, for the harvest gathering.

Lifted up and kissed by great aunts in bonnets and shawls and great uncles with calloused hands and prickly whiskers was a bewildering event for a child, but I was compensated by meeting my cousins who were the same age as myself.

The men moved back all the furniture in the parlour and erected trestle tables using snowy white linen sheets for tablecloths. Well-scrubbed benches were brought in from the barn, where they had been all the summer, being made grubby by the old corduroys of casual labourers who travelled from farm to farm seeking work. The females bustled about in the large stoneflagged kitchen, "best" clothes covered with long white aprons.

Plates set to warm on the black shiny fender were piled high with turkey, goose or chicken. A massive pink succulent ham was sliced to a loud lament from Great Uncle bemoaning the demise of his prize pig. I had the feeling, young as I was, he begrudged the small portion on my plate. I've always detested ham since then. Great Aunt Bertha knew the menfolk well, the pudding was always Spotted Dick. With fish kettles and saucepans of every size used to cook the mountains of floury and waxy potatoes, sweetcorn, swede, sprouts and runner beans taken from the salt used to preserve them, there was only one place left to cook the pudding. The copper.

Cheers greeted this monster horseshoe-shaped pudding stripped of its cloth, and Great Uncle brandishing a knife would solemnly ask who wanted the ends. With the exception of one uncle all refused, so the steaming monster was cut in two. One half for Uncle, the other for himself. We'd all protest by turning our plates face down and banging the base with our spoons. No one was rebuked for bad table manners, it was as much a ritual as the whole harvest gathering.

With the pudding suitably shared the meal was rounded off by the adults with home-made wines; wheat, parsnip, beetroot, elderberry and dandelion, while the children had lemonade. When I was six I refused mine and asked for cherry brandy because it was "so pretty". I never lived it down.

Grandmother presided over the whole gathering and would take the opportunity to criticise or advise her family as to their future prospects or recent behaviours.

Sadly there were few gatherings left to enjoy, for in 1919 my father came home from the war and we moved to Hurstpierpoint. When Great Uncle died the farm was sold. Years after, each time the kin met, one subject was guaranteed to raise a laugh – the monster Spotted Dick being hauled manfully from the copper.'

GUY FAWKES NIGHT

'One big celebration every year at Parbrook, Billingshurst, was on 5th November, Bonfire Night. This was recognised by many villages around. There was a popular fancy dress competition which was judged in the old village hall in late afternoon. In the early evening everyone assembled outside The King's Arms to start a torchlit procession led by Billingshurst Band, and bands from other villages.

The guy was carried on a cart of torches. Fireworks were let off – squibs, bangers and jumpers – as the procession wound its way around the village, calling at one or two big houses and the Station Hotel and returning to the field at Alicks Hill, which is now Hillview Garage and a housing estate. Here there was a very large bonfire. Someone would climb to the top of the ladder to recite the bonfire prayer and position the guy, after which the fire was lit by torches. This was a major village occasion between the wars.'

CHRISTMAS

'Christmas was a joy. As young children we were taken into Worthing when the lights were on. There was one shop owned by two ladies who only sold dolls, and to our delight each and every doll, large and small, was dressed as a fairy. Just imagine how marvellous this was to young eyes. Opposite was a butcher whose shop was also decorated. The whole shop front was hung with birds, from larks to turkeys. The two pork butchers dressed their window with piglets in party clothes at a table fully laid, with a boar's head in pride of place.'

'I paid into a Christmas Club and saved in the Halfpenny Club at Strettington. It came to about 30 shillings and in the 1920s that was a fortune. I did all my Christmas shopping out of that. We made all our own decorations – paper chains and such like. I'd save up all my bits of silver paper . . . we made our own Christmas. The boys only had one good present, and they'd have an apple, an orange and sweet knick-knacks. We did eventually get a second-hand gramophone with a trumpet and a few records.'

'Flour which came from a bakery near Chichester had a coupon on each packet which Mother saved and at Christmas they were exchanged for an iced Christmas cake, the size depending on how many coupons had been saved. Our Christmas stockings always contained a little sugar mouse, either pink or white.'

'Christmas Day in the 1930s, for me, meant a day spent at Granny's. Father hired a car to take us to Milland with the food Mother had prepared. We also took a portable wireless, hired from a local shop, so that we could listen to the King's broadcast. Granny didn't have a wireless and neither did we at that time, so it was really exciting to have one for a few days.

When we arrived dinner was already cooking, sometimes a chicken or occasionally a pheasant. The pudding Mother made was put on to boil, then we opened our presents, one for each person. Everything took place in the kitchen, I don't remember the sitting room being used at all. There were two or three wooden armchairs, the rest were Windsor type chairs, some with a cushion on. A large scrubbed table filled the centre of the room, with a small table under the window, and a large dresser holding crockery at one end and the coal range at the other end.

There were no Christmas decorations or Christmas tree, yet the room was warm and friendly.

We sat round the table, now covered by a spotless white cloth. There would be Granny, Grandad, Father, Mother, myself and sometimes my two aunts (father's sisters), ready for our special Christmas Dinner. Our plates were filled with chicken, roast potatoes, greens, carrots or parsnips and gravy. This was followed by the pudding, a flame burning on the top as it was put on the table – this was always a mystery to me. When we each had our piece of pudding we probed carefully with our spoon to see if we could find a silver threepenny piece. Sometimes I was lucky. Custard was poured over the pudding before we ate it, then we felt so full up we could hardly move.

After the meal the ladies washed up and then we sat round the fire having a cup of tea ready to listen to the King's Christmas Message. It seemed like magic to think he was sitting in his castle miles away talking to us in Granny's kitchen. What a fine voice he had although, to me, he seemed so old. There was a big picture of the King and Queen on the wall and I looked at it while he talked.

While the grown ups talked, I played with Granny's button box or a word game in a tin tray. The letters were all jumbled up and filled the box, except for one space, and by pushing the letters up, down, or across one at a time it was possible to make a sentence. It kept me occupied for a long time.

For Christmas tea we had bread and butter, and what tasty butter it was too, fresh from the farm, it was a pity to put jam on it. Also there were some of Granny's special crumbly scones, no one else has ever made them of the same texture. She made one for me in the shape of a cottage loaf. Then there was my special favourite, Christmas cake with marzipan and white icing. I always hoped for a big piece. Tea was in special china cups, white with a thin gold band.

As it got dark Granny lit the oil lamp hanging from the centre of the ceiling, then she closed the shutters over the window and put the bolt through.

Later they drank Granny's home-made wine: parsnip, dandelion or whatever else she had in the cellar. It was very strong I believe. I was not allowed to have any, but as a special treat had a small glass of ginger wine. They told stories about my father as a little boy, always up to mischief. Then Grandfather would sing *The Village Blacksmith*, *A Miner's Dream of Home* and other old favourites, and we all joined in the chorus.

Eventually it was time to go home, so we put our coats on, kissed everyone goodbye, collected up our presents and the precious wireless and got in the car.

It was only five miles so it didn't take long, but it was unusual for me to be out so late and I looked eagerly at the dark countryside. It was a lovely Christmas Day and so long to wait till next year's.'

'Before the Second World War, as a member of the church choir, I remember the fun we had for a week, just before Christmas, when we sang carols around Pulborough village. Each evening one house (home of a choir member) was our refreshment stop. My mother's cakes, mince pies and coffee plus, if wished, my father's mulled home-made elderberry wine were thoroughly enjoyed. The war stopped this practice as most of the men were called up and many of the women were Mobile Red Cross and also on call, but the congregational church led by Mr Chantler continued to carol sing throughout the war, and all the offerings collected were sent to Great Ormond Street Hospital.

One lovely Christmas Eve we walked the mile to Midnight Service, a brilliant, starry, moonlit night, with the road, house-roofs, everything sparkling with hoar frost, but no bells, just silence broken by our footsteps on the frozen road, no peal ringing out from the bell-tower (that was reserved as a warning of an invading enemy landing). We opened the door into church.

Faerie, angelic bells ringing softly! The captain of the tower, his wife, other bellringers and friends were playing carols on the handbells, beside the large Christmas tree!'

'I was born in Boxgrove in 1940 during the war and lived in a house attached to the village club which my parents ran. My father worked for Goodwood Estate as a forester, working long hours felling trees and then replanting, often coming home wet through after a day in the woods with his horse pulling out the timber to be taken to the sawmills.

One of my happiest memories was Christmas parties at Goodwood House, to which the wives and children of estate workers were invited each year. A bus would pick us up in all the local villages and take us to Goodwood House where we were all welcomed by the Duchess of Richmond, talking to everyone as we entered. Then on to the ballroom for a lovely tea with Christmas crackers, what fun, then into another room to see either a conjuror or cartoon film show before Father Christmas arrived with a sack of presents for all the children. How anxious I was waiting for my name to be called by Father Christmas and I was never disappointed with my present, whether book, doll or puzzle they were wonderful. Then back to the ballroom again for ice cream. What bliss, and the end to a perfect day.'

'Mrs Skaife was a doctor's wife in Chichester in the early 1920s and lived in a very large house in North Street where the Ship Hotel is now. My aunt was her companion and she had three other servants.

I went to stay there on many occasions. I was given six pennies in a bank bag every week. This was a lot of money. You could buy two ice cream cones for a penny. I was allowed to attend some of her dinner parties and when they had wine I had a special glass with milk and soda water.

At Christmas time I was given a large party and was allowed to invite my friends. A car was hired from Adcocks and all the children were picked up from their respective homes. I stood in the hall and greeted them. We had lovely food and a silk name tag and crackers were on the table. The dining room was big and the table very long and wide. This was cleared after tea and then we had games.

Something was made to put all the presents in. One year it was a wishing well, another year it was a huge car and so on. Before presents were given out my mother and father and all the staff, gardener and his wife, stable boy etc came in. My father dressed up in some appropriate attire and gave out the presents in the presence of Mrs Skaife.

Then the car came to collect all my friends and take them home. The end of another happy day. When I think about it now, I always had plenty of friends about this time of year.'

Index